Dialectical Behavior Therapy

Theories of Psychotherapy Series

Theories of Psychotherapy Series
Matt Englar-Carlson, Series Editor

Dialectical Behavior Therapy

Alexander L. Chapman and
Katherine L. Dixon-Gordon

 AMERICAN PSYCHOLOGICAL ASSOCIATION

Published by
American Psychological Association
750 First Street, NE
Washington, DC 20002
https://www.apa.org

Order Department
https://www.apa.org/pubs/books
order@apa.org

In the U.K., Europe, Africa, and the Middle East, copies may be ordered from Eurospan
https://www.eurospanbookstore.com/apa
info@eurospangroup.com

Typeset in Minion by Circle Graphics, Inc., Reisterstown, MD

Printer: Sheridan Books, Chelsea, MI
Cover Designer: Beth Schlenoff Design, Bethesda, MD

Library of Congress Cataloging-in-Publication Data

Names: Chapman, Alexander L. (Alexander Lawrence), author. | Dixon-Gordon, Katherine L., author.
Title: Dialectical behavior therapy / Alexander L. Chapman and Katherine L. Dixon-Gordon.
Description: Washington, DC : American Psychological Association, [2020] | Series: Theories of psychotherapy series | Includes bibliographical references and index.
Identifiers: LCCN 2020000549 (print) | LCCN 2020000550 (ebook) | ISBN 9781433831454 (paperback) | ISBN 9781433831461 (ebook)
Subjects: LCSH: Dialectical behavior therapy.
Classification: LCC RC489.D48 C43 2020 (print) | LCC RC489.D48 (ebook) | DDC 616.89/142—dc23
LC record available at https://lccn.loc.gov/2020000549
LC ebook record available at https://lccn.loc.gov/2020000550

http://dx.doi.org/10.1037/0000188-000

Printed in the United States of America

10 9 8 7 6 5 4 3 2 1

To all of the DBT clients who have taught me so much.
—*Alexander L. Chapman*

To my mentors and colleagues in the DBT community—
thank you for building a foundation of compassionate,
evidence-based care for our clients.
—*Katherine L. Dixon-Gordon*

Contents

Series Preface

Matt Englar-Carlson

Some might argue that in the contemporary clinical practice of psycho-therapy, the focus on evidence-based intervention and effective out-come has overshadowed theory in importance. Maybe. But, at the same time, it is clear that psychotherapists adopt and practice according to one theory or another because their experience (and decades of empirical evidence) suggests that having a sound theory of psychotherapy leads to greater therapeutic success. Theory is fundamental in guiding psycho-therapists in understanding *why* people behave, think, and feel in certain ways, and it provides the guidance to then contemplate *what* a client can do to instigate meaningful change. Still, the role of theory in the helping process itself can be hard to explain. This narrative about solving problems may help convey theory's importance:

> Aesop tells the fable of the sun and wind having a contest to decide who was the most powerful. From above the earth, they spotted a person walking down the street, and the wind said that he bet he could get the person's coat off. The sun agreed to the contest. The wind blew, and the person held on tightly to his coat. The more the wind blew, the tighter the person held onto his coat. The sun said it was his turn. She put all of her energy into creating warm sunshine, and soon the person took off his coat.

What does a competition between the sun and the wind to remove a person's coat have to do with theories of psychotherapy? This deceptively simple story highlights the importance of theory as the precursor to any effective intervention—and hence to a favorable outcome. Without a guiding theory, a psychotherapist might treat the symptom without understanding the role of the individual. Or we might create power conflicts with our clients and not understand that, at times, indirect means of helping (sunshine) are often as effective—if not more so—than direct ones (wind). In the absence of theory, a psychotherapist might lose track of the treatment rationale and instead get caught up in, for example, social correctness and not wanting to do something that looks too simple.

What exactly *is* theory? The APA *Dictionary of Psychology, Second Edition*, defines theory as "a principle or body of interrelated principles that purports to explain or predict a number of interrelated phenomena" (VandenBos, 2015, p. 1081). In psychotherapy, a theory is a set of principles used to explain human thought and behavior, including what causes people to change. In practice, a theory frames the goals of therapy and specifies how to pursue them. Haley (1997) noted that a theory of psychotherapy ought to be simple enough for the average psychotherapist to understand but comprehensive enough to account for a wide range of eventualities. Furthermore, a theory guides action toward successful outcomes while generating hope in both the psychotherapist and client that recovery is possible.

Theory is the compass that allows psychotherapists to navigate the vast territory of clinical practice. In the same ways that navigational tools have been modified to adapt to advances in thinking and ever-expanding territories to explore, theories of psychotherapy have evolved over time to account for advances in science and technology. The different theoretical schools are commonly referred to as waves: the first wave of psychodynamic theories (i.e., Adlerian, psychoanalytic), the second wave of learning theories (i.e., behavioral, cognitive–behavioral), the third wave of humanistic theories (i.e., person-centered, gestalt, existential), the fourth wave of feminist and multicultural theories, and the fifth wave of postmodern and constructivist theories (i.e., narrative, constructivist). In many ways, these waves represent how psychotherapy has adapted and responded to changes in psychology, society, and epistemology, as well as to changes in the nature of psychotherapy itself. The wide variety of theories is also testament to the different ways in which the same human behavior can be conceptualized depending on the view one espouses (Frew & Spiegler, 2012). Our theories of psychotherapy are also challenged to expand beyond the primarily Western worldview endemic in most psychotherapy theories and the practice of psychotherapy itself. That revision and correction requires theories and psychotherapists to become more inclusive of the full range of human diversity in order to reflect an understanding of human behavior that accounts for a client's context, identity, and intersectionality (American Psychological Association, 2017). To that end, psychotherapy and the theories that guide it are dynamic and responsive to the changing world around us.

It is with these two concepts in mind—the central importance of theory and the natural evolution of theoretical thinking—that the *APA Theories of Psychotherapy Series* was developed. This series was created by my father (Jon Carlson) and me. Though educated in different eras, we both had a love of theory and often spent time discussing the range of complex ideas that drove each model. Even though my father identified strongly as an Adlerian and I was parented and raised from the Adlerian perspective, my father always espoused an appreciation for other theories and theorists—and that is something I picked up from him. As university faculty members teaching courses on the theories of psychotherapy, we wanted to create learning materials that not only highlighted the essence of the major theories for professionals and professionals in training, but also clearly brought the reader up to date on the current status of the models, future directions with an emphasis on the inclusive application of the theories with clients representing the range of identities. Often in books on theory, the biography of the original theorist overshadows the evolution of the model. In contrast, our intent was to highlight the contemporary uses of the theories, as well as their history and context— both past and present.

As this project began, we faced two immediate decisions: which theories to address and who best to present them. We assessed graduate-level theories of psychotherapy courses to see which theories were being taught, and explored popular scholarly books, articles, and conferences to determine which theories drew the most interest. We then developed a "dream list" of authors from among the best minds in contemporary theoretical practice. To that end, each author in the series is one of the leading proponents of that approach as well as a knowledgeable practitioner. We asked each author to review the core constructs of the theory, bring the theory into the modern sphere of clinical practice by looking at it through a context of evidence-based practice, and clearly illustrate how the theory looks in application.

There are 24 titles planned for the series, and many titles are now in their second edition. Each title can stand alone or can be put together with a few other titles to create materials for a course in psychotherapy theories. This option allows instructors to create courses featuring the approaches they believe are the most salient today. APA Books has also developed a video for each of the approaches that demonstrates the theory in practice with a real client. Many of the videos show psychotherapy over six sessions with the same client. For a complete list of available videos, visit the APA website (http://www.apa.org/pubs/videos).

When my father and I first began strategizing about the different theories for the series, we knew that we needed to address the seminal approaches, but we were also excited to include more contemporary approaches (e.g., narrative therapy, acceptance and commitment therapy) that we were learning about and our students were asking to learn. At the top of that list was dialectical behavior therapy (DBT). A true integrative approach, DBT involves individual sessions and a skills group, and it uses mindfulness, processing negative emotions, emotional regulation, and an interpersonal component to support clients in making true change with presenting concerns that are often difficult to treat. In this monograph, Alexander L. Chapman and Katherine L. Dixon-Gordon elucidate the DBT theory and approach beginning with a comprehensive review of DBT origins and thoughtful explanations of the DBT's core tenets. As you read deeper into the monograph, it becomes clear how the clinical process and focus of DBT offers a compassionate clinical approach towards clients who often present with challenging concerns. Finally, the authors translate the wealth of empirical literature supporting the effectiveness of DBT into a manageable framework that the reader can clearly understand.

How to Use This Book
With APA Psychotherapy Videos

Each book in the *Theories of Psychotherapy Series* is specifically paired with a video that demonstrates the theory applied in actual therapy with a real client. Many videos feature the author of the book as the guest therapist, allowing students to see an eminent scholar and practitioner putting the theory they write about into action.

The videos have a number of features that make them excellent tools for learning more about theoretical concepts:

- Many videos contain six full sessions of psychotherapy over time, giving viewers a chance to see how clients respond to the application of the theory over the course of several sessions.
- Each video has a brief introductory discussion recapping the basic features of the theory behind the approach demonstrated. This allows viewers to review the key aspects of the approach about which they have just read.
- Videos feature actual clients in unedited psychotherapy sessions. This provides a unique opportunity to get a sense of the look and feel of real psychotherapy—something that written case examples and transcripts sometimes cannot convey.
- There is a therapist commentary track that viewers may choose to play during the psychotherapy sessions. This track gives unique insight into why therapists do what they do in a session. Further, it provides an in

vivo opportunity to see how the therapist uses the model to conceptualize the client.

The books and videos together make a powerful teaching tool for showing how theoretical principles affect practice. In the case of this book, the video *Dialectical Behavior Therapy*, which features author Alexander L. Chapman as the guest expert, provides a vivid example of how this approach looks in practice.

Dialectical
Behavior Therapy

1

Introduction

When we first heard about borderline personality disorder (BPD), we had more questions than answers. One of us (ALC) probably first heard about BPD during my undergraduate course in abnormal psychology, while the other (KDG) read books that referred to BPD while in middle school. What stood out to both of us at the time was the image of someone who was unpredictable and out of control, with intense emotions and fears of abandonment. The term *borderline* seemed confusing, like people with BPD had some kind of mysterious or undefined syndrome. And what resonated with us was the prevailing notion that this condition may not be treatable.

A few years after my first encounter with BPD as an undergraduate, I (ALC) started working at a transitional mental health facility for patients who had been hospitalized and needed more residential support before returning home. Many of these patients had attempted suicide, harmed

http://dx.doi.org/10.1037/0000188-001
Dialectical Behavior Therapy, by A. L. Chapman and K. L. Dixon-Gordon

themselves, or experienced flare-ups of psychotic or mood symptoms. After they received some treatment in the hospital and their medications were stabilized, they stayed at the facility I worked at for a few days to a couple of weeks. I was a junior mental health clinician and knew very little about what I was dealing with, but I certainly encountered patients with BPD. As it turned out, they weren't scary or unpredictable. They were often emotionally up and down and distraught about the state of their lives, and many had seriously harmed or tried to kill themselves. At the same time, they were sensitive, empathetic, and fun to work with, and they desperately wanted help.

At the time, at least in my area, the kind of help they needed was not easy to get. People with BPD and other complex mental health problems often need a comprehensive, structured, evidence-based treatment. Not only were programs offering this kind of treatment hard to find, but clinicians often avoided patients with BPD because they either did not know how to help them or were put off by stigmatizing attitudes (i.e., the idea that BPD patients are impossible to treat, angry, unpredictable, and out of control). This combination of stigma, a lack of appropriate services, and a general unwillingness of clinicians to help those with BPD made it difficult for people to maintain hope for recovery.

Our introduction to Marsha Linehan's work indelibly shifted our views related to BPD and its treatment. I (ALC) learned about dialectical behavior therapy (DBT) during one of my graduate courses on the treatment of adult mental health problems, and later, in a course on the treatment of BPD. We had to read the main DBT text (Linehan, 1993a) and skills training manual (Linehan, 1993b), and I remember writing a paper comparing and contrasting DBT with more psychoanalytic approaches to the treatment of BPD. At around the same time, I had started to see some of my first clients, one of whom happened to have BPD. She was a bright young woman who had been harming herself for several years. I was teaching her DBT skills while another student clinician provided individual DBT weekly. I was learning DBT skills while I was teaching them to this client, so I had more homework to do each week than

4

she did! Over the course of a year or so, she stopped harming herself, started to improve her relationships, got back into school, and began to piece together the key ingredients of a life worth living. Throughout this process, I became fascinated with the treatment of clients with BPD and changed the direction of my research, focusing on BPD for my dissertation, completing an internship focused on DBT, ultimately working with Dr. Marsha Linehan as a postdoc for 2 years at her research and treatment center, the Behavioral Research and Therapy Clinics at the University of Washington (UW).

Likewise driven to understand this seemingly mysterious, painful, and difficult-to-treat condition, I (KDG) also wrote a paper on BPD in college. Yet it was only when I began seeking an undergraduate research experience that I learned about the work being done by Marsha Linehan to treat BPD at my very own school, UW. When I saw how behavioral principles could be harnessed to effectively treat this unfairly maligned, heartbreaking condition, I dedicated myself to the study of DBT. I was lucky enough to complete my graduate studies under the supervision of ALC. DBT and research on BPD and related problems have since been a major focus of our careers.

CASE EXAMPLE

To understand the problems DBT aims to solve, consider the case of "Mandy." Mandy is a 25-year-old Caucasian woman who lives off and on with her partner. She currently works at a local coffee shop while taking some classes at the community college and wishes to eventually go into social work. Mandy grew up in a large city in the Northeast, with her parents and two older brothers. She described her upbringing as "difficult." When asked to elaborate, she became tearful and eventually disclosed that she had always felt like the black sheep in the family. Unlike her older brothers, who were straightlaced, into sports, and seemed to take everything in stride, she was always the emotional one. Her family called her "moody Mandy," as she had so many ups and downs. She was also a little on the impulsive side, had difficulty focusing at school, and gravitated toward rougher crowds from a fairly young age—kids who smoked, drank, and experimented with drugs as early as junior high school. Mandy reported that her parents were very caring but often seemed fed up with her and her problems (emotional ups and downs, getting in trouble at school, and so forth). In her early teens, she started to experience depressive episodes following an attempted sexual assault by an acquaintance, and she began to drink more, experiment with drugs, and engage in risky sex. Over the next couple of years, Mandy became increasingly depressed, started self-injuring, and was hospitalized for the first time following a suicide attempt at age 15. She attempted suicide two or three more times following the index attempt and continued to self-injure. Throughout high school, Mandy often seemed to be in a crisis of some sort. Her relationships with friends were up and down, she seemed to choose the wrong guys to date, and she often skipped classes and failed to prepare for tests or complete assignments. Mandy was very bright, but she had tremendous difficulty organizing herself, and her emotional ups and downs made it nearly impossible to function consistently. Eventually, she dropped out of school, later receiving her high school equivalency and beginning college in her early 20s. Before she came to treatment, Mandy already had seen five or six other therapists. She reported that some of her previous therapists were very helpful but that she tended to get overly attached, had difficulty keeping up with therapy (often missing sessions or dropping out prematurely), and regrets some of the things she said or did during past therapy sessions. In the month before her intake, she had withdrawn from her courses for the semester and made a serious suicide attempt, following which she was hospitalized for a week. Mandy desperately wants help and wishes her life could be different. She wants to finish college, work as a social worker helping underserved and disenfranchised clients, have a stable and happy relationship, and mend fences with her family (from whom she is currently alienated). She has told her therapist that she is going to give therapy "one last chance" before she packs it in and decides life isn't worth the constant struggling and suffering.

DIALECTICAL BEHAVIOR THERAPY

"Mandy" is fairly representative of the types of complex suicidal clients that Dr. Marsha Linehan (whom we will periodically refer to as Marsha throughout this book, as we know her well) set out to help when she began developing DBT (Linehan, 1993a) in the late 1970s and early 80s. Marsha's primary goal in developing DBT was to find a way to help highly suicidal individuals learn how to build lives that were worth living. In Mandy's case, a life worth living would involve better relationships with her family, at least one close, supportive relationship with a friend or romantic partner, and meaningful work helping others. Despite her many strengths, her extreme emotional ups and downs, difficulty with impulse control, and sensitivity in relationships kept getting in her way. She often became demoralized and began to believe that it was impossible to achieve her goals, as she just couldn't trust her "incredibly emotional brain" to stop dragging her down time and time again.

Through challenges in her work applying standard cognitive behavior therapy (CBT) with clients like Mandy, Marsha quickly realized that something new was needed. One challenge that emerged was that many of the clients she was treating had BPD, with its accompanying instability in emotions, relationships, cognition and identity (American Psychiatric Association, 2013). Forming effective therapy relationships with clients whose emotions were often dysregulated and who vacillated between loving and hating their therapists was sometimes a daunting task. Standard cognitive therapy strategies were hard to employ, given intense emotional ups and downs that made it difficult for clients to reflect on and change their thinking patterns. In addition, like Mandy, clients often presented with myriad difficulties, and therapists needed to find a way to structure and address many treatment targets at once. The co-occurrence of many clinical problem areas made it challenging to use any specific CBT protocol. When applying treatment for panic, for example, other problems such as self-injury, substance use or disordered eating often rose to the top of the priority list, taking therapy in another direction. The solution to this problem was to develop a structured way to organize and prioritize problem areas, discussed in detail in Chapter 4.

The heavy focus on cognitive and behavioral change in standard CBT also did not fit well with these clients. The message of standard CBT was that clients needed to change their thinking and behavior and learn new coping skills, and this was probably true. Marsha discovered, however, that clients needed therapists who were able to deftly balance acceptance of the client with efforts to help the client make difficult changes (e.g., face painful emotions, learn how to navigate relationships differently). She also discovered that clients needed to learn how to accept themselves before they were able to change. Mandy, for example, needed to accept that she was a sensitive person who had an emotional system that was fairly turbulent and complex. Rather than engage in futile efforts to suppress or numb her emotions, or punish herself for feeling at all, what Mandy needed to do was to learn how to navigate her own brain, recognize and manage her emotions, and curb impulses that often led her astray. In this way, DBT evolved into a "dialectical" treatment, involving the balance and synthesis of acceptance and change, with the acceptance end of the dialectic including a nonjudgmental and validating therapeutic stance that often runs counter to prevailing pejorative and stigmatizing views of clients with BPD.

Additionally, through her work with clients like Mandy, Marsha learned that complex, highly suicidal clients did not have many of the skills they needed to improve their lives. Through a combination of having a highly emotional temperament and growing up in an environment that invalidated their emotions, highly suicidal clients with BPD had not learned how to understand and manage their emotions. They often had difficulty tolerating overwhelming emotions without engaging in harmful behavior (e.g., self-injury, suicidal behavior, and other reckless or risky behaviors) and getting their needs met while maintaining healthy relationships. Clients needed concrete, practical tools that they could use to attend to the present moment (i.e., what was happening both inside and outside of them), recognize and manage emotions, deal with other people in ways that maintained or enhanced their relationships, tolerate distress, and avoid behaviors that made things worse. DBT, therefore, evolved into a skills-oriented therapy. Standard DBT consists of a combination of individual treatment, structured skills training, telephone consultation (geared toward helping clients transfer skills they are learning in therapy to their everyday lives), and a therapist consultation team.

Regarding the team, Marsha recognized that clinicians seeing complex, often suicidal clients needed support and help maintaining their skills and motivation. DBT includes a consultation team consisting of therapists who meet weekly to help one another maintain the skills and motivation needed to help their clients build lives worth living. Each team member takes some responsibility both for the well-being of their teammates and that of all clients seen on the team. In this way, DBT is best considered a community of therapists treating a community of clients.

OVERVIEW OF THIS BOOK

Our aim in writing this book is to provide a clear and concise description of the theory, research, and practice of DBT. Our hope is that seasoned clinicians and students alike will find this book to be a helpful resource, whether they are practicing full, standard DBT, or simply trying to incorporate some DBT principles, strategies, or skills into their everyday practice. As with other books in the Theories of Psychotherapy Series, this book includes chapters on the history of the approach, the theoretical foundations of DBT, the treatment's structure and primary interventions, research evidence, and mechanisms of change, or how and why DBT might work. Clinicians who wish to make DBT a focus of their practice will still need to be familiar with the original DBT text (Linehan, 1993a) and the DBT skills training handouts (Linehan, 2015a) and manual (Linehan, 2015b) and should ideally seek additional training through clinical workshops, and possibly ongoing supervision or consultation. Next, we briefly describe the focus of each chapter.

Chapter 2 provides a discussion of the history of DBT. In this chapter, we expand the discussion we began in this chapter to illustrate how Dr. Marsha Linehan developed DBT, why it is called "dialectical" behavior therapy, and how the struggles of applying standard CBT to complex clients formed the impetus for the development of a comprehensive treatment program. We also discuss issues related to training and dissemination, some elements of the evolution of the research on DBT (although this is discussed much more thoroughly in Chapter 5), and how DBT has changed, adapted, and expanded to populations other than suicidal individuals with BPD.

Chapter 3 details the theoretical underpinnings of DBT. Within this chapter, we discuss the dialectical world view underlying DBT and the influence of Zen practice on the treatment. As DBT, at its core, is a behavioral treatment, we also discuss behavioral principles for understanding the causes and maintaining factors for human behavior. Additionally in Chapter 3, we describe the biosocial developmental theory (Crowell, Beauchaine, & Linehan, 2009; Linehan, 1993a) of the development of BPD. These theoretical elements come together to inform a treatment that (a) balances acceptance and change in terms of therapeutic style, core interventions, and skills training; (b) focuses on the function or purpose of client behavior and the need to ameliorate skill deficits in key areas; and (c) emphasizes the role of dysregulation in the emotion system in the many behavioral problems that often accompany BPD and other complex mental health difficulties (e.g., suicidal behavior, self-injury, drug and alcohol use, other harmful behaviors).

In Chapter 4, we describe the goals, structure, and process of DBT. DBT is a comprehensive, cognitive–behavioral treatment program with several key aims, including (a) improving client skills and capabilities, (b) improving client motivation to change, (c) ensuring that clients generalize what they learn in therapy to their everyday lives, (d) structuring the treatment environment and the client's natural environment to promote positive change, and (e) maintaining therapist skill and motivation. Standard DBT accomplishes these aims through weekly individual therapy, group skills training, telephone consultation, and a therapist consultation team. DBT also occurs in stages, with different types of treatment targets emphasized in each stage. Additionally, as DBT was developed with clients who often had difficulty navigating therapy relationships and getting the most out of their treatment, DBT also includes principles and strategies to address problems that interfere with therapy. Clinicians who are wondering what DBT looks like, what to focus on in the initial stages of therapy, how to navigate the flow of activities in an individual therapy session, the focus and importance of a therapist consultation team, the role of telephone consultation in DBT, and how to structure skills training, will find this chapter to be a helpful, concise resource.

In Chapter 5, our focus is on the research supporting the efficacy and effectiveness of DBT. This chapter provides a contemporary, thorough snapshot of the state of the research on DBT, recognizing, of course, that the research is always evolving. From the beginning, when a small randomized trial showed that highly suicidal clients with BPD could be treated effectively (Linehan, Armstrong, Suarez, Allmon, & Heard, 1991), research on DBT has proliferated, expanding well beyond its the initial focus. Although the strongest evidence for DBT still has to do with the treatment of problems characteristic of BPD, growing evidence suggests that DBT and its elements (e.g., DBT skills training) are probably helpful for a range of clinical problems. When people ask us whether they should consider using DBT with their clients, we often tell them that it may be most helpful with clients who (a) are multiproblem and multidiagnostic, (b) are suicidal or self-injurious, (c) have BPD or significant BPD features, or (d) present with significant emotion dysregulation and risky or harmful behaviors. We discuss these and other important points about the application of DBT in Chapter 5 and in various places in other chapters in this book.

Having established in Chapter 5 that DBT works, our emphasis in Chapter 6 is on mechanisms of change, or how and why DBT works. In this chapter, we focus broadly on (a) treatment elements that may be essential to the effectiveness of DBT, and (b) changes in the client that may account for the effects of DBT. Although much research remains to be done to understand the precise mechanisms of change in DBT, findings have emphasized the importance of skills training as a key element of the treatment, skills practice as a potential mediator of treatment outcome, and changes in brain regions related to emotions and emotion regulation as potentially important within-client mechanisms of change. We also illustrate how these mechanisms may play out in therapy, using illustrative clinical examples.

Finally, in Chapter 7, we pull together what we have presented in the previous chapters to provide a summary of DBT. In this chapter, we return to the case example of Mandy to briefly illustrate the theoretical under-pinnings of DBT, the structure and process of treatment from start to finish, and some of the core interventions and skills used in DBT. We also discuss future directions for the development and practice of DBT.

2

History

Dialectical behavior therapy (DBT) arose from attempts to apply evidence-based cognitive and behavioral interventions to highly suicidal clients, many of whom met criteria for borderline personality disorder (BPD). It soon became clear that complex, severe, and multi-diagnostic clients required an approach that balanced change-oriented strategies, therapeutic styles, and skills with acceptance-oriented strategies, styles, and skills. DBT evolved into a comprehensive cognitive–behavioral approach for complex clients with emotion regulation problems. Over the years, DBT has been adapted and adopted in many settings and has garnered considerable evidence for its efficacy. In this chapter, we describe and discuss the origins and history of DBT, as well as the efforts to disseminate and adapt this treatment, along with the influence of this work on awareness and care of people with BPD and related problems.

http://dx.doi.org/10.1037/0000188-002
Dialectical Behavior Therapy, by A. L. Chapman and K. L. Dixon-Gordon
Copyright © 2020 by the American Psychological Association. All rights reserved.

THE ORIGINS OF DBT

A combination of lived experience, science and theory, and clinical trials and tribulations informed Dr. Marsha Linehan's development of DBT. In her youth, Marsha (because we know her well, we often refer to Marsha Linehan as "Marsha" rather than "Linehan" throughout this book) experienced personal struggles with severe mental illness, including suicidal behavior and other difficulties, and she spent considerable time in inpatient psychiatric facilities. A brilliant, compassionate, and creative woman, Marsha persisted and climbed her way "out of hell" through a combination of treatment and spiritual practice. She resolved to go back in and bring others like her out of hell. Her mission was to find the people who were suffering the most and help them build lives worth living. Marsha reasoned that the most intensely suffering members of the mental health community were those who had tried many times to end their own lives. Therefore, she set out on a journey to develop an effective treatment for highly suicidal clients with complex mental health concerns.

The first leg of this journey involved gathering clinical and empirical wisdom wherever it could be found. Marsha's graduate training was not originally in clinical psychology, but rather, in social psychology. She realized she needed to learn to do stellar research to help long-suffering clients learn to build lives worth living. At the time, she was advised to consider pursuing a degree in social psychology. Social psychologists are incredibly careful and creative with research design and often have benefited from not having to focus on clinical populations, who are complex and hard to recruit and retain in research. Moreover, therapy is at least, in part, a process of social influence. Where better to learn key principles of social influence than from social psychology? Indeed, some of the key interventions in DBT derive largely from research on social influence, particularly the commitment strategies (Linehan, 1993a), discussed in Chapter 3.

It was in her postdoctoral studies in the early 1970s that Marsha dove into clinical psychology, and she had some catching up to do. She has often described her postdoctoral fellowship with Drs. Gerald Davison and Marvin Goldfried at the State University of New York at Stony Brook as pivotal in her development as a clinician and her understanding of core principles of behavior change as they apply to real-world clinical work. Marsha subsequently began her position at the University of Washington (UW), where she continued her work in the fertile intellectual terrain of luminaries developing innovative and influential theories and treatments for problems such as alcohol and substance use (e.g., Alan Marlatt), and couple discord (e.g., John Gottman and Neil Jacobson), among others. She has credited many of these individuals, along with many other colleagues as well as her early graduate students and fellows, for influencing her thinking on DBT (Linehan, 1993a).

The next leg of the journey was to find intensely suffering people, bring them to UW, and begin the arduous, trial-by-fire process of figuring out how to help them. To do this, Linehan developed a center for the development and evaluation of treatments, the Behavioral Research and Therapy Clinics (BRTC) at UW, staffed by herself and her trainees, fellows, and graduate students. Over the ensuing years, BRTC became a fertile center for the training of students and other professionals in the treatment of complex clients. Marsha sought the most complex, suffering, and suicidal clients she could find, often exclaiming that she aimed to find the most "super-duper suicidal clients" and use empirically supported approaches to help them.

The Trials and Tribulations of CBT With Highly Suicidal, Complex Clients

Given the high risk nature of this population, it was critical to develop treatment with a strong empirical foundation. This was not a group of clients with which to roll the dice and use unproven techniques. As she often has claimed, Marsha plundered the best available treatment approaches and manuals, and from these she garnered key interventions and principles to use with long-suffering, suicidal clients. Existing interventions with empirical support largely involved cognitive and behavioral therapy approaches, including skills training, contingency management, exposure and related procedures (e.g., systematic desensitization), and cognitive restructuring. These cognitive and behavioral strategies (henceforth referred to as CBT) already had amassed considerable evidence for various anxiety and mood disorders, but little research had directly addressed (or even included) clients who were suicidal. Notwithstanding, CBT was a good place to start.

Marsha and her students and fellows quickly learned, however, that standard CBT as it existed in the 1970s and 1980s was woefully inadequate for the clients she was trying to help. At the time, Marsha did not realize that many of the clients she was helping met criteria for BPD, the hallmark features of which included a combination of interpersonal/relational disturbance, impulsivity, and affective dysregulation (Skodol et al., 2002; Trull, Tomko, Brown, & Scheiderer, 2010). Many of these clients experienced extremely painful and intense emotions, did not have the skills to understand or manage them, and had extensive histories of invalidation and sometimes abuse or trauma. They had no idea how to navigate healthy relationships in their daily lives or in therapy. The existing mantra of CBT was that to get better, clients needed to learn new coping skills and change their thinking and behavior. Marsha's clients experienced this message as invalidating and as an overly simplistic prescription to "cure" their complex and long-standing suffering.

Clients became disillusioned with therapy, felt emotionally distraught, and had difficulty benefitting from change-oriented interventions. Experiencing heightened emotional arousal (a common reaction to invalidation) that interfered with their ability to think and to solve their problems, her clients had difficulty learning anything new in therapy. This was a significant barrier to progress, as CBT (like DBT) is a learning-oriented therapy, where the aim is for the client to learn new thinking and behavioral patterns and skills. Clients were effectively blinded by the invalidating context of therapy, unable to see their way forward.

Therapy also seemed to be off target much of the time. No matter which direction Marsha went with therapy, her clients often conveyed that it was the wrong direction. When Marsha identified a problem to work on (e.g., substance use), the client would say it's the wrong problem, so she tried to switch gears and go with the problem the client wanted to work on (e.g., relationships). Then the client would change her mind, want to work on something else, or shut down. When she tried to tackle as many of the client's problems as she could at once, she and her clients felt overwhelmed, and the clients often felt blamed and misunderstood.

So, Marsha switched tactics. She tried to simply listen, accept, and understand the client's experience. This strategy backfired as well. Simply listening and accepting was like a forest ranger saying to a person trapped in quicksand, "Boy, it looks hard to get out of there. Look, you're sinking even deeper! That must be awful." When Marsha moved toward change, the client wanted more acceptance, and when she moved toward acceptance, the client wanted more change. Therapy was like trying to balance oneself on a teeter totter with a partner who keeps moving back and forth.

DBT, Acceptance, and Zen Practice

Marsha knew she needed to find a way to balance acceptance of clients' history, thoughts, feelings, and circumstances with the problem-solving needed to help them develop lives worth living. As change-based interventions were abundantly available in CBT, to gain a deeper understanding of acceptance, she sought guidance from the practice of Zen. Despite its spiritual history, which had the potential to deter some clients and clinicians, Zen was appealing in its simplicity, its focus on the concrete experience of the here and now, and its relative absence of constructs. Indeed, Marsha often has told a story wherein she kept getting caught up in ideas and concepts during her Zen practice, such as the meaning of the practice and all of the suffering she was experiencing, and so forth. In response, her Zen master would exclaim, "Concepts, Marsha! Concepts!" The practice of Zen is deceptively simple: attending to and experiencing the sensations of the moment, letting go of judgments and attachment (i.e., without clinging to a desired state of reality; Suzuki, 1970, 2011). To learn more about Zen practice, Marsha spent months at Shasta Abbey in California and began working with Zen masters (Willigus Jaeger) in Germany and later in Arizona (Fr. Pat Hawk, Roshi), attending retreats to gain personal experience with the ins and outs and trials and tribulations of Zen practice.

Zen practice is rigorous practice in acceptance. Sitting hour after hour on a cushion or chair attending to one's breath or some other point of focus is intensive practice in acceptance of all sorts of experiences— pains; limbs that have fallen asleep; distressing thoughts, memories, and images; and desires and urges to move, talk, eat, drink, and do pretty much anything but sit on a cushion and experience all of this. Zen retreats are arduous, with set schedules and routines, often starting before 5 o'clock each morning and ending late in the evening. To survive and benefit from these experiences, students must let go of their attachment to what they want (e.g., when and what they want to eat; what type of schedule they want to have; when to work, relax, or sleep; and so on). Through this experience, Marsha believed she had found exactly what her clients needed: to take the radical step of completely accepting the reality of the present moment, and for some, the reality of unbearable past moments.

Although Marsha was heavily influenced by her Zen practice, she also noticed the parallels between many tenets of Zen and other spiritual practices around the world. She started to work closely with her Zen teachers to filter out most of the religious connotations, rituals, and traditions that some clients or clinicians may object to and distilled the practice of Zen into concrete behavioral skills that therapists can teach their clients. These efforts contributed to a treatment that is acceptable and aligned with diverse cultural and religious contexts. There were a few bumps in the road, however, such as when she tried to have her clients remove their shoes or sit and meditate, and they all refused. Another time, she instructed her clients in a slow walking meditation and had walked a fair distance only to turn around and realize she was the only one walking! Notwithstanding, when Marsha framed mindful practice as a set of concrete behavioral skills (largely involving nonjudgmental attention to and participation in present-moment experience) that anyone can do, clients responded well and found the skills helpful. This work formed the foundation of the core DBT mindfulness skills, along with reality acceptance skills in the distress tolerance skills module (Linehan, 1993b, 2015a, 2015b). It was not sufficient, however, to simply teach clients how to accept themselves and their experiences in the present moment.

Therapists also needed to accept their clients and convey genuine understanding and acceptance. The primary way for therapists to do this in DBT is by validating clients' experiences, or conveying that the client's responses are understandable (Linehan, 1993a, 1997). Validation, reflective listening, and empathy have long been core features of most psychosocial treatments, including the 1970s and 1980s version of CBT that formed the backbone of DBT. It would be impossible to help a client with a phobia, posttraumatic stress disorder (PTSD), or depression, for example, without understanding and accurately reflecting the client's emotions and behaviors and conveying that these responses are understandable on some level. Validation, however, had yet to be clearly operationalized and systematized in CBT. Linehan realized that if her treatment were to be effectively disseminated to a range of clinicians, she would need to operationalize the therapist behaviors that fall within the category of validation so that clinicians can learn these behaviors, much like clients learn behavioral skills in treatment. Described in Linehan (1993a) and further updated and elaborated in Linehan (1997), DBT includes seven forms or levels of validation, all involving specific ways to convey understanding and acceptance of the client. We discuss and illustrate these forms of validation later in Chapter 3.

DBT as a Dialectical Treatment

Once acceptance and change-oriented interventions were clearly operationalized and incorporated into her treatment, Marsha and her students and trainees needed to find a way to effectively balance acceptance and change-oriented strategies in therapy sessions with complex clients. In her experiences with clients who vacillate between wanting or needing acceptance and wanting or needing change, Linehan realized that therapy with complex clients is often a *dialectical* process. A dialectical world view holds that reality consists of opposites, that there is tension between these opposites, and that change occurs when opposites balance and synthesize. Often associated with Marxism, dialectics has been present in one form or another for many centuries (Bopp & Weeks, 1984; Kaminstein, 1987) and is often used to describe a process of persuasion. In the dialectical process of persuasion, a thesis (e.g., "The sun is good for you") generates an antithesis ("The sun is bad for you"), and a synthesis of thesis and antithesis contains the elements of truth inherent in both positions ("The sun provides Vitamin D, and excessive sun exposure can cause skin cancer"). In DBT, the primary opposites to be synthesized are acceptance and change. Intensely suffering, suicidal clients need to both accept and change their lives to achieve a life worth living.

Long-suffering suicidal clients' lives often are so unbearable as to be experienced as not worth living. The experience can be much like a severely burned client experiencing chronic, unrelenting pain and envisioning a future consisting of much of the same. It would be hard to imagine how such a life could be worth living. Clients, understandably, have tremendous difficulty accepting things as they are and are often drawn to what they perceive as the escape hatch (suicide). Much of the research on the functions, motivations, and reasons for suicide has suggested that the vast majority of people report attempting suicide to escape emotional pain (e.g., Brown, Comtois, & Linehan, 2002). For treatment to progress, the therapist must understand that clients experience their lives as so unbearable that death sometimes seems more attractive than life. Just as a client with severe burns or the diagnosis of a chronic illness must accept the current state of affairs before change (e.g., treatment) is possible, severely suicidal clients must learn to accept where they are before they can move forward.

To overcome their suffering, suicidal clients need to accept themselves, be accepted by their therapists, and take steps to change their lives. On the one hand, acceptance with no change would be like treating a severely burned client with empathetic listening. On the other hand, change in the absence of acceptance risks invalidating the client's pain or moving too quickly into a treatment causing further damage and suffering. Both of these options are imbalanced and ineffective.

Another imbalanced option would be to focus only on keeping the client alive. This is often the focus of family members, loved ones, and treatment providers when faced with severe suicide risk. Their radars are tightly calibrated to the signs of suicide risk, and their aim (understandably) is to keep the client "safe." When helping suicidal clients, it can be tempting to remain focused on crisis and suicide risk management, but this is much like trying to help the client establish a life worth living on life support. This is, of course, understandable. A dead client can't develop a life worth living. At the same time, establishing a life worth living (by solving the problems generating misery and moving toward meaningful goals) is the only way to stay alive.

The central paradox and dialectic in DBT is that clients need to stay alive to develop a life worth living, and they need to develop a life worth living to stay alive. Resolving this paradox is an ongoing process throughout treatment. Because the stakes are sometimes so high (literally life and death), for the therapist, entering into and engaging with the dialectic of acceptance and change can be much like walking a tightrope. To stay balanced, Marsha developed and incorporated several strategies into a treatment that seeks to balance acceptance and change in terms of therapeutic interventions (e.g., validation vs. change-oriented techniques like skills training, exposure, contingency management, and cognitive therapy), style (e.g., irreverence vs. reciprocity, warmth, and responsiveness), and behavioral skills.

DBT as a Skills-Oriented Treatment

On the change end of the dialectic, Marsha realized that the complex clients she was treating often had not learned the behavioral skills or tools they needed to start piecing together a life worth living. The biosocial theory underlying DBT is a sociodevelopmental model proposing that the emotional, behavioral, and cognitive features of BPD reflect a disordered emotion regulation system, characterized by deficits in a range of behavioral skills. Within this framework, clients with BPD are considered to be temperamentally predisposed to *emotional vulnerability*, consisting of a low threshold for emotional activation, intense emotional responses, and delayed return to baseline emotional arousal. Additionally, in more recent iterations of the biosocial theory, a predisposition toward trait impulsivity is considered a key vulnerability factor for the development of BPD (Crowell, Beauchaine, & Linehan, 2009; 2014). The sociodevelopmental aspect of the biosocial theory consists of the invalidating environment. An *invalidating environment* consistently rejects or criticizes the individual's communication of emotions and thoughts, oversimplifies the ease of solving difficult or upsetting problems, and intermittently reinforces emotional escalation. Within this framework, emotional vulnerability transacts with an invalidating environment to influence the development of core BPD features. The emotionally vulnerable child elicits invalidating behaviors from caregivers, who are often bereft of the skills to manage their own emotions or those of the child. Invalidation exacerbates emotional vulnerability, and the child fails to learn key skills to understand and regulate emotions. Within DBT, this deficit in emotion regulation capacities is considered a core problem influencing the other behavioral and relational difficulties often observed among those with BPD. The individual with BPD lacks the skills to understand or regulate emotions; manage interpersonal conflict and effectively communicate needs, concerns, or fears within relationships; tolerate emotional distress without acting on impulse and exacerbating already stressful situations (e.g., self-injuring, attempting or threatening suicide); and disengage from emotionally evocative events and responses. DBT, therefore, includes a weekly skills training group to address these key skill deficits. This skills training is embedded in a treatment program that includes individual therapy to sustain motivation throughout this complex treatment program and to directly target maladaptive forms of coping such as self-injury. Taken together, behavioral principles, dialectical theory, and the biosocial model informed a comprehensive treatment program for suicidal and self-injuring individuals.

THE EVOLUTION AND DISSEMINATION OF DBT

Perhaps the first clear words of hope for often maligned and stigmatized clients with BPD began to appear in academic publications around the end of the 1980s.[1] The first publications on DBT appeared in 1987, with the seminal article appearing in the *Journal of Personality Disorders*, describing the theory and practice of this emerging treatment (Linehan, 1987a), followed by another article on this topic that same year (Linehan, 1987b). Meanwhile, at the BRTC, Marsha was wrapping up the first randomized controlled trial (RCT) of DBT, focused on suicidal women with BPD. Although her interest always had been in treatment for suicidal women, as mentioned, many of her clients also met criteria for BPD. Ironically, grant funding at the time was easier to attain for treatment studies attached to a psychiatric diagnosis (e.g., BPD) rather than a behavioral (and life or death) problem such as suicide. Notwithstanding, the key characteristics of clients with BPD heavily influenced both the theory and practice of this developing treatment; thus, focusing on BPD and suicide was a good synthesis.

The first RCT on DBT was published in *Archives of General Psychiatry* in 1991 (Linehan, Armstrong, Suarez, Allmon, & Heard, 1991), consisting of a study comparing 12 months of DBT to treatment as usual (TAU) for 44 parasuicidal women with BPD. Findings indicated that compared with TAU clients, DBT clients engaged in fewer parasuicide acts (including both suicide attempts and nonsuicidal self-injury) and had lower medical severity of parasuicide acts, had fewer psychiatric inclient days, and were less likely to drop out of treatment. These findings were striking and created ripples in the field, contradicting common lore that persons with BPD were intractable and untreatable, and indicating that the most severe and problematic behaviors occurring among those with BPD (suicidal

---

[1] This is not to disregard the work by Otto F. Kernberg, John F. Clarkin, and others in the development of a psychodynamic approach to BPD, which began in the mid-1970s and culminated in perhaps the first volume blending theory and practice with a focus on BPD (and narcissistic personality disorder), from an object relations viewpoint (Kernberg, 1984). Since then, this approach has evolved into transference-focused psychotherapy and has demonstrated promising evidence (Doering et al., 2010; Giesen-Bloo et al., 2006). Likewise, general psychiatric management has demonstrated itself to be a useful treatment for BPD (Gunderson & Links, 2014; Links, Ross, & Gunderson, 2015; McMain, Guimond, Streiner, Cardish, & Links, 2012).

and self-injurious behavior) can be treated. Further, later findings based on a cost analysis of DBT from the original trial suggested that, although comprehensive, DBT was less costly than treatment as usual. The cost savings primarily came from a reduced rate of psychiatric hospitalization in DBT. Therefore, not only did treatment work, but it was cost-efficient and reduced the revolving door of hospitalization and its detrimental effects on client functioning and well-being. Following the landmark Linehan et al. (1991) trial, a number of secondary publications emerging from this first trial appeared over the next few years (Linehan & Heard, 1993; Linehan, Heard, & Armstrong, 1993; Linehan, Tutek, Heard, & Armstrong, 1994; Shearin & Linehan, 1992, among others). Some of these studies showed beneficial effects of DBT on interpersonal outcomes (Linehan et al., 1994) as well as sustained effects over a 12-month follow-up period (Linehan et al., 1993).

Dissemination of DBT

Riding the wave of these positive findings, the early 1990s saw key efforts to begin to disseminate this promising treatment. In 1993, Guilford Press published what became the primary clinician manual or text on DBT, *Cognitive Behavior Therapy of Borderline Personality Disorder* (Linehan, 1993a), along with the manual for the skills training component of DBT, *Skills Training Manual for Treating Borderline Personality Disorder* (Linehan, 1993b). Although the actual name of the treatment was DBT, the publisher was concerned that including "dialectical" in the title would reduce the appeal of the original text among clinicians who may be unfamiliar with the concept of dialectics. Clinicians, however, were well aware of the growing popularity and empirical evidence for CBT; thus, the notion that a CBT approach had promise in the treatment of BPD had widespread appeal. Many years later, these manuals remain bestsellers, having been published in several languages.

The publication of a treatment manual is no guarantee of the uptake of a new treatment or of clinician fidelity to the manual. Recognizing the need to disseminate this multifaceted, nuanced treatment to front-line clinicians, Marsha and colleagues developed a training organization with the mission to facilitate the dissemination of DBT to the clinicians treating complex clients in need of evidence-based care. Ideally, training in DBT would also help clinicians to overcome their misconceptions, judgments, and reluctance to treat suicidal people with BPD. Marsha's new training organization originally was called the Linehan Training Group, then the Behavioral Technology Transfer Group, and now Behavioral Tech, LLC.

The first major training in DBT occurred in 1993, consisting of an "intensive" workshop provided by Marsha and three of her graduate students: Heidi Heard, Henry Schmidt, and Darren Tutek. The intensive training consisted of an initial 5 days of training, typically starting at 8 a.m. and running well into the evening, followed by a second 5-day training occurring about six months later. Part 1 of the first intensive DBT training occurred over 5 days at Duke University Medical Centre from March 24 to 28, 1993, with Part 2 occurring at New York Hospital, Westchester Division, in White Plains, New York from September 24 to 28, 1993.

Some of the attendees of this original two-part training began the first standard DBT programs outside of the BRTC or were instrumental in the development of organizations focused on DBT or BPD. Dr. Clive Robins and Dr. Lindsey Tweed, for example, started the Duke DBT program, which is still operating at Duke University Medical Center, offering treatment as well as training for psychology interns and psychiatry residents. Dr. Charles Swenson was already offering an inpatient DBT program when he attended the intensive training and has continued to provide DBT as well as consultation and training over the years. In 1996, Dr. Swenson helped to found and chaired the first meeting of the International Society for the Improvement and Teaching of DBT (ISITDBT; https://www.isitdbt.net), the first international organization devoted to the study and teaching of DBT. Dr. Perry Hoffman, who also attended the first training, later founded the National Education Alliance for BPD (NEA-BPD; https://www.borderlinepersonalitydisorder.com), an organization devoted to education and outreach for BPD, with an emphasis on programs to support those with BPD and their families and loved ones.

Since the original intensive training, the scope and reach of DBT training has broadened considerably. Behavioral Tech, LLC and its predecessors have provided workshop training to over 55,000 clinicians, including over 1,400 teams that have received intensive training. Further, these trainings have occurred in more than 15 countries. Taking into account other organizations offering DBT training, it is likely that 60,000 to 70,000 clinicians have received in-person DBT training workshops. Many others have read the DBT manuals or other DBT books, watched webinars or taken online courses.

DBT has been disseminated and implemented in many countries around the world. Currently, more than 30 countries have comprehensive DBT programs, and many others have developing programs or programs offering components of DBT. There are training organizations offering DBT training in Canada, the United States, the United Kingdom, Germany, Argentina, and New Zealand, among other countries. When DBT training began in the early 1990s, computer-based learning often was restricted to activities such as typing (one of us owes a lot to Mavis Beacon in this regard!); however, over the past several years, online training has ballooned, and online DBT training is beginning to keep pace. Training organizations have adapted and developed online training in various components of DBT (e.g., chain analysis, validation, exposure-based interventions, DBT skills training, and more recently, comprehensive online training in DBT [see https://behavioraltech.org/training/online-training-courses-2/]). Just as it is not always clear how well in-person training translates into changes in practice, whether clinicians can actually learn DBT through online learning methods is an important empirical question.

The reach of DBT training and implementation has expanded into a variety of practice settings, often influencing practice standards. In Canada, for example, DBT has become an integral component of training for psychiatry residents, and many predoctoral clinical psychology internship training programs offer significant DBT rotations. There has been significant interest in DBT in correctional and forensic settings, given that inmates often show elevated rates of BPD, suicidality, self-injury, and various harmful forms of impulsivity (Chapman & Cellucci, 2007; Chapman & Ivanoff, 2018; Chapman, Specht, & Collucci, 2005; see also Sheppard, Layden, Turner, & Chapman, 2018, for a review of the research on DBT in forensic and correctional settings). Nearly all of the women's correctional institutions in Canada, for example, have DBT-oriented programs, and a growing number of institutions in the United States, Europe, and elsewhere offer DBT to forensic and correctional populations. In one project we are involved in, the entire state of South Dakota is engaged in a multiyear, widespread implementation of DBT in corrections and community mental health. The primary aims of this implementation are (a) to help inmates transition smoothly into evidence-based care in the community and (b) for community mental health clients to improve their lives and avoid adverse outcomes, such as incarceration, repeated hospitalization, and so forth.

To address the need for clients to know whether the DBT they are receiving meets reasonable standards and to increase transparency and encourage the coverage of DBT by insurers and other payers, Marsha and her colleagues founded the DBT Linehan Board of Certification and Accreditation (https://dbt-lbc.org) in 2014 and certified the first cohort of clinicians in 2015. This organization provides certification for individuals in DBT (including DBT more broadly and group skills training specifically) as well as accreditation for programs offering DBT. The development of certification and accreditation by the founder of the treatment is an important step in ensuring consumer awareness of the likely quality of their DBT services. Many times, we have seen clients who have said, "DBT doesn't work. I did it a few years ago." Upon further assessment, it becomes clear that the client did not actually receive DBT or just received elements of DBT, or that even those elements did not appear to be provided with fidelity to the DBT model. Although certification and accreditation are perhaps most relevant to countries with a multiple payer/insurance-based healthcare system, the benefit of knowing that your clinician has met some minimal standard for DBT practice is applicable to any client seeking DBT.

Possible Effects of DBT on Awareness and Research on BPD

In addition to expansion in the dissemination of DBT, research on and awareness of BPD has seen somewhat of a renaissance since the publication of the initial RCT and DBT treatment manuals. Preceding 1993, publications with "borderline personality disorder" in the title numbered around 200 at most in any given year, whereas by the end of 2017, 500 to 700 publications per year was the norm. There is no way to know whether this increase is attributable to the dissemination of DBT; however, DBT likely has had a significant influence on the research on BPD. The biosocial theory (Linehan, 1993a) was the first theory of BPD to make emotion dysregulation a central factor underlying the disorder. Perhaps as a result, many lines of productive research have examined the characteristics and treatment of emotion dysregulation in BPD using a variety of methods (e.g., self-report, ecological momentary assessment, laboratory manipulations, neuroimaging studies; see Goodman et al., 2014; Soler et al., 2012, for some examples of this research; see also Carpenter & Trull, 2013; Chapman, 2019; Dixon-Gordon, Weiss, et al., 2015, 2017; Hope & Chapman, 2019; Santangelo, Bohus, & Ebner-Priemer, 2014, for recent chapters and articles reviewing the issue of emotion dysregulation in BPD). We believe that the widespread dissemination and popularity of DBT has at least influenced this increased interest in BPD and related problems (e.g., self-injury, suicidal behavior), resulting in innovative research that will ultimately improve how we help people with these difficulties.

Additionally, over the past 20 years, educational efforts and organizations geared toward raising awareness of BPD have developed, with notable examples including NEA–BPD (mentioned previously) and Tara4BPD (an organization focused on support for family members). Further, the U.S. House of Representatives passed (by a vote of 414 to 0) House Resolution 1005 to make May BPD Awareness Month. Self-help and other books on BPD from both professional and personal perspectives have expanded in recent years, and websites have been developed to raise awareness of BPD and effective coping skills for people with BPD and related problems. Again, we can't fully attribute these important developments to the emergence of DBT; however, we believe the evidence for DBT, along with this treatment's emphasis on nonpejorative, non-judgmental ways of understanding people with BPD and its widespread popularity have stimulated widespread interest in BPD.

Growing Research, Extensions and Adaptations of DBT

Returning now to the growing research on DBT, following the publication of the DBT treatment manuals, research on DBT proliferated, and adaptations began to emerge in the literature. In the 1990s, there were approximately one to 16 publications per year with "DBT" or "dialectical behavior therapy" in their titles (based on a search conducted on August 20, 2018), in 2000 to 2010, the range was 15 to 92 per year, and since 2010, the range has been 72 to nearly 150 per year. When the original treatment manuals were published, there was only one existing RCT examining the efficacy of DBT, whereas to date, there have been over 30 published RCTs examining standard, comprehensive DBT, and over 20 RCTs examining DBT skills training. Although these numbers may not sound tremendously high, the majority of studies have included clients who are very difficult to recruit and retain (e.g., those with BPD, other severe or co-occurring disorders, substance use problems) and have been costly and resource-intensive to implement (often requiring considerable grant funding in a climate of funding scarcity).

Early studies of DBT focused primarily on clients with BPD and related difficulties, but in the later 1990s, DBT expanded into different realms. One of the first extensions and adaptations of DBT focused on clients with substance use disorders (SUDs). A few factors likely influenced the expansion of DBT into the realm of SUDs. First, many highly suicidal clients with BPD also met criteria for an SUD (up to two thirds), with substance use problems interfering with therapy and quality-of-life goals. Second, the funding climate in the 1990s was more fertile for grants focused on substance use problems compared with personality disorders. With funding from the National Institutes of Drug Addiction, Marsha and her colleagues, therefore, began to examine the efficacy of standard DBT for substance using clients with BPD (Linehan et al., 1999, 2002).

This work resulted in what was perhaps the first systematic attempt to adapt standard DBT to a specific population, with adaptations largely including the monitoring of substance use via the DBT diary card (and regular urinalysis, concurrent drug replacement pharmacotherapy, and skills focused on substance use difficulties). The adapted skills have been used in various studies of DBT for substance using clients but were not published in a treatment manual until the publication of the second edition of the *Dialectical Behavior Therapy Skills Training Manual* in 2015 (Linehan, 2015b).

In the late 1990s and early 2000s, the first published RCTs conducted outside the BRTC began to appear. The first published RCT conducted outside of the BRTC included a small study of 6 months of DBT for women veterans with BPD ($N = 20$; Koons et al., 2001), conducted through the Durham VA Hospital, in collaboration with investigators at Duke University Medical Center. Findings suggested that DBT had promise for the reduction of parasuicidal acts (an aggregate category including both nonsuicidal self-injury and suicide attempts), anger, and dissociation in this population. This study was noteworthy, in that it was also the first to examine a briefer version of DBT (6 months). The need for briefer and more efficient forms of DBT is underscored many years later by the challenges inherent in implementing a comprehensive, long-term treatment into resource-strapped practice settings, the proliferation of studies examining DBT skills training alone for various mental health problems (Valentine, Bankoff, Poulin, Reidler, & Pantalone, 2015), and efforts underway to examine the efficacy and cost-effectiveness of briefer forms of comprehensive DBT (McMain et al., 2018).

Among the first studies of an adapted version of DBT outside of the BRTC was a nonrandomized trial published by Rathus and Miller (2002), comparing DBT for adolescents, or DBT-A ($n = 29$) to supportive psychodynamic therapy ($n = 82$). Findings were promising, with DBT-A clients having fewer psychiatric hospitalizations and a lower dropout rate than the clients in the control condition. The adaptations incorporated into DBT-A included modifications to the DBT skills, the length and composition of group skills training (including caregivers in the group), and other adaptations to make the treatment more acceptable for adolescents.

This early work generated considerable enthusiasm for the application of DBT to adolescents, who often seem to have borderline tendencies even when they do not meet criteria for any specific disorder. Until recently, however, the reach of DBT-A probably exceeded its grasp, as much of the dissemination of this adaptation predated the first RCTs (discussed further in Chapter 4), which indeed have strongly supported the efficacy of DBT-A (McCauley et al., 2018; Mehlum et al., 2014, 2016). A clinician guide (Miller, Rathus, & Linehan, 2017) and a skills training manual (Rathus & Miller, 2014) have since been published, outlining the DBT-A approach.

Other adaptations of DBT have emerged over the past couple of decades. DBT approaches have been adapted and investigated for inmates in correctional and forensic settings (as mentioned earlier; Ivanoff & Marotta, 2019), persons with eating disorders (Bankoff, Karpel, Forbes, & Pantalone, 2012), college students (Chugani, Ghali, & Brunner, 2013; Uliaszek, Rashid, Williams, & Gulamani, 2016), children (Perepletchikova et al., 2011, 2017), older adults with depression and personality disorders (Lynch, Morse, Mendelson, & Robins, 2003), among others, and emerging work is being done with bipolar clients and other populations (Goldstein et al., 2015). We summarize much of this work in Chapter 4.

Recent work has examined how to incorporate evidence-based treatment for PTSD into DBT for suicidal clients with BPD. Harned and colleagues (Harned, Korslund, Foa, & Linehan, 2014) have incorporated several adaptations to standard DBT, including two weekly individual therapy sessions (one standard individual therapy session and another exposure therapy session) in addition to skills group, as well as a number of contingencies and strategies to ensure that prolonged exposure for PTSD is conducted safely and effectively with this high risk population (we discuss some of the findings on this approach in Chapter 4). This work is particularly noteworthy given the high rates of past abuse, trauma, and current PTSD among persons with BPD (50%; Harned, Rizvi, & Linehan, 2010; Zanarini, Frankenburg, Hennen, Reich, & Silk, 2004), the desire among clients to receive help for symptoms related to past trauma, and the need to undertake this difficult work without increasing clients' suicide risk.

Although the majority of the applications and adaptations of DBT have focused on client populations with problems related to emotion dysregulation, a new treatment has been developed and tested that addresses excessive self-control or overcontrol. Radically Open DBT (RO-DBT; Lynch, 2018) grew from efforts to apply standard DBT to depressed older adults with personality disorders (Lynch et al., 2007; Lynch et al., 2003;). Lynch and his colleagues discovered that a subset of these clients did not fit the common emotionally intense and dysregulated profile that DBT addressed so effectively. Instead, these clients were constricted in their emotion expression (and sometimes, experience), had strong inhibitory control (i.e., the ability to curtail or inhibit behavior and avoid impulsive behavior, self-discipline, self-regulation), and did not resonate with the therapeutic rationale (often advanced in standard DBT) that they needed to learn how to understand and manage their strong emotions. This group of "overcontrolled" clients appeared to be on the opposite pole of many of the BPD clients often seen in DBT. Perhaps resulting from their excessive control over emotional expression, over-controlled clients often had difficulty establishing emotionally intimate relationships and often were lonely and disconnected from others. In contrast to standard DBT, which posits emotion dysregulation as the core problem for BPD and similar problems characterized by insufficient regulatory control, RO-DBT contends that emotional loneliness secondary to social signalling deficits represents the core problem for disorders of overcontrol (Lynch, 2018). RO-DBT includes a biosocial model of the development of over-controlled characteristics, modified skills (e.g., a module focused on "radical openness") and individual therapy strategies, as well as changes to the stylistic (therapist manner and demeanor) aspects of therapy, and an emphasis on social signalling, or the ways in which clients communicate their thoughts, emotions, and preferences to others. RO-DBT differs enough from standard DBT to be considered a new treatment but also retains some of the core elements of DBT (a dialectical and biosocial theory, roots in behavioral principles, and some of the core DBT skills). Preliminary evidence suggests that RO-DBT has promise in the treatment of disorders characterized by emotional overcontrol (e.g., anorexia—Lynch et al., 2013; refractory depression—Lynch et al., 2018, 2019).

At present, given the scope and variability of the existing applications and extensions of DBT and the growing empirical support for them, it is probably safe to say that, much like CBT, DBT has become a treatment paradigm rather than a specific treatment for a particular disorder. DBT has many forms but contains unifying principles that are unique to DBT and particularly helpful for complex, multidiagnostic clients primarily characterized by emotion regulation problems, and in the case of RO-DBT, emotion overregulation.

CONCLUSION

The beginnings of DBT can be traced back to the mental health struggles experienced by the treatment developer, Dr. Marsha Linehan, earlier in her life, as well as her diligent efforts to apply evidence-based principles to the care of complex clients. Her personal experiences inspired her to find a way to help clients who were suffering so severely that they had attempted, often many times, to end their own lives. Through formative personal and professional experiences, Marsha began to piece together a treatment with roots in evidence-based CBT, Zen practice, and an overarching dialectical framework guiding therapists to balance and synthesize acceptance and change. The resulting treatment, DBT, consists of a combination of individual therapy, skills training, telephone consultation (often referred to as phone coaching) to help clients apply therapy to their everyday lives and challenges, and a consultation team to maintain dialectical balance and therapist effectiveness and motivation. Since the publications of the first articles and early studies with promising findings, the field of DBT has flourished, resulting in a substantial body of research, systematic efforts to disseminate and implement this treatment around the world, and extensions and adaptations of DBT to new populations. At present, DBT is best conceptualized as a treatment paradigm with key principles and strategies that can be flexibly applied across different populations and settings, well beyond where DBT began, with the outpatient treatment of suicidal individuals with BPD.

3

Theory

In this chapter, we discuss the theoretical underpinnings of dialectical behavior therapy (DBT). As with other psychological treatments, theory forms the foundation of DBT. Theory helps provide a coherent story regarding why people do what they do, how problem areas develop, and what to do to ameliorate those problems (Laska & Wampold, 2014; Norcross & Prochaska, 2003; Wampold, 2019). Theory also helps to guide the therapist's case conceptualization. In the case of DBT, which is a behavioral treatment based on the notion that emotion dysregulation is central to many of the difficulties experienced by persons with borderline personality disorder (BPD), case conceptualization tends to emphasize the functions of and role of emotions in client behavior. Theory also provides the therapist and client with a common understanding of the client's problems and goals and a common language to describe this understanding. Ideally, if the client understands their problems in a

http://dx.doi.org/10.1037/0000188-003
Dialectical Behavior Therapy, by A. L. Chapman and K. L. Dixon-Gordon

similar way to the therapist, they will be able to use this understanding to guide their continued use of skills and strategies well beyond therapy.

The theoretical underpinnings of DBT are nonpejorative and non-judgmental, directly countering the long-standing legacy of stigmatizing views of BPD and related problems. Prior to the emergence of DBT, it was widely believed that personality disorders (PDs) simply were not amenable to change (Lewis & Appleby, 1988). Indeed, individuals with PDs historically were thought of as manipulative and annoying, and the defining symptoms of PDs were considered deliberate attempts to get attention (Lewis & Appleby, 1988). We have worked in settings where "Axis II" and "characterological" were thrown out whenever a client was particularly challenging to treat or to get along with. Compounding this problem, work with chronically suicidal clients has been described as a key ingredient in the recipe for burnout (Fox & Cooper, 1998), let alone work with chronically suicidal clients with a PD characterized by inter-personal difficulties that often manifest in therapy. Even more recently, reviews of the literature suggest that many negative views of BPD persist among medical professionals (Ross & Goldner, 2009). The notions that clients with BPD are manipulative, resistant, or engage in problematic behaviors on purpose can further dissuade clinicians from working with this population and lead to ineffective care.

Pushing against this tide, the theory underlying DBT purports that persons with BPD (and other mental health problems) have under-standably developed maladaptive ways to meet their needs through a complex transaction of environment and biology. Many behaviors that create long-term problems for clients with BPD or that stress out clinicians are either natural consequences of a dysregulated emotional system or function to regulate dysregulated emotions (Linehan, 1993a). Further, from a DBT perspective, the best way to help people with BPD is to balance compassionate understanding and acceptance with a steady focus on change, using core, evidence-based behavioral and cognitive behavioral principles. Accordingly, the structure, goals, and focus of DBT emphasize the clear and precise prioritization and target-ing of the client's presenting problems, the balancing of acceptance and change in terms of therapy style and strategies, and the building of key behavioral skills.

THEORY IN DBT

For the purposes of this book, and in considering the role of theory in different aspects of DBT, it can be helpful to think of theory in DBT on three key levels, ranging from broad to more specific (see Figure 3.1). Most broadly, on Level 1, is DBT's philosophical perspective on the nature of truth and reality, which in turn, influences the therapist's style and the timing and selection of intervention strategies. In DBT, this level consists of dialectical theory, the guiding philosophy about the nature of truth and reality that informs many aspects of DBT, as well as Zen theory and practice. On Level 2 is theory regarding the factors causing and maintaining human behavior (both adaptive and maladaptive). At this level, DBT is based on behavioral theory, particularly that of *social behaviorism* (Staats, 1975). Level 3 is more narrow and disorder specific, consisting of theory regarding the development and maintenance of the clinical

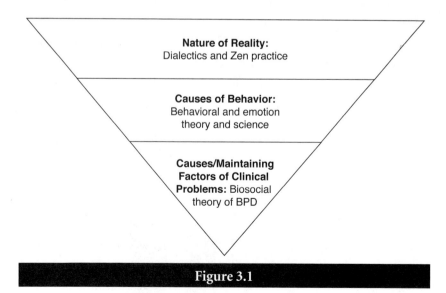

Figure 3.1

Levels of theory in dialectical behavior therapy.

problems that are the focus of DBT. This level consists of the biosocial theory of BPD (Crowell, Beauchaine, & Linehan, 2009; Linehan, 1993a), but as BPD is not the only focus of DBT, this level also includes biosocial theories of other relevant clinical problems (e.g., suicidality, self-injury, depression, substance use problems, and so forth). As the biosocial theory emphasizes the role of emotions and emotion regulation in BPD, basic emotion theory and science also influence theory at Level 3. Below, we discuss the key theoretical elements of DBT at all three levels and illustrate how they influence DBT practice.

THE NATURE OF REALITY: DIALECTICS AND ZEN

A dialectical philosophy (Marx & Engels, 1970) informs the balance of behavioral principles of change and Zen practices of acceptance in DBT. As described in Chapter 1, this volume, this innovation to the treatment arose in response to Marsha's impression of being on a teeter-totter with clients, constantly adjusting and bringing perceived opposites into a synthesis to help clients remain in balance (Linehan, 1993a). Dialectical philosophy infuses DBT in several ways. First, dialectics stresses the interrelated, holistic view that underlies DBT. This perspective acknowledges that individuals are embedded within and transact with systems, cultures, subcultures, and so forth. Second, dialectics suggests that reality consists of polar opposites, such as positive and negative charges, good and bad, right and wrong, and thesis and antithesis. There is tension between polar opposites because each lacks a critical element contained by the other, and reality changes when poles are balanced and synthesized. Applying this viewpoint to perspectives or positions, the idea is that truth exists in both thesis and antithesis, and each side is incomplete on its own, without the recognition of the truth in an opposing side. For instance, there is often function within the dysfunction among clients with BPD, as with self-injury, which is maladaptive in many ways but also functions to help clients bereft of coping skills to regulate overwhelming emotions. A synthesis of the notions that self-injury is dysfunctional and functional might be to help the client reduce or eliminate self-injury while teaching her new ways to cope with misery. The dialectical perspective results in a more complete and effective treatment by encouraging the clinician to seek the validity in seemingly opposing positions and to work with the client to find a synthesis. In turn, each synthesis can have its own polar opposite, forming a new dialectical tension to be resolved. Third, dialectical philosophy notes that reality, in its holistic, interconnected, and oppositional nature, is also subject to continuous change, whereby opposing forces arise and are synthesized, generating new opposing forces, and so on. Reality consists of a continual, dynamic interplay of opposing forces, and a synthesis in which polar positions are integrated leads to a more balanced, harmonious state or understanding of reality. The dialectical philosophy in DBT encourages therapists to continually move towards a more complete, balanced view of the client's problems and the solutions needed to overcome them. Thus, dialectical philosophy guides the therapist and client to continually examine what is missing from their current understanding of the problem.

Through a dialectical lens, many of the client's problems can be seen as dialectical dilemmas. In particular, one of the presenting problems seen in BPD is the failure to integrate opposing views (Linehan, 1993a). The goal in DBT is for both the therapist and client to recognize these opposing forces and work together to reconcile polarities to form a more balanced and flexible stance. In DBT, there is dialectical tension between the need to accept the client as is and its opposition, the desperate and urgent need to help the client make changes to improve their quality of life. Treatment addressing only one of these poles (acceptance or changing the client's life) is likely to be imbalanced and ineffective. The therapist focusing predominantly on the need for the client to change her thoughts or behavior may inadvertently invalidate the client's self-view or communicate that they are not acceptable the way they are. Conversely, only accepting the client and their life as it is would likely result in continued misery and suffering, as complex, chronically suffering clients must make changes to build lives worth living. Moreover, not helping the client change is like watching the client sink into quicksand and simply offering empathetic words (e.g., "It's scary to keep sinking deeper no matter what you do!"); the client is likely to feel invalidated and misunderstood. Furthermore, absent efforts to change, the client may think change is hopeless and that the therapist thinks the same.

Dialectical theory reminds the DBT therapist to keep at least a few key principles in mind:

- Maintain a dialectical worldview.
- Balance and synthesize positions, strategies, and styles.
- Accept natural change.

These principles help therapists maintain a dialectical stance throughout therapy and can help the therapist and the client become unstuck when polarization occurs. We often have turned to these principles when, for example, we have locked horns with clients, asserting the need for the client to commit to staying alive throughout therapy, while the client pushes back and says they can't or won't make such a commitment. Maintaining a dialectical stance and working through polarization can sometimes literally be a life-or-death proposition.

Maintaining a Dialectical Worldview

One key principle, perhaps the most important one, is for the therapist to maintain a dialectical worldview, as described previously. Maintaining the viewpoint that truth is both relative and absolute, that the universe is constantly changing, and that the therapist's aim is to recognize and help balance opposite forces arising in therapy, can be invaluable when difficulties arise. Along with this worldview is the notion that when polarization occurs, it is helpful to seek a synthesis. In the dilemma whereby the client and therapist are polarized around the commitment to stay alive during therapy (an essential commitment at the beginning of DBT; Linehan, 1993a), the dialectically oriented therapist recognizes that there is truth in both perspectives. From the therapist's perspective, the client must take suicide off the table to throw her efforts into building a life worth living. From the client's perspective, having suicide on the table as a possible escape from unbearable pain sometimes helps her bear such pain, just as knowing that chemotherapy will end one day can help a cancer client bear the accompanying illness and discomfort. Also, from the client's perspective, it might seem absurd to commit to staying alive when neither the therapist nor the client can foretell the future or ensure that the client's life will be worth living. Recognizing the inherent validity in both the client's and therapist's position helps the therapist validate the client's perspective and work toward a synthesis. One such synthesis, for example, is that the client will commit to building a life worth living and taking suicide off the table, and the therapist will commit to helping the client maintain this commitment and learn how to build a life worth living.

Balancing and Synthesizing Strategies, Positions, and Styles

A second key principle is that the therapist continually seeks to *balance and synthesize treatment strategies, positions, and styles*. DBT individual therapists and skills trainers often seek to balance their therapeutic style, sometimes using a *reciprocal* style, characterized by warmth and responsiveness to the client, and at other times, using an *irreverent* style, characterized by a matter-of-fact demeanor, the use of humor or direct confrontation, off-the-wall or unexpected statements, and so forth (Linehan, 1993a). Consider the example of an unemployed client suffering from social anxiety and depression who says, "It's hopeless, I can't get a job. I'm panicking about this interview, and there's no way I'll get through it without embarrassing myself. It's pointless to try, I might as well kill myself." A therapist using a reciprocal style might say something like, "I know the interview process is very scary, especially as it's hard enough to be around people altogether, let alone people you know are evaluating you! I want to find a way to help you prepare and cope with the interview, but first, let's talk about your suicidal thoughts. . . ." A therapist using an irreverent style, in contrast, might say something like, "Well, if you kill yourself, you definitely won't get the job." Alternatively, another irreverent riposte could be, "I thought you agreed not to quit therapy," as a natural consequence of suicide is that the client is out of therapy. Irreverence often involves unexpected statements that highlight different perspectives or implications or consequences of behavior that the client hasn't considered, or that capture the client's attention (Linehan, 1993a; Lynch et al., 2006).

Across both individual therapy and skills training, DBT therapists also seek to balance the core strategies of *validation* and *problem-solving*, both conveying understanding of the client's experiences and problems and helping her change and solve them. Clients may not have caused their problems, and they still need to solve them. The clinician seeks to both validate the client's experiences and help the client solve problems and change his or her life. Problem-solving in DBT consists of standard problem-solving skills and strategies as well as an overarching focus on the use of interventions to systematically solve the problems contributing to the client's misery. Often, the solutions to the client's difficulties involve any of an array of interventions drawn from standard cognitive behavior therapy (CBT) or other evidence-based practices, as discussed further in Chapter 4. The DBT therapist balances these often change-oriented approaches with validation, or conveying that the client's experiences, emotions, thoughts, and actions are understandable. Although the use of validation in therapy is hardly unique to DBT, one unique aspect of validation in DBT is that Marsha has operationalized seven different types of therapist behaviors that fall within the broader category of validation (Linehan, 1993a; 1997), and we describe these levels in Figure 3.2.

Dialectical Balance in Skills Training and Coaching

DBT skills training and coaching also involve the balancing of acceptance and change. Some DBT skills focus primarily on acceptance, such as the mindfulness and distress tolerance skills, and other skills focus primarily on change, such as the interpersonal effectiveness and emotion regulation skills. Also, within primarily acceptance-based skill modules, there are skills to help clients change their experiences (e.g., the distress tolerance TIPP skills for down-regulating extreme emotions; Linehan, 2015a, 2015b), and within the primarily change-oriented skills, there are skills to help clients accept their experiences (e.g., the skill of

Validation level	Description
1	Appearing interested and listening to the client; expressing interest; listening in an active and unbiased manner
2	Accurately reflecting the client's thoughts, emotions, and actions
3	Articulating thoughts or emotions the client has not fully expressed
4	Explaining how client reactions make sense in view of pathology, disease, or learning history
5	Explaining how client reactions make sense in view of the current context or normative functioning
6	Interacting with the client in a genuine, caring, non-role-prescribed manner
7	Cheerleading: Communicating belief in the client and their capacity for wisdom and to change and achieve valued goals

Figure 3.2

Levels of validation in dialectical behavior therapy. Data from Linehan (1993a, 1997).

mindfulness of current emotion in the emotion regulation skills, and the skill of validation in the interpersonal effectiveness skills; Linehan, 2015a, 2015b). In ad-hoc skills coaching occurring in individual therapy or during phone coaching calls, the therapist also strikes a balance of coaching clients in primarily change or primarily acceptance oriented skills. A therapist might coach a client struggling with sadness after a breakup in skills to accept and mindfully attend to sadness (e.g., radical acceptance and mindfulness of current emotion) as well as interpersonal effective as skills to seek support or build new relationships. A therapist might help a client accept that he lives with an unbearably rude roommate while also coaching him in skills to ask the roommate to change or find a new apartment. A therapist might help another client who struggles with loneliness to learn to accept and make the most of being alone and use skills to seek support and connect with others.

Dialectical Balance in Case Management

Additionally, the DBT therapist strikes a balance between an approach to case management characterized by *environmental intervention* or *consultation to the client.* Environmental intervention involves actively intervening in the client's environment to reduce aversive or stressful events or remove reinforcement for dysfunctional behavior. One of us, for example, saw a client who attended therapy religiously, always did her homework, and was a role model for other group members. When she experienced a crisis, however, all of her skills fell apart. She ended up in the psychiatric inpatient unit, engaging in all sorts of behavior that stressed the staff and other clients (e.g., writing about death on her door, yelling, screaming, threatening suicide). One approach to this scenario, following the consultation to the client principle, would be to consult with the client on how to use skills to reduce dysfunctional behavior, interact effectively with the staff, and communicate her wishes to be discharged. Environmental intervention, in contrast, would involve talking with the mental health staff about ways to effectively interact with the client, skills that she might find particularly helpful, and strategies to manage her behavior. Sometimes a DBT clinician may choose to use a combination of both strategies, but in this case, the therapist opted to consult with the client, who fortunately was amenable to the suggestion that, if she keeps this behavior up, she will end up stuck on the unit with a bunch of staff members who can't stand being around her. In DBT, therapists usually emphasize consultation to the client strategies except in cases of serious imminent harm or when the client lacks the skills or social position (i.e., is in a low-power position) to enact change.

Accepting Natural Change

A third key dialectical principle is that the therapist should be willing to *accept natural change* as it occurs and switch tactics when interventions are not working. This principle is consistent with the notion that reality is constantly changing. What might work with one client might not work with another, and what worked with a client last week (or 5 minutes ago) might not work with the same client this week (or right now!). We have seen several clients with whom we thought we were making excellent progress. Things seemed to be going so well, and then the client came in the following week and exclaimed, "Therapy isn't working!" Other clients encounter major life problems requiring a reorienting of priorities (e.g., a client who experiences a traumatic event mid-therapy), present with new or different clinical problem areas to focus on (e.g., a client who appears to have previously unnoticed psychotic features or an eating or substance use disorder), and so forth. Complex clients also sometimes have serious relationship difficulties that manifest in the therapy relationship, requiring the therapist to switch tactics and find a way to keep the relationship healthy and help the client continue to piece together a life worth living. The therapist sometimes has to turn on a dime, address a new problem area, and use different strategies. The process of doing this—flexibly switching tactics as needed, using a variety of strategies, taking positions wholeheartedly (e.g., stating, "Avoidance is your mortal enemy!" "We need to get suicide off the table") and so forth—is often called *movement, speed, and flow* in DBT and is considered an essential characteristic of the effective treatment of complex clients.

Dialectical Dilemmas

Dialectical theory also helps the therapist attend to polarized behavioral patterns that commonly emerge with complex clients. In DBT with adult clients, we tend to focus on three of these polarized behavioral patterns, often referred to as *dialectical dilemmas* or *secondary targets*. At times, the therapist fails to recognize these patterns until they begin to interfere with treatment; thus, it is helpful to think of dialectical dilemmas as representative of assessment failures. Often, when therapists recognize dialectical dilemmas and help clients work toward a middle path or synthesis, problems interfering with the effectiveness of therapy can be overcome.

Below, we discuss dialectical dilemmas for adult clients, but we recognize that many readers may see youth as well. For those clinicians working with youth, some of the dialectical dilemmas discussed below are still relevant, but others may be more applicable, given adolescents' developmental level and the various transactions occurring between parents and caregivers and the youth. One example is the polarity between the tendency to try to control the child's behavior and the tendency to let go and be excessively lenient (e.g., authoritarian control versus excessive leniency). Space does not permit a detailed discussion of these dialectical dilemmas for youth, so we refer the reader to Rathus and Miller (2000).

One adult dialectical dilemma involves the client vacillating between *apparent competence* and *active passivity*. Apparent competence occurs when the client appears more competent than he is, either in general (e.g., across social relationships, job functioning, coping with stress) or in some specific life domain (e.g., at school). The problem with apparent competence is that the client's presentation of competence often belies a desperate need for help, leading the therapist and loved ones with the impression that the client is doing just fine. As a result, people do not recognize the urgency of the client's need for help and do not provide adequate or timely support. The situation is akin to an otherwise healthy young adult presenting with symptoms of stroke that emergency room staff overlook and thereby fail to provide timely, life-saving intervention.

Active passivity, in contrast, involves the client's passively addressing their own problems but actively recruiting others to help solve them. "William," for example, was intensely lonely and felt alienated from his family. He was anxious about uncertain social situations and avoided situations where he might meet new people, but he had a large team of health and mental health professionals and met with at least one of them several times per week. These individuals temporarily alleviated William's loneliness and worked considerably harder than he did to find ways to connect him to others. In contrast with apparent competence, where the client appears well-functioning, when actively passive, the client often appears unable to function without others' support. Clients engaging in active passivity risk burning out their support networks and exacerbating beliefs that they are unable to take care of themselves and miss opportunities to learn to actively solve problems. Common problems arising in therapy include the client frequently emailing, texting, or calling for various forms of help and support and burning out the clinician. Key goals for clients presenting with active passivity and apparent competence are to (a) learn how to take an active approach to problem-solving and reduce demands on others; and (b) accurately express emotions, describe difficulties, and effectively seek help.

Another dialectical dilemma is that of *emotion vulnerability* and *self-invalidation*. On the one pole, the client experiencing and expressing emotion vulnerability is caught up in the storm of her emotions, feels and presents as out of control of her feelings and behaviors, and may appear fragile and may feel bitter and blame others for her problems. In contrast, the client on the self-invalidation pole often blames themselves or feels self-hatred, dismisses their own suffering, and has unrealistic expectations about their ability to overcome challenging problems. The primary goals for clients who end up on these poles are to help them learn to regulate or modulate extreme emotions and validate their own emotional pain. Emotion regulation and distress tolerance skills, as well as the modeling of validation strategies, are particularly helpful in this regard.

The third dialectical dilemma is that of *unrelenting crisis* and *inhibited grieving*. When caught up in unrelenting crisis, the client seems to have a pattern of nearly continual crisis and dysfunction. The client may, for example, be evicted from his apartment, be involved in a domestic violence situation, arrive at work drunk or hungover, and attempt suicide—all in the week between therapy sessions. The state of unrelenting crisis feels out of control, and the client often engages in crisis generating behaviors (e.g., getting drunk, initiating interpersonal conflict, failing to fulfill work or financial obligations, spending time with harmful friends or partners) that exacerbate the client's problems. On the other pole is inhibited grieving. In this case, the client actively avoids or blocks intolerable or unwanted emotional states, passively avoids emotions through dissociation, suppression or other methods, and avoids experiencing the emotional pain related to highly distressing events (e.g., the aforementioned crisis situations, or the loss of a relationship or loved one). Consequently, the client misses the opportunity to work through emotional pain, digest it, and learn from it. Goals for clients presenting with unrelenting crises and inhibited grieving are to help them (a) reduce crisis generating behaviors and exercise realistic judgment, and (b) experience emotional pain without escaping or avoiding it.

Dialectical Strategies

Along with key dialectical principles and dialectical dilemmas, specific dialectical strategies are used in DBT to help balance and synthesize polarities, magnify tension, and facilitate change. We have included a list and brief description of these strategies in Figure 3.3 and will briefly discuss a couple of them here. One key dialectical strategy is called *entering the paradox*. Clients, therapy, and life often present seemingly incompatible polarities. At times, the DBT therapist's aim is to notice these polarities when they arise and help the client see that seemingly opposing or contradictory ideas can coexist. One example is the assumption that clients are doing the best they can and have not caused all of their problems and that they still have to do better, try harder, and solve their problems. Another example, discussed in Chapter 1, is that clients

Dialectical strategy	Description
Extending	Magnifying tension between positions by making statements conveying that the therapist is taking the client's communication more seriously than the client intended
Making lemonade out of lemons	Highlighting the opportunity in a crisis or stressful situation
Playing devil's advocate	Magnifying tension between positions by arguing against desired change
Entering the paradox	Presenting two seemingly contradictory ideas without resolving the contradiction for the client
Using metaphors, stories, similes, analogies, and so forth	Using language devices that help the client recognize and understand key ideas, concepts, or patterns more clearly

Figure 3.3

Dialectical strategies in dialectical behavior therapy. Data from Linehan (1993a).

must let go of suicide to build a life worth living *and* must build a life worth living to let go of suicide. Clients ultimately need to both accept and change themselves and their lives in order to become free from suffering.

Another common dialectical strategy is *making lemonade out of lemons*. While this strategy may seem like a version of a grandmotherly admonition that every cloud has a silver lining, making lemonade out of lemons has roots in Zen practice and is a way to search for synthesis. In Zen, there is a saying that "the Dharma gates are countless," as well as a vow to "wake to them." This means that each moment, sensation, event and experience presents the opportunity to experience reality as it is. Waiting in line; being criticized for poor work performance; having a knock-down, drag-out fight with someone; or simply walking down the street and feeling the sun on one's face all are opportunities to awaken to the nature of reality. Similarly, making lemonade out of lemons is a way to help clients perceive the opportunity in a crisis. The opportunity might be to learn something new; practice and become more proficient at DBT or other skills; and to grow, change, and move closer to a life worth living. The therapist's challenge is to skillfully point out the opportunity in a stressful event or crisis without completely invalidating the client's pain and suffering. A couple of examples include the following statements to a client working with a difficult boss who is incredibly punitive and critical: "As painful as it is to work with your boss day in and day out, if you can learn to use interpersonal effectiveness skills with her, you will be able to use them with anyone," or "This boss is the universe's gift to you. You are going to get such amazing practice with distress toler- ance and interpersonal effectiveness!" Effectively making lemonade out of lemons requires the skillful balance of acceptance (validation of the client's pain) and change (providing a new perspective by highlighting an opportunity).

Zen Principles and Practices in DBT

As mentioned in Chapter 1, Linehan incorporated Zen principles and practices in DBT as a way to balance and synthesize the heavily change- based approach of CBT. Zen practice does not necessarily need to adhere to any specific religious system, such as Buddhism. The fundamental practice of Zen, known as *zazen*, involves attending to the experience of the present moment, often through meditative practices, such as sitting and observing one's breathing or other sensations. Zen practice is the practice of experiencing the reality of the present moment; seeing things as they are; letting go of attachments to needs, preferences, or desires; and shedding misconceptions and delusions. One key principle guiding Zen practice is that the universe is fundamentally interconnected. In a dialectical manner, all beings are both separate *and* one with the rest of the universe. The practice of zazen is considered an expression of this fundamental principle or truth about reality (Suzuki, 1970, 2011).

Zen principles and practices are consistent with those of behavioral theory and science. In Zen, there is an emphasis on direct observation, data, and experience. Similarly, behavioral science emphasizes empirical evidence gleaned through observation. Zen also emphasizes that a common contributor to suffering is attachment to a particular state of being, such as attachment to the state of permanence (given that the universe is constantly changing), or to particular emotions, thoughts, sensations, or situations. From a Zen perspective, attachment to wants, needs, and preferences and avoidance of reality lead to suffering. From the perspective of contemporary CBT and behavioral theory, many clinical problems and maladaptive behaviors are maintained by avoidance or escape from particular experiences or situations (e.g., Abramowitz, Deacon, & Whiteside, 2011; Chapman, Gratz, & Brown, 2006; Hayes, Strosahl, & Wilson, 1999; Hofmann, 2007), and avoidance/escape often result in increased long-term suffering.

Zen principles and practices have also influenced the development of the skills of mindfulness and radical acceptance in DBT. In Zen, there is a saying that everything is "perfect" as it is. Given the nature of cause and effect and all of the causes and forces that have contributed to the present state of the universe, things could not be different than they are, and in essence, the present reality is complete and "perfect" exactly as it is. Zen practice involves experiencing the present moment as it is, without delusion, while acting effectively (using "expedient means"). Accordingly, in DBT, mindfulness practice involves attending to (observing), describing, and participating in the present moment nonjudgmentally, one-mindfully (doing one thing at a time), and effectively (i.e., like the Zen notion of using "expedient means"). Radical acceptance similarly involves the complete acceptance of reality as it is in the present moment (Linehan, 1993b, 2015a, 2015b). Clients are taught that refusal to accept pain (e.g., emotional or physical discomfort) generates suffering, similar to the Zen notion that suffering arises from attachment.

CAUSES OF BEHAVIOR: BEHAVIORAL THEORY IN DBT

The DBT conceptualization of what causes and maintains human behavior is rooted in behavioral theory. As with many behavioral frameworks, DBT therefore emphasizes the effect of learning history, recent reinforcement contingencies, and the current environmental context in guiding behavior in the moment.

In particular, DBT is most consistent with *social* or *psychological behaviorism* (Staats, 1995). In contrast with other schools of behaviorism, psychological behaviorism explicitly integrates behavioral approaches with other fields of knowledge within psychology, including developmental, biological, and personality psychology. Therefore, psychological behavioral frameworks view the transactions between learning history and environmental events as critical to the development of the basic behavioral repertoire that constitutes an individual's personality (Staats, 1995). From this vantage point, DBT considers client behaviors (whether motor or overt actions; or cognitive–verbal, including thoughts or physiological responses) to be governed by complex, dynamic interactions between biological predispositions, the present environment, and learning histories.

For instance, a client with a predisposition towards intense emotional responses and who has been reared in an invalidating environment may have experienced intense distress in response to perceived rejection. Further, this client may have been intermittently heard (and thereby reinforced) for emotional outbursts in the past in such situations. Thus, they may have acquired a behavioral repertoire in response to perceived rejection that involves emotions such as shame, anger, and intense emotional expressions. In the absence of accumulated learning of adaptive skills to respond to such situations, the client may have skills deficits. A DBT therapist would therefore work to develop alternative behavioral response sets to situations in which the client is likely to perceive rejection. For instance, the DBT therapist may teach the client mindfulness, cognitive reappraisal, or *checking the facts* to reduce the inaccurate perception of rejecting environments. In addition, the client may learn strategies to reduce the occurrence of rejection, such as interpersonal effectiveness skills. Further, the client may be taught skills such as distress tolerance crisis survival skills to manage intense emotions in the moment without engaging in impulsive expressions of emotion, and finally the client may learn to express emotions and requests more effectively. Over the course of treatment, the ultimate goal is to help clients cultivate more adaptive behavioral repertoires to respond to many of the situations that elicit problem behaviors.

With these firm behavioral roots, DBT is primarily a learning-oriented treatment. Thus, many of the elements of treatment are in the service of identifying contexts in which clients have narrow or maladaptive behavioral repertoires and ameliorating clients' skills deficits to provide them with the skills they need to build a life worth living. This often begins with developing a behavioral formulation of the problem behaviors. Important variables to consider in such a formulation include the *antecedents* or conditions that precede the problem; *person variables* such as temperament or learning history; *behaviors* including emotions, thoughts, and actions; and *consequences*, or events that increase (reinforce) or decrease (punish) the likelihood that the behavior will recur (Farmer & Chapman, 2016; see also the S-O-R-C model first described by Goldfried & Davison, 1976). One of the ways in which DBT therapists identify contexts associated with problematic behavioral repertoires is to identify the links that precipitate and follow specific problem behaviors, with the aim of understanding how the behaviors function within the context of the client's biological characteristics, learning history, and contingencies in the environment.

Consider, for example, Marita, who frequently thought about and planned suicide while driving home from work. A careful microlevel behavioral analysis of a particular instance of suicidal ideation (termed a *chain analysis* in DBT; Linehan, 1993a) revealed several antecedents. Some of these antecedents included Marita being excluded from a lunch with coworkers, feelings of shame, loneliness, and sadness, and thoughts about how she will never connect with the folks at work or establish a close friendship. In terms of person variables, Marita was bullied severely for her weight and appearance in high school and had two older siblings who spent most of their time with same-age friends and did not pay much attention to Marita. This type of learning history might have made Marita particularly sensitive to perceived social exclusion. The behavior of suicidal ideation and planning thereafter had several consequences. In the short term, suicidal ideation and planning were comforting to Marita, distracting her and providing relief from feelings of shame and loneliness, thereby providing both positive and negative reinforcement (in this case, internal or "automatic" positive and negative reinforcement; Nock & Prinstein, 2004). Over time, chain analyses of Marita's suicidal ideation and planning revealed consistent patterns, showing that she was particularly prone to think about and plan suicide in situations involving perceived social rejection or interpersonal conflict (e.g., with her mother or siblings). Further, suicidal ideation and planning consistently alleviated loneliness and sadness. As a result, therapy focused on reducing her suicide risk, addressing her tendency to readily perceive rejection (e.g., through the skill of "checking the facts"; Linehan, 2015a, 2015b), improving her current relationships and expanding her social network, and increasing her skills in regulating and tolerating sadness and loneliness.

To expand clients' behavioral repertoires and address skills deficits, skills are taught formally in structured skills training groups (Linehan, 1993a; 2015b). Yet the therapist and client may identify specific skills deficits that do not align neatly with the skills training curriculum. Therefore, DBT augments the acquisition of skills that occurs in DBT skills groups with idiographic skills training in individual therapy. For instance, the therapist may coach the client in imaginal and in vivo exposure to driving and the emotions arising during this activity, while preventing suicidal or other harmful escape or avoidance behaviors. Alternatively, if together they determined that the client had a deficit in skills to down-regulate panic, the therapist might coach the client in other strategies to manage her distress, such as deep breathing.

UNDERSTANDING THE DEVELOPMENT OF PARTICULAR DISORDERS: THE BIOSOCIAL THEORY

Having discussed some of the dialectical and behavioral underpinnings of DBT, we now zero in on DBT's theoretical understanding of clients with BPD and other related, complex mental health problems. The *biosocial theory* (Linehan, 1993a) proposes that BPD emerges as a result of dynamic transactions of a biologically based, temperamental vulnerability to heightened emotionality (called *emotion vulnerability*) and early experiences of invalidation. Emotion vulnerability and the invalidating environment transact to produce the cognitive, emotional, and behavioral patterns characteristic of BPD. The biosocial theory is a *transactional* rather than additive or interactional model. As such, it is not the additive effect of an emotional temperament on top of adverse or invalidating childhood experiences that produces BPD. Moreover, the biosocial theory is not like a diathesis-stress model, whereby the emotionally vulnerable temperament predisposes the child to experience adverse outcomes from an invalidating or adverse environment. In contrast, the biosocial theory proposes that there is a mutual interplay between emotion vulnerability and the invalidating environment, whereby each factor amplifies and exacerbates the other, often having a snowball effect over time, resulting in severe emotional and behavioral dysfunction.

Temperamental or Biological Vulnerabilities

The temperamental or biological vulnerability to heightened emotionality—emotion vulnerability—has three key components. One component is *emotional sensitivity*, whereby the child has a low threshold for emotional arousal. It does not take as much to elicit an emotional response from sensitive individuals as it does from less sensitive individuals. A voice tone, the look on someone's face, a minor disappointment, distance or exclusion from others that most people might not perceive, and so forth, may reliably elicit an emotional response. The second component, *emotional reactivity*, has to do with the intensity of the individual's emotional responses. Theoretically, emotionally reactive people experience very intense emotional responses in terms of both physiological and subjectively perceived emotional arousal. An emotionally reactive client, for example, might become enraged when someone cuts in front of them in line, whereas a less reactive individual might become mildly frustrated. The third component of emotion vulnerability is *slow return to emotional baseline*, involving delayed recovery from emotionally evocative events. It is quite likely that slow return to baseline sometimes masquerades as emotional reactivity. The child who has a hard time recovering from stressful events at school might, for example, appear to be flying off the handle about minor disappointments (e.g., having a disliked item for dinner). In reality, however, the child never recovered from the stressful events at school and thus appears to be overreacting to the disappointing dinner, when this is not the full story. Conversely, it is possible that emotional reactivity contributes to slow return to baseline. Very intense emotional reactions might take longer to subside. As with other components of the biosocial theory, the three components of emotion vulnerability likely influence and amplify one another.

Sociodevelopmental Factors

The sociodevelopmental factor considered to contribute to BPD (in transaction with emotion vulnerability) is called the *invaliding environment*. The invalidating environment has three key components. One component is that the environment *indiscriminately rejects the child's communication* of thoughts and emotions. Regardless of how valid the child's feelings or thoughts are, the environment conveys that they are inappropriate, pathological, or not what they seem. A second component is that the environment *oversimplifies the ease of problem-solving*, or makes it seem like it should be easier than it is for the child to manage or recover from stressful events. The third component of the invalidating environment consists of the *intermittent reinforcement of emotional escalation*, whereby the environment periodically and inconsistently provides attention and support in response to highly escalated behavior (e.g., tantrums, aggression, yelling, screaming, self-harming). As a result, the child learns that extreme behaviors sometimes garner help and support. Some of our clients have said that this pattern contributed to feelings of worthlessness or insignificance, as it took such an extreme behavior (e.g., a serious suicide attempt resulting in intensive care) before people were willing to attend to their needs. These environmental experiences of invalidation may range from caregivers or loved ones who do not understand their child's sensitivity, all the way through more extreme forms of invalidation such as severe abuse or neglect. Of note, the larger societal context may also contribute to invalidating messages as well, through stigmatizing messages about people with BPD and social mores suggesting that it is normal to be happy or unemotional. For instance, many of our clients with minority sexual orientations or nonbinary gender identities received stigmatizing messages at the societal level that amplified experiences of invalidation.

As mentioned, within the biosocial framework of DBT, emotion vulnerability and invalidation transact to produce characteristic BPD features over time. At the level of genes, it is possible that parents pass down genes contributing to a propensity toward an emotionally vulnerable temperament. If both the parents (or caregivers in the case of children raised by nonbiological parents) and the child are emotionally vulnerable, the parents may find the child's emotionality to be particularly aversive and difficult to cope with and respond dysfunctionally to shut it down. Coercive and punitive tactics to curtail intense emotional expression would be expected to exacerbate the child's emotionality, further contributing to an interplay of intense emotionality and invalidation. Even when caregivers and children do not share genes or traits related to emotion vulnerability, emotional children may require stronger parenting skills than less emotional children, or an adverse and invalidating childhood environment may amplify what would have been normal-range emotionality by directly or indirectly influencing the development of neurological and biological systems underpinning emotions. In addition, sometimes, the transaction is between an emotional child and a seemingly normal caregiver environment, where the child gets the sense that they are the only emotional person in the family and feels set apart or pathological. The calm or "normal" family sometimes inadvertently communicates that there is something wrong with the child or amplifies the child's sense of separateness by becoming even more calm or "normal" to maintain equilibrium (Linehan, 1993a).

In response to perceived recurring invalidation, children may alternate between inhibiting their emotions or escalating emotional expressions. After finding their emotions met with perceived invalidation or punishment, children may learn to distrust their own emotional responses, or at least to hide them. At times, however, the child may lose the ability to contain his or her emotional expressions, and may erupt in an emotional outburst, possibly resulting in the pattern (described above) of intermittent reinforcement of emotional escalation. Furthermore, without the type of support and care that facilitates emotion regulation capacities, emotionally vulnerable children in invalidating environments have difficulty learning effective ways of managing their emotions. Over time, this type of caregiver–child relationship may instantiate emotion dysregulation. According to the biosocial theory, this emotion dysregulation leads to impulsive efforts to manage emotions, an unstable sense of self, and rocky interpersonal relationships, thereby paving the way for the development of BPD.

Updated Biosocial Developmental Model of BPD

When the original version of Linehan's (1993a) biosocial theory was published in her treatment manual, the empirical literature on the development of BPD and on emotions and emotion regulation was still fairly scant. The field of emotion regulation had yet to receive widespread attention or to be influenced by a unifying theoretical framework (Gross, 1998, 2015; Thompson, 1994). Developmental psychopathology literature existed on the effects of abuse and trauma, and there was a growing and influential literature on syndromes of disinhibition (Patterson & Newman, 1993), such as attention-deficit/hyperactivity disorder, child and adult conduct problems (e.g., conduct disorder and eventual antisocial personality disorder; e.g., Patterson, DeBaryshe, & Ramsey, 1989). The basis of Linehan's (1993a) biosocial theory, therefore, consisted of clinical observations, findings on the effects of childhood maltreatment, and existing emotion and behavioral science.

Capturing developments in the field of developmental psychopathology more broadly and BPD and emotion regulation more specifically, Crowell and colleagues (Crowell et al., 2009, 2014, see also Beauchaine, Hinshaw, & Bridge, 2019) proposed an updated biosocial model of the development of BPD. Crowell et al.'s (2009) model similarly emphasizes the transaction of biological and environmental factors in the development of BPD as well as the important role of familial socialization of emotion regulation and dysregulation. Compared with Linehan's (1993a) original biosocial theory, which emphasizes a biological disposition toward emotion vulnerability, Crowell et al. (2009) more strongly emphasize the role of trait impulsivity as a key, biologically based heritable factor that makes the child particularly vulnerable to developing emotion dysregulation in the context of adverse environments. The vulnerable child with high trait impulsivity is at risk of developing a constellation of child behavioral problems, such as oppositional defiant disorder, attention-deficit/hyperactivity disorder, and others. Impulsivity also confers a particular vulnerability to the negative effects of invalidation, abuse, and coercive behavioral control processes that reinforce emotional escalation and dysregulation. Over time, the child's emotional lability and dysregulation worsen. Alongside this process, impulsive youth often spend time with deviant or impulsive peers, and peer modeling of dysfunctional coping can set the stage for the development of dysfunctional coping strategies such as substance use and self-injury in early adolescence.

Within this framework, self-injury, in particular, is a key predictor of escalating self-damaging behavior (e.g., suicide attempts) and the development of BPD in later adolescence. Therefore, taken together, the original and updated versions of the biosocial theory emphasize the importance of transactions between heritable vulnerabilities (trait impulsivity, and possibly emotion vulnerability, or more broadly, neuroticism; see Chapman, 2019, for a detailed discussion of research and theory on the development of emotion dysregulation and BPD) and adverse, invalidating rearing environments. Clinically, the biosocial theory forms the backbone of a solid DBT-oriented case conceptualization. Further, to ensure that clients understand their difficulties in the same way that therapists do, clients often are oriented to the biosocial theory during the early phases of DBT individual therapy and skills training.

The Role of Emotions and Emotion Regulation in DBT

A biosocial developmental conceptualization of BPD highlights emotion dysregulation as a key treatment target in DBT. As such, the aim of reducing emotion dysregulation and increasing emotion regulation capacities underpins many facets of this treatment. Consistent with that of other theories of emotion and emotion regulation, the DBT model emphasizes that emotions (a) are multicomponent, systemic processes; (b) occur in motivationally relevant situations (i.e., situations that are relevant to an individual's needs or goals); and (c) serve important social and behavioral functions (Ekman, 1992; Levenson, 1994) The components of the emotion system include (a) physiological responding (e.g., sympathetic and parasympathetic arousal, changes in blood chemistry and brain activity, awareness of changes in physiological activity), (b) cognition (including perception, awareness, and appraisals of emotionally relevant events), and (c) behavior (e.g., the desire or "action urge" to engage in actions consistent with an emotional state, specific actions, and emotional expressive tendencies). *Emotion regulation* is the process by which individuals influence any of these components and can occur through automatic or implicit processes (e.g., physiological or neurological down-regulation) or explicit, conscious efforts (Beauchaine, 2015; Gross, 1998; 2015; Thompson, 1994).

From a DBT perspective, *emotion dysregulation* involves "the inability, even when one's best efforts are applied, to change *in a desired way* emotional cues, experiences, actions, verbal responses, and/or nonverbal expressions under normative conditions" (p. 511). From this perspective, a client who appears to be overreacting to a seemingly small event (e.g., someone forgetting a coffee date) would be considered emotionally dysregulated if they were unable to modulate their emotional responses in a manner that is consistent with their goals. The client who, for example, tried but was unable to lessen their rage and ended up yelling at the friend or felt extreme sadness and sat on the couch binge drinking and self-injuring throughout the evening, would likely be considered emotionally dysregulated. Presumably, yelling at the friend contravenes the goal of maintaining a healthy relationship, and self-injuring and binge drinking undermine important therapy goals.

At the level of case conceptualization, the DBT therapist attends to the important role of emotions and emotion dysregulation in clients' presenting problems. To illustrate how this emphasis on emotions differentiates DBT from standard CBT, consider the example of Sandra. Sandra struggles with persistent depression, has little social support aside from her sister and mother, is on psychiatric disability, and is working toward increasing behavioral activation (a common goal in the beginning of CBT for depression). When her alarm clock goes off in the morning, she wakes up and thinks, "There's no point in getting up this morning. Today will be just as miserable as yesterday. I just can't face the day and get through coffee with my sister." She feels sad, lethargic, despondent, and anxious about getting up, getting groceries, and meeting her sister for coffee. She turns off her alarm, goes back to sleep, and misses her coffee date. In standard CBT with Sandra, the therapist's conceptualization of these events would likely emphasize her thinking patterns, characterized by poor outcome expectancies (the day will be miserable) and low self-efficacy (she "can't" do what she needs to do today), and resulting interventions would help her make useful behavioral changes (e.g., stimulus control, moving the alarm clock further away, graduated behavior change, such as starting with simply getting out of bed) and cognitive changes (e.g., evaluating the evidence or utility of her thoughts about herself and the day, considering more adaptive thinking). All of these factors would be emphasized and addressed in DBT as well, but the DBT therapist also would attend closely to the role of emotions and emotion regulation in this scenario. The therapist might attend to and assess the antecedent emotions (sadness, anxiety) and related sensations, thoughts, and action urges. The therapist also would assess any expectations the client might have had about emotion regulation (e.g., the expectation that certain emotions would increase or decrease if she were to stay in bed or get up). In addition, the therapist would attend to the possible emotion regulatory consequences or functions of turning off the alarm and remaining in bed, both in the short term (e.g., reductions in sadness or anxiety) and long term (e.g., relief at not having to see anyone; guilt about missing the coffee date with her sister).

The emphasis on emotions in terms of case conceptualization paves the way for interventions that are also focused on emotion regulation and reducing emotion dysregulation. In individual therapy, these interventions sometimes occur in the form of behavioral plans to avoid future problems, such as plans to help Sandra avoid staying in bed. Interventions might help Sandra attend mindfully to her emotions upon awakening, learn to tolerate these emotions while engaging in effective behavior (e.g., sitting up in bed), experience and ride out urges to turn off the alarm, and make changes to emotion-based expressions (facial expressions, body language) or engage in behaviors inconsistent or "opposite" to those related to the current emotional state (e.g., the skill of opposite action; Linehan, 1993b, 2015a, 2015b). In other cases, emotion-oriented interventions in individual therapy occur in an ad-hoc manner as opportunities arise during therapy sessions. With a client struggling with anger management, the individual DBT therapist might look for opportunities to help the client observe, describe, and manage anger in the moment in therapy sessions. Such opportunities can include instances when the client becomes angry in the session about other topics or toward the therapist. In these cases, the therapist might often help the client attend to sensations, thoughts, and urges associated with anger, and coach the client on skills to regulate anger and avoid engaging in ineffective behavior (e.g., yelling, storming out of the office). With a different client experiencing anxiety or sadness, who appears to be switching topics or engaging in other behavior functioning to avoid or escape these experiences, the individual therapist might orient and coach the client in the strategy of *informal exposure* to emotional states. This intervention, involving mindful experiencing of the various components of an emotional state, can be particularly useful for clients who are "emotion phobic" (Linehan, 1993a), helping them learn that emotions do not foretell or result in dangerous or harmful consequences. Additionally, the primary individual therapist often coaches clients during ad-hoc phone coaching calls in how to regulate or tolerate strong emotions without engaging in behavior that will likely worsen the situation (Chapman, 2018; Linehan, 1993a). Indeed, given the brevity of phone coaching calls (usually under 10–15 minutes), the primary goal of most of these calls is to help the client apply skills to regulate or tolerate emotions until they can use other strategies (e.g., problem-solving to address a serious relationship difficulty or make decisions about a work situation) to address and solve problems over the long run.

In DBT skills training, the focus on emotion regulation is more explicit and structured, occurring primarily via skills aimed at helping clients tolerate or regulate emotional experiences. The emotion regulation skill module (DBT-ER) most explicitly addresses emotion regulation, containing skills to understand, recognize, label, regulate, and accept emotional experiences. Some of the DBT-ER skills involve emotion regulation through behavior change, such as by engaging in behavior that is opposite to the action urge associated with an emotion (opposite action), whereas others involve cognitive strategies to modify interpretations and appraisals of emotional events (e.g., checking the facts). Other skills involve strategies to reduce vulnerability to emotional events (e.g., the ABC PLEASE skills) or modify emotionally evocative situations (e.g., problem-solving skills). Distress tolerance also addresses emotion regulation through strategies aimed at helping clients switch their attention from emotionally evocative events to other experiences (e.g., distraction, improving the moment), soothe or dampen physiological arousal (e.g., self-soothing and skills to modify physiological arousal by changing body temperature, engaging in intense exercise or relaxation or breathing strategies), or accept current emotional experiences (which sometimes is a focus of the skill of radical acceptance). Finally, mindfulness skills also indirectly address emotion regulation by helping clients attend to current emotional experiences while letting go of judgments and acting wisely.

CONCLUSION

The bedrock of DBT is composed of several philosophical and theoretical perspectives at multiple levels. Both dialectical philosophy and Zen inform the DBT views of the nature of reality. Dialectical philosophy highlights the dynamic interplay of opposing tensions and guides DBT therapists to seek the truth in such polarities to achieve a synthesis. Zen contributes to a view of the universe as unified and all beings as both interconnected and unique. In addition, Zen infuses DBT with a range of acceptance-oriented strategies, and emphasizes acceptance of each moment without judgment and forms the backbone of mindfulness and reality acceptance skills. When it comes to explaining client behavior, DBT largely draws on behavioral principles. Thus, DBT views client behaviors in any given situation as the result of a dynamic interaction between temperament, learning history, and the current circumstance. Ultimately, DBT aims to augment existing behavioral repertoires to align with client goals and values. These behavioral and dialectical views inform the biosocial theory (Linehan, 1993a) of the development of emotion dysregulation, especially in BPD. The biosocial theory proposes that BPD emerges as a result of dynamic interactions of temperamental emotion vulnerability and early experiences of invalidation. Thus, dialectical philosophy infuses this model, such that neither temperament nor environment alone are sufficient to lead to emotion dysregulation— it is the ongoing, transactional influences between the individual and their environment that ultimately set the stage for emotion dysregulation. These perspectives guide the case conceptualization and treatment planning for clients throughout their treatment in DBT.

Functions, Structure, and Core Interventions

Dialectical behavior therapy (DBT) is a comprehensive treatment program designed to address the needs of complex, multidiagnostic clients. Rather than a single intervention (e.g., exposure therapy) or package of interventions (e.g., exposure therapy, cognitive restructuring, and anxiety management skills for posttraumatic stress disorder), DBT is a treatment program consisting of a community of therapists treating a community of clients (Linehan, 1993a). As discussed later, many programs offer certain components of DBT, but not others. What is often referred to as *standard DBT* consists of four primary modes of intervention: (a) weekly individual therapy, (b) weekly group skills training, (c) telephone consultation, and (d) a therapist consultation team (discussed and further elaborated below and shown in Figure 4.1). These four modes address five important functions of comprehensive treatment for complex, multidiagnostic clients: (a) enhancing client

http://dx.doi.org/10.1037/0000188-004
Dialectical Behavior Therapy, by A. L. Chapman and K. L. Dixon-Gordon

Mode	Function
Individual therapy	Improve motivation, generalize treatment gains, solve life problems, build a life worth living
Group skills training	Increase capabilities (mindfulness, distress tolerance, interpersonal effectiveness, emotion regulation, self-management/regulation)
Telephone consultation	Generalize new behaviors to relevant situations
Consultation team	Maintain and improve therapist motivation and capability

Figure 4.1

Dialectical behavior therapy modes and functions. Data from Linehan (1993a).

motivation to change, (b) enhancing client capabilities, (c) generalizing gains to the natural environment, (d) structuring the environment, and (e) maintaining and enhancing therapists' motivation and skills. In this chapter, we begin by reviewing the five functions and four primary modes of DBT.

In this chapter, we also discuss core intervention strategies used in DBT. Core interventions occurring within DBT are guided by evidence-based principles and practices, dialectical and behavioral theory, the biosocial developmental theory of BPD, and the therapist's formulation of the maintaining factors for individual clients' problem areas. Clients receiving DBT typically have multiple problem areas (e.g., one client may present with a combination of suicidality, substance use problems, disordered eating, relationship discord, panic attacks, and so forth), making the application of the many potentially relevant evidence-based protocols (e.g., protocols for the treatment of panic disorder, depression, etc.) challenging. To maximize efficiency and allow for the flexibility needed to address multiple problem areas at various points in treatment, DBT therapists take a principle-based approach, incorporating protocols and aspects of protocols as needed, based on an individualized case formulation.

THE FIVE FUNCTIONS OF DBT

Complex, multidiagnostic clients need comprehensive treatment addressing several key areas. First, treatment must *enhance client motivation.* Without motivation to change, the other functions are doomed to remain unfulfilled, much like teaching a client who has not considered quitting smoking ways to avoid lighting up. In DBT, we assume clients want their lives to be different *and* need to become more motivated to change. Clients experiencing persistent suffering often desperately want their lives to change and have difficulty establishing or maintaining motivation to make the painful changes needed to develop a life worth living (e.g., eliminating self-injury or suicidal behavior; reducing problematic substance use; addressing key interpersonal vulnerabilities; experiencing painful and often avoided emotions, such as sadness and shame). DBT includes strategies to assist clients in developing and maintaining motivation and commitment to change. Individual therapy is the primary DBT mode that addresses this function.

Second, treatment must *increase client capabilities*, or help clients learn the skills they need to establish and maintain a life worth living. As mentioned in Chapter 3, DBT is partially based on a skills deficit model, whereby complex clients often have not had sufficient environmental scaffolding, support, and/or modeling to develop skills to modulate and tolerate emotions and navigate relationships effectively. DBT provides training in four core skill areas (mindfulness, distress tolerance, interpersonal effectiveness, and emotion regulation) in the context of a structured weekly group skills training session. Outside of skills training, DBT more broadly is a learning-oriented therapy; thus, individual therapists often address skill deficits (e.g., job interview skills, couples communication skills, anxiety or anger management strategies) as needed.

Third, treatment must *generalize* what the client is learning in therapy to all relevant contexts, including challenging everyday situations. One of the four modes of DBT, telephone consultation (often referred to as *phone coaching*; Chapman, 2018), involves the therapist being available by phone or other methods to coach the client in the use of skills in everyday life situations. Generalization is the primary goal of phone coaching in DBT. Other examples of ways to generalize learning in therapy to everyday life include encouraging clients to practice new skills in all relevant contexts and helping clients establish stimulus control strategies, reminders, or prompts that encourage the practice of skills in daily life (see Chapman, 2018, for other examples of skill generalization strategies).

Fourth, comprehensive treatment should *structure the environment* to promote and maintain progress. The environment is structured in a couple of key ways. First, the individual therapist structures the treatment environment to ensure the client has all necessary treatment components. Second, often, the individual therapist also helps the client change her natural environment in ways that reinforce effective behaviors and promote progress. The therapist of an adolescent client, for example, whose parents may inadvertently reinforce depressive behavior by bringing her breakfast in bed, might help the client and parents to change the contingencies around depressive behavior.

Fifth, comprehensive treatment for complex, high-risk, challenging clients should *enhance therapist motivation and capabilities.* The DBT consultation team, involving a weekly meeting of DBT therapists, serves this function by supporting therapists in their work with often challenging clients who engage in worrisome (e.g., repeated, severe suicide attempts) or distressing behaviors (e.g., behaviors that interfere with therapy or burn out the therapist). Therapists often need this kind of ongoing support, consultation, and practice in order to maintain effective work with complex, challenging clients.

THE STRUCTURE OF DBT

The four primary DBT modes of intervention that serve these functions include individual therapy, group DBT skills training, telephone consultation, and the therapist consultation team. Each of these modes serves a unique (but sometimes overlapping) function in the treatment. DBT also may include additional modes of intervention as needed, such as ancillary pharmacotherapy, couples or family based treatment, or case management. Next, we describe the structure of the four primary modes of DBT programs.

Individual Therapy

Individual therapy typically consists of weekly meetings with a primary individual therapist. This individual is considered the client's *primary* individual therapist because she or he is responsible for developing and implementing the client's treatment plan, and ensuring that the appropriate functions of treatment are met and all of the necessary modes of DBT are in place. The primary individual therapist, for example, tries to ensure that the client begins and sustains skills group attendance and (where needed and appropriate) coordinates care with other professionals. In some cases, the client may have other individual therapists, counselors, occupational or recreational therapists, and so forth, and the primary individual DBT therapist must ensure that the client's DBT services are coordinated effectively with these other services.

During individual therapy sessions, typically occurring weekly for 50 to 60 minutes, the primary individual therapist aims to help clients improve motivation and modify behavior in ways that help them pursue meaningful goals and build lives worth living. In this way, individual therapy helps clients to connect the skills that they learn in other DBT modes (typically DBT group skills training) to their treatment goals. Individual DBT sessions are structured very similarly to standard CBT sessions. Typically, after greeting the client, the therapist and client review the client's *diary card*, a standing homework item involving the monitoring of relevant emotions and actions daily over the course of the week (examples of the diary card used in standard DBT can be found, among other resources, at the University of Washington's Behavioral Research and Therapy Clinics website: http://depts.washington.edu/uwbrtc/wp-content/uploads/NIMH4-S-DBT-Diary-Cards-with-Instructions.pdf).

The diary card typically includes rows for each day and columns for various behaviors and urges to engage in those behaviors. The standard

DBT diary card, for example, includes a section on urges to engage in substance use, self-harm, or suicidal behavior, columns asking clients to rate the intensity of various emotional states on each day, and columns asking clients to indicate whether they engaged in any of various behaviors (e.g., self-harm, suicidal behavior, drug or alcohol use). The diary card provides the client and therapist with a snapshot of the client's life over the past week, highlighting important topics to put on the agenda for that session.

Accordingly, following the review of the diary card, the client and therapist collaboratively set an agenda for the session. Individual DBT therapists try to balance a week-to-week focus on emergent behavioral targets (e.g., the self-injury that a client engaged in on Tuesday) with an ongoing focus on goals and factors contributing to client difficulties (e.g., reducing suicidality, depression, or emotional avoidance; improving relationships; addressing deficits in functioning; achieving important social or occupational goals). Treatment targets are identified collaboratively on the basis of how these behaviors lead to problems in the context of the client's daily life. As a result, individualized treatment targets take into account clients' values and the social and cultural contexts in which clients are embedded. The key targets for each session are arranged in a hierarchy, with more time and effort spent on items higher on the hierarchy. The DBT individual therapy hierarchy is as follows:

- *Life-threatening behavior:* any intentional harm of self or others, suicidal crises, thoughts of harming self or others, suicidal/aggressive/homicidal urges, nonsuicidal self-injury, suicide attempts, suicide-related affect, cognition, or actions (e.g., planning for suicide).
- *Therapy-interfering behavior:* any behavior on the part of the clinician or client(s) that interferes with the process or outcome of therapy or the therapy relationship.
- *Quality-of-life-interfering behavior:* behaviors that hamper the client's ability to attain or sustain a reasonable quality of life or reach important goals. Common examples include severe psychiatric symptoms or episodes (e.g., major depressive episode) that impair functioning,

disordered eating, substance use, interpersonal discord, and problems with social or occupational functioning.

- *Skill deficits:* deficits in key behavioral capabilities needed for the client to establish and maintain a life worth living, such as deficits in interpersonal skills needed to connect with others, establish and maintain effective relationships, or get one's needs met (interpersonal effectiveness); distress tolerance skills needed to ride out urges to engage in self-destructive behavior; skills needed to identify and modulate emotions (i.e., emotion regulation skills); skills to pay attention and focus on the present moment (i.e., mindfulness skills), and so forth.

- *Secondary targets:* polarized behavioral patterns or "dialectical dilemmas," in which the client vacillates between extremes. These secondary targets were discussed in Chapter 3.

Also toward the beginning of the session, the client and therapist may review homework from the previous session if applicable. Typically, they set an agenda for the session at the beginning and then actively work on problem areas and goals during the middle of the session. Toward the end of the session, there are a few common activities, including reminding the client that the session is coming to a close soon, summarizing and reflecting on the session, discussing homework, and so forth. Figure 4.2 provides a description of the structure and flow of activities for a typical DBT individual therapy session.

The middle of the session is the crux of where the action happens to help clients reduce problem behaviors and move toward their goals. In terms of content and core interventions, the therapist draws from the broad armamentarium of evidence-based assessment and intervention strategies. Typically, once the therapist has conducted a *functional analysis* (called a *chain analysis* in DBT; Linehan, 1993a; see also Rizvi, 2019) to understand antecedents and consequences surrounding particular problem behaviors, the therapist and client work collaboratively to address these problems using appropriate interventions. For example, a therapist working with a client who has self-injured (a life-threatening behavior) the day prior to the current therapy session

Beginning	• Review diary card. • Prioritize emergent and ongoing targets. • Review homework. • Check on or debrief other modes of therapy (e.g., skills training, phone coaching). • Set agenda.
Middle	• Assess high-priority target areas, often using chain analysis. • Problem-solve problem areas, using various cognitive behavior therapy and DBT interventions. • Obtain a commitment to enact solutions, skills, or behavioral plans or homework related to problem areas/targets. • Troubleshoot client's commitment to various solutions.
End	• Provide notice that the session is soon coming to an end. • Discuss and summarize session activities and discussions. • Discuss and troubleshoot homework, if applicable. • Plan for next session. • Remind client of continued availability for phone coaching, etc.

Figure 4.2

Structure and flow of activities in dialectical behavior therapy (DBT) individual therapy sessions. Data from Linehan (1993a).

would conduct a chain analysis to illuminate factors preceding the self-injury as well as consequences or potential functions of self-injury (e.g., negative reinforcers such as emotional relief, or positive reinforcers such as attention and support from others). During or following the chain analysis, the client and therapist would discuss ways that the client could use behavioral skills to prevent self-injury in similar circumstances in the future (e.g., distress tolerance or emotion regulation skills to reduce emotional distress; communication skills as an alternative means to obtain support). With a client who has arrived late for the third session in a row (a therapy-interfering behavior), the therapist and client would most commonly engage in a chain analysis and address the problems contributing to lateness. With a college student working on social anxiety, the session might involve cognitive strategies to reappraise situations involving speaking up and asking questions during a seminar class, imaginal or in-vivo exposure to anxiety-provoking situations in class, and perhaps a behavioral assignment to ask questions in class, make conversation with fellow classmates, or attend a social function. With a client who reports on the diary card that they went on a bender, used drugs, or misused prescription medications, the DBT therapist would most commonly conduct a chain analysis of factors contributing to these behaviors and use interventions that are effective for the treatment of substance use problems. Sometimes, the same client will present with all of the aforementioned problems (self-injury, lateness, social anxiety, drug and alcohol use), and in these cases, the therapist and client rely on the DBT target hierarchy to delineate the highest priorities for that session. In this example, the client and therapist would most likely address the self-injury and the lateness, and if time permits, the substance use. In these ways, DBT follows a case formulation-driven, modular approach to individual treatment (Farmer & Chapman, 2016; Persons & Tompkins, 2007), rather than a predetermined protocol. Figure 4.3 provides a general guide to the types of interventions that an individual DBT therapist may consider to address particular problem areas.

Group DBT Skills Training

The primary aim of group DBT skills training is to increase client capabilities (skills) in several key areas. The skills training group is like a class, and individual therapy and the client's everyday life are like the lab, where the client gets to apply new skills to important situations (C. R. Swenson,

Problem area	Possibly helpful intervention
Motivational deficit	Commitment or motivational strategies
Skill deficit	Skills training
Contingencies reinforce problem behavior	Contingency management strategies
Excessive fear or inhibited grieving	Exposure-based strategies, acceptance/mindfulness
Cognitions contribute to misery or problem behavior	Cognitive strategies, acceptance/mindfulness

Figure 4.3

Matching intervention strategies with problem areas. Data from Linehan (1993a).

personal communication, January 26, 2020). In DBT, skills training is separated from individual therapy and occurs in a group, primarily because trying to teach behavioral skills in a structured manner in individual therapy with highly suicidal clients would be much like trying to give cooking lessons to a student who keeps taking the food off the stove, fighting with the sous chef, lighting fires in the kitchen, pouring salt into the cake batter, or leaving to use drugs. In a treatment that must address urgent and complex challenges, it is difficult to consistently teach skills, and in a skills-only treatment, it is difficult to address individual client's challenges. The class-like structure of the DBT skills group allows for consistency in skills training and helps clients feel connected to a group of other people who are struggling with similar difficulties.

The DBT skills training group typically occurs weekly, for approximately 1.5 to 2.5 hours, with shorter groups typical in the treatment of adolescents (1.5 hours), and longer groups typical in the treatment of adults (e.g., 2–2.5 hours). Groups typically include between 4 and 12 clients—our preference is usually somewhere between 6 and 10, as this allows for optimal time to get through the review of homework and the teaching of new skills. We have found that groups that are much larger than 12 are challenging to navigate, leaving little time to review each client's homework in a helpful manner.

The DBT skills group is structured like a class, with a predetermined flow of activities and a set curriculum. The group normally begins with a brief mindfulness exercise to strengthen clients' skills in mindfulness over time, followed by the review of homework (to practice new skills) from the previous week, a break, teaching of new skills, assigning of homework, and a brief wind-down exercise at the end. Teaching and homework assignments focus on the four skill modules of DBT: mindfulness, distress tolerance, interpersonal effectiveness, and emotion regulation. Although not a formal skills module in DBT, the skills trainers weave in ad-hoc teaching on behavioral self-management and self-regulation, often including discussion of the use of contingencies to promote behavior change in oneself (e.g., rewarding oneself after using skills or going for a period without problem behaviors) or others (e.g., by observing limits in relationships with others, avoiding reinforcing the abusive or problematic behavior of others). Clients in DBT often have received the message that they simply need to "try harder" to overcome their problems, but in reality, they lack the self-management skills to do so. Figure 4.4 describes the structure and flow of activities for a typical DBT group skills training session.

DBT skills groups are taught by a leader and a coleader. The leader's role usually is to run the group, keep discussions on track, review homework, and teach skills. The leader is the key agent of change, whereas the coleader balances this change focus by observing the group process, providing validation and clarification as needed. The coleader is also available to assist and coach distressed or dysregulated clients in skills to tolerate distress during group. In some groups, the leader and coleader alternate roles week-to-week or even within particular sessions: one therapist serves as the leader for the first half of group (the mindfulness and homework review portion) and the other therapist serves as the leader for the latter half (teaching new skills, assigning homework, and leading the wind-down activity).

Sometimes, the leader, coleader, or both are also primary individual therapists for some of the clients in the group, although this does not have to be the case. When a leader or coleader also functions as a group client's

| 5–10 minutes before group: Group leaders arrive, set up and interact with clients. |
| Leader leads clients in and debriefs mindfulness exercise (~5 minutes). |
| Leader reviews clients' homework from last week, seeking opportunities to coach in new skills. |
| Break |
| Leader teaches new skills for that week, using active teaching strategies and encouraging practice. |
| Leader assigns and troubleshoots homework for that week (usually, specific worksheets). |
| Leader leads wind-down exercise, often involving brief observations of the group session. |

Figure 4.4

The structure and agenda for dialectical behavior therapy skills training group sessions. Data from Linehan (1993a).

individual therapist, it is helpful for the individual therapist to orient the client to the different roles the therapist will play in group versus individual therapy, and to discuss relevant issues pertaining to confidentiality (i.e., does the client wish to keep the identity of their individual therapist confidential from other group members?).

As with individual therapy, a hierarchy of behavioral targets guides the focus of the DBT skills training group. This hierarchy is different from that of individual therapy, in that life-threatening and quality-of-life-interfering behaviors are not part of the hierarchy. This is because the skills group leaders do not directly target life-threatening behavior in group. If a client is suicidal, the group leaders will conduct a reasonable risk assessment and connect the client to their individual therapist or (if needed) crisis or hospital services. Life-threatening behavior, however, is not a common topic of discussion in group, and clients are discouraged from discussing the specifics of any self-damaging behavior during group (to avoid behavioral contagion). Quality-of-life-interfering behavior likewise is not a focus of group, except insofar as applicable quality-of-life issues emerge during discussions of skills during the homework review or teaching portion of the group. A client may, for example, describe efforts to apply interpersonal effectiveness skills during arguments with a partner, and the discussion of this would center on how to use specific skills.

Target Hierarchy

The target hierarchy for skills training includes three primary targets. The highest priority target in skills training, if applicable, is *therapy-destroying behavior*, consisting of any behavior on the part of the client (or therapists) that makes it nearly *impossible* for the group to function or for the clients to benefit from skills training. Therapy-destroying behavior typically is rare, but it does happen, and examples include verbal or physical aggression toward other group members or the group therapists, out of control yelling or screaming during group, physical damage of property, the offering or selling of drugs to other group members, and so on. When therapy-destroying behavior occurs, the skills group leader and coleader must attend to it immediately, help the client cease the behavior, and if it is severe enough, consider a repair for the group (e.g., an apology or some kind of gift or action to repair the damage to the group), a therapy vacation, or termination (very much a last resort). The next highest priority target in group skills training is *skill acquisition*. Assuming no therapy-destroying behavior is occurring, the leader and coleader spend the majority of the group either coaching clients in skills (in the homework review portion of group) or teaching skills (in the teaching portion). Finally, the third highest priority target is *therapy-interfering behavior*, with common examples including homework noncompliance, lateness, absences, off-task or distracting behavior (e.g., texting, falling asleep, dissociating), lack of participation, talking out of turn or in a tangential manner, and so forth. Often, the leader and coleader will either ignore therapy-interfering behavior or address it directly by highlighting it and redirecting the client to engage in an alternative behavior, coaching the client in a helpful skill (e.g., a distress tolerance skill, if the client is emotionally overwhelmed during group), or conducting a chain analysis or a missing links analysis (Linehan, 2015b), which is a structured, abbreviated version of a chain analysis. Most commonly, skills group leaders will use chain or missing links analyses with clients who have not completed their homework. In addition, there are some specific rules and norms for DBT skills groups, and violating the rules would constitute therapy-interfering behavior. In our groups, however, we often tell clients that DBT skills groups are not no-mistakes-allowed groups. When clients don't do their homework, show up late, have difficulty staying present during group, or engage in other behaviors, we let them know we want to help them get back on track so they and others can get the most out of group. Only in exceptionally rare circumstances are clients asked to leave a group based on therapy-destroying or interfering behavior.

DBT Skills Modules

DBT skills training teaches four distinct modules of skills, across mindfulness, interpersonal effectiveness, distress tolerance, and emotion regulation. The standard format involves 2 weeks of mindfulness training, followed by 6 weeks of another module followed by 2 weeks of mindfulness training, with the exception being that the emotion regulation module usually takes 8 weeks to complete. Thus, each of the other three modules alternates with mindfulness. Following this schedule, it takes approximately six months to teach all the modules of the skills.

Mindfulness skills are considered a core skill set in DBT. The goal of this module is to help clients identify when their behaviors are governed by emotional urges ("Emotion Mind") or logic without considering emotions ("Reasonable Mind"), with the aim of spending more time in a state of mind in which they are aware of emotions and the facts of the situation, and are able to intentionally choose behaviors in line with their values ("Wise Mind"). In the service of spending more time making mindful, intentional choices, clients are taught *What* skills of mindfulness, involving *observing* sensations, *describing* or adding a label to these sensations, and *participating* fully in the present moment. The *How* skills teach clients to adopt a *nonjudgmental* stance, in which clients are coached to let go of value-laden interpretations and focus on describing the facts. In addition, these skills teach clients to be *one-mindful* of the present moment. Finally, clients are taught that mindfulness involves acting *effectively* in the present moment, focusing on doing what works in the moment.

Interpersonal effectiveness skills are focused on helping clients to improve their ability to maintain adaptive relationships. The therapist coaches clients to consider their priorities in a given interpersonal interaction as a guide to what skills might be useful. Borrowing from classic assertiveness training, DBT teaches clients steps to ask for what they need and say no to unwanted requests. In addition, DBT teaches skills for sustaining relationships, in part by validating others. Further, there are skills to help clients interact in a manner consistent with their values to maintain self-respect even in the context of difficult interactions. The latest skills manual also incorporates strategies for building new relationships and ending destructive relationships.

Distress tolerance skills help clients get through a crisis situation without resorting to behaviors that may make the situation worse. This module teaches clients that sometimes pain is unavoidable, and yet can be tolerated through a number of strategies, including distracting, self-soothing, and focusing on small ways to improve the present moment. In addition, this module includes reality acceptance skills that help clients observe distress without acting on urges and focus on acceptance of unavoidable pain. Ultimately, the goal is to help clients survive unavoidable pain without engaging in impulsive behaviors such as self-injury, substance use, or conflictual behaviors that may make the situation worse.

Emotion regulation skills are intended to improve emotional awareness and reduce overall emotional lability. Clients are taught to identify their emotions, including paying attention to how these emotions might convey important information about the environment. For instance, fear may signal a need to protect oneself, or sadness may signal a desire for social support. This psychoeducation counters much of clients' early learning that emotions are bad or wrong. In addition, clients are taught to identify when emotions fit the facts of the present moment, serving as signals that are responsive to the present circumstances, versus when emotions may be disproportionate to the present situation, or may be elicited by thoughts or memories. For instance, a client with frequent intrusive thoughts regarding a past traumatic car accident may experience fear or anxiety when riding as a passenger in the car, even if there is no danger in the present environment. In the case that emotions are prompting ineffective behaviors or do not fit the facts of the present situation, clients are encouraged to identify the urges that go along with the emotion (e.g., escape or avoidance of cues that elicit memories of a past trauma) and practice *opposite action*, which in this case might be to approach (safe) car rides. Conversely, in the event that emotions are signaling appropriate information about the environment, often problem-solving the event that is eliciting the emotion is warranted. For instance, if a client notices fear when driving a vehicle that is unsafe, problem-solving efforts might include a trip to the mechanic. Clients are also taught strategies for reducing vulnerability to intense emotions by engaging in regular self-care behaviors (e.g., maintaining stable sleep and exercise), engaging in valued activities, and building positive emotional experiences.

These elements of DBT skills training have been modified in several ways to make them more accessible to a range of cultural contexts. For instance, in an effort to increase the accessibility of interpersonal effectiveness skills to a Latinx client, one therapist added values of family unity to DBT skills training (Mercado & Hinojosa, 2017). Likewise, another clinician added a focus on indirect, harmonious communication to interpersonal effectiveness skills training for an international student from China (Cheng & Merrick, 2017). Although such modifications have not been tested experimentally, the DBT skills training format lends itself to the modular application of skills that work in a given context. Skills trainers also encourage clients to use skills in ways that are aligned with their values and effective in their social and cultural contexts. We have seen clients, for example, who have said the interpersonal skills seem far too "American," (i.e., direct and assertiveness-based) and that, in their cultures, more indirect communication is most effective. In those cases, we work with clients to help them use principles underlying the skills (e.g., balancing one's own needs with those of others; being clear about wants and needs; considering and validating the other person's perspective) in ways that work with their friends and loved ones.

Telephone Consultation, or Phone Coaching

The primary aim of *phone coaching* is to help clients generalize what they are learning in therapy to their everyday lives. The therapist is available between sessions for as-needed communication to coach the client in skills they can use to navigate challenging everyday life situations. Typically, phone coaching occurs over the phone, but increasingly, DBT therapists have been using various forms of electronic communication for phone coaching, with their attendant conveniences and challenges (for a discussion of these issues, see Chapman, 2018). The key focus of phone coaching is on which skills the client can use and how to use them. The therapist is also available when the client needs to discuss reactions to the therapist or therapy sessions that would simmer over the course of the week without the opportunity to express them and receive help with skills coaching. In addition, phone coaching sometimes focuses on resolving suicidal crises and emergencies, although it is more ideal for clients to call earlier for help with skills to avert crises (Chapman, 2018).

In terms of structure, phone coaching calls are brief, focused, and emphasize skills. These calls are typically initiated by the clients to address issues as they arise in the clients' daily lives. Calls typically are brief (usually 5–15 minutes, although there is no set time frame for the calls), are focused primarily on skills the client can use, and are not therapy sessions over the phone. Most commonly, the therapist will begin phone coaching calls by asking the client about the current problem, what skills they have tried so far, and what kind of help they need. The discussion then centers on how the client can effectively use various skills. Subsequently, time permitting, the therapist may secure a commitment to a plan to use these skills, help the client troubleshoot factors that might interfere with the plan, and end the call. Sometimes the therapist will schedule a future check-in call or remind the client of the therapist's continued availability for phone coaching.

It is always important for therapists to remember that phone coaching is not individual therapy. To avoid allowing phone coaching to turn into individual therapy on the phone, the clinician should clearly orient the client at the beginning of therapy to the purpose and structure of phone coaching, remind the client that the focus is on short-term ways to use skills to navigate everyday situations (most commonly, skills to regulate or tolerate difficult emotions in the short term), and redirect the client to focus on skills during the call. For example, with a client who begins talking at length about relationship difficulties, the therapist might say something like, "I know these challenges with your partner have been incredibly stressful and demoralizing, and I want to spend more time trying to work on this problem. For now, we only have a few minutes, and the best we can do is focus on skills to make the situation a little more bearable until we can meet and spend more time on it."

As with individual therapy and group skills training, there is a hierarchy of targets for DBT phone coaching calls (Figure 4.5 describes the hierarchy of targets across DBT modes). The top of the hierarchy is *life-threatening behavior*, and when acute suicide risk is present, phone coaching calls aim to reduce risk and help the client use skills to manage emotions or situations contributing to suicidality (or desires to engage in self-injury or harm someone else). The next highest priority, and the primary focus of most phone coaching calls, is *skill generalization*, whereby the therapist helps the client apply skills learned in therapy to the current, challenging situation. If a client, for example, calls because they are distressed about losing their job, the therapist would provide coaching on how to manage the most distressing emotions arising in this situation, tolerate these emotions, avoid worsening the situation (e.g., by drinking or self-harming behavior), and so forth. Similarly, a client calling after a distressing break up would receive coaching in how to use skills to manage or tolerate emotions (e.g., sadness, guilt) related to this loss. Addressing joblessness or relationship issues in the long run would be deferred for individual therapy sessions, when the client and therapist have more time to discuss and problem-solve these longer-term issues. Finally, the third highest priority is to reduce the client's *sense of alienation from the therapist*. In these cases, clients might call when they

Individual therapy	Group skills training	Phone coaching
Life-threatening behavior	Therapy-destroying behavior	Life-threatening behavior
Therapy-destroying or therapy-interfering behavior	Skill deficits	Skill generalization
Quality-of-life-interfering behavior	Therapy-interfering behavior	Sense of alienation from clinician
Skill deficits		
Secondary targets (dialectical dilemmas)		

Figure 4.5

Target hierarchies for different dialectical behavior therapy modes. Data from Linehan (1993a).

feel disconnected or alienated from the therapist or when distressing events have arisen in therapy sessions, and a brief heart-to-heart talk and discussion of skills to tolerate or manage related emotions would make it easier to cope while waiting to address these issues more thoroughly in the next session.

DBT Consultation Team

The primary aim of the DBT consultation team is to fulfill the function of maintaining and enhancing therapist motivation and skill. The team typically meets weekly for a duration that largely depends on the size of the program and number of clients and clinicians on the team (most commonly 45 minutes–2 hours). Team members may be from different disciplines (e.g., psychology, psychiatry, social work, counseling) but all must be actively engaged in some element of DBT. The consultation team is a group of peers who consult, support, and help one another, and as such, team members must be willing to be vulnerable enough to discuss emotional and other challenges occurring in their work. When power differentials are present (e.g., a supervisor, director, or manager is on the team), the team strives to treat all members as equals and discourages supervisors or administrators from acting as such during team meetings.

In terms of the team structure and roles, two members help to lead each meeting, with one member acting as the meeting leader and another acting as the observer, with a third member serving as a note taker. In many DBT teams, the meeting leader, observer, and note taker roles rotate regularly to allow clinicians to gain experience in each role. At the DBT Centre of Vancouver, for example, we rotate these roles each month. The leader position rotates in alphabetical order. The person who served as the leader the previous month is the observer the next month, and the person who took notes the previous month is the leader the next month. The meeting leader starts the meeting by leading a mindfulness exercise, reads aloud an agreement emphasizing a key principle of DBT, helps to set the agenda, and ensures that team discussions stay on track. The leader often decides upon a mindfulness exercise from among many common exercises that appear in the DBT skills training manual (Linehan, 2015b), other books on mindfulness, or among the many mindfulness exercises that have been passed down or shared among people in the DBT community or during trainings. The leader may choose which agreement they feel like reading or may choose an agreement that is particularly germane to issues facing the team. A team, for example, that is regularly arguing or becoming polarized about various issues could benefit from a reminder of the *dialectical agreement* to work to understand the truth in both positions and work toward a synthesis. See Linehan (1993a) for a list and description of each of the DBT consultation team agreements.

The observer is an active participant in the meeting (i.e., brings up agenda items of their own to discuss) but remains alert for any behavior on the part of a therapist that should be addressed, such as a therapist expressing judgment about themselves or their clients, coming to the meeting unprepared, not participating, becoming defensive in response to suggestions or feedback, or other behaviors considered contrary to the principles of DBT. The observer highlights these behaviors when they occur, and the team works together to get back on track. Most commonly, the observer quickly highlights a therapist's behavior, and things move on. If a therapist calls themselves stupid for something said or done during a session, for example, the observer might say, "Hey, stupid is a judgment. Describe what happened without judging yourself." The observer also tries to maintain the dialectical focus of the team by noticing when discussions become polarized and helping the team work toward synthesis. Usually, consultation teams also have a note taker, who actively participates in team discussions and takes relevant notes for documentation purposes.

In most of the teams we are familiar with, and in the teams that operated at Dr. Linehan's center, the agenda usually follows the hierarchy of client targets and most commonly addresses the following (in order of importance): (a) imminent risk of harm to self or others; (b) out of town coverage (e.g., for phone coaching or in-person individual or group sessions); (c) risk of dropout; (d) life-threatening, therapy-interfering, and quality-of-life-interfering behavior, among other relevant targets. Although the agenda usually follows this client-oriented hierarchy, the team functions much like "therapy for the therapists" in that discussions do not center on client behavior or pathology but rather on therapist challenges in working with clients. A therapist, for example, requesting help with a client who is habitually late or absent, might seek suggestions on how to assess or intervene as well as how to cope with irritation or frustration about repeated lateness or absences. A therapist encountering difficult client behavior (e.g., hostile criticism, repeated suicidal crises, frequent calls) might seek help to reduce the likelihood of impending burnout. In this case, the team might help the therapist practice ways to bring up the problem behavior with the client and collaboratively work to solve it. Another therapist with a client at imminent risk of suicide might seek suggestions on how to reduce the client's risk or ask for help thinking through the pros and cons of hospitalization or other courses of action. As with individual DBT sessions, well-functioning teams look for opportunities to "drag out" new behavior on the part of the therapist, using strategies such as modeling effective behavior, and encouraging the therapist to practice this behavior in a role-play during the team meeting. Teams that spend the whole hour or two simply discussing problems or trying to solve administrative or programmatic issues have drifted from the purpose of the consultation team, which is to support therapists and help them maintain motivation and skill with challenging clients. To maintain the focus on therapist needs and help meetings run smoothly and efficiently, many teams encourage therapists to identify what kind of help they need from the team before the meeting. Four areas are often emphasized: (a) assistance assessing a problem, (b) assistance solving a problem, (c) validation of the therapist's challenges, and (d) assistance increasing or maintaining empathy for the client.

In some practice settings, it can be challenging to implement the DBT consultation team. We have worked with teams in which clinicians are geographically separated, there are too few DBT clinicians to form a team, rotating work shifts and demands hamper regularly scheduled team meetings, and so forth. It is beyond the scope of this chapter to address all of these problems. In some cases, teams have benefitted from the use of remote communication technology to form virtual teams with clinicians in other places. When work shifts and obligations threaten team functioning, some teams have successfully lobbied for protected time for consultation team meetings or reduced caseloads to allow for productivity credit. DBT is not an approach we would recommend for solo practitioners, as it is a team-based program, and solo practitioners offering an element of DBT (e.g., individual therapy only) would benefit from seeking ways to connect with other local DBT clinicians. For more discussion of these and other issues, see Sayrs and Linehan (2019).

THE FIVE STAGES OF DBT

DBT includes five primary stages of treatment:

1. *Pretreatment* focuses on orienting the client to treatment and eliciting a commitment to engage in therapy.
2. *Stage 1* focuses on helping the client attain control over their behavior and learn skills.
3. *Stage 2* often focuses on helping the client experience and accept difficult emotions and continue to work toward building the foundations of a life worth living.
4. *Stage 3* involves helping the client solve ordinary problems in living faced by people without significant mental health concerns, such as occupational or relationship difficulties, stress management, and so forth.
5. *Stage 4* usually addresses the client's capacity for joy and freedom, as well as meaning and fulfillment.

To illustrate some of the strategies used in some of these stages, we have included an example of the hypothetical client, "Mario."

> Mario is a 45-year-old, married, cisgender Italian American man who presented for help with anger management, relationship problems, and depression. He has been married to his wife, Georgia, for 15 years and has two preteen boys. At intake, standard cognitive behavioral

therapy, possibly supplemented with couples therapy, seemed appropriate, but later, Mario disclosed a history of multiple prior suicide attempts and related hospitalizations, as well as problematic alcohol use. He had great difficulty tolerating and managing anger and frustration, particularly toward his wife, children, or coworkers, and his anger has caused problems at work (disciplinary reports) and at home (in his relationship with his wife and children). When he first came in for treatment, he was not in a depressive episode, but he did express strong suicidal ideation and stated that he did not think there was any point trying to work on his problems, as he'll just "end ruining everyone's life" or "back in the hospital again." Nevertheless, he did report that his relationship with his wife and children was his "lifeline," and that he desperately wants to get his anger under control so he can earn their respect and trust.

We will return to "Mario" when we illustrate various principles and strategies throughout the remainder of the chapter.

The first stage, pretreatment, is when the client initially presents for help and is undergoing an intake assessment and their initial therapy sessions, which are focused on assessment, orientation, and commitment to moving forward with the treatment. Often, the pretreatment stage lasts approximately four sessions, in addition to any intake assessment sessions.

In Stage 1, the primary aim is to help the client attain behavioral control. Clients in Stage 1 often present with reckless, out of control or self-destructive behavior, serious risk of suicide or NSSI, and severe instability in their interpersonal relations and/or living situation. Many clients lack the behavioral skills they need to avoid exacerbating their problems through self-destructive behaviors or actions that harm relationships or impair their functional capacity (e.g., substance use, reckless spending). Skills training addresses these deficits, and individual therapy aims to improve behavioral control and help clients begin to work toward developing a life worth living. Stage 1 is perhaps the most commonly implemented stage of DBT. As increasing behavioral control and reducing life-threatening behaviors are prerequisites to developing a life worth living, in this chapter, we emphasize Stage 1 more so than other stages.

In Stage 2, clients often have learned how to avoid making their problems worse and begun to piece together a life worth living but may still experience posttraumatic stress symptoms, inhibited grieving, emotional avoidance, or a sense of alienation from others. As such, Stage 2 may focus on PTSD treatment, acceptance strategies to increase emotional experiencing and tolerance, interventions to address damage to relationships, and ongoing work to increase the client's level of functioning (findings suggest persisting functional impairment in BPD, even in the presence of symptom remission; Gunderson et al., 2011; Soloff & Chiappetta, 2017; Zanarini, Frankenburg, Reich, & Fitzmaurice, 2010; see also Biskin, 2015).

Stage 3 addresses ordinary problems in living, such as general life or work stress, relationship difficulties, health and well-being, mood, anxiety, or mild substance use problems, among other normative difficulties. By the time clients reach Stage 3, they have a fairly stable life and are able to work on improving and enhancing life and reducing factors that generate stress or dissatisfaction.

Finally, Stage 4 tends to be more existential, focused on issues of meaning and fulfillment and the cultivation of freedom and the capacity for joy. Freedom in DBT generally refers to freedom from having to do what one's thoughts, urges, and emotions dictate and instead to follow a valued life path. By Stage 4, clients are better able to devote their efforts to increasing their capacity for joy and fulfillment. Stage 4 may also address issues of meaning, purpose, values, and spirituality. These stages are not fixed and linear, in that a Stage 1 client, for example, may at times work on Stage 3 problems, and a Stage 3 client may fall back into Stage 1 patterns from time to time.

Primary Pretreatment Strategies

In the pretreatment stage, the primary goal is to help the client understand and commit to treatment. The emphasis is on assessment, orientation, and commitment strategies. In this stage, the primary individual therapist orients the client to the theory, philosophy, and practicalities of DBT, conducts assessment of current and prior psychosocial functioning (broadly defined, including psychiatric symptoms, history of suicidal or self-injurious behaviors among other important targets, social and occupational functioning, and so forth), and helps the client commit to treatment. The individual therapist often describes the DBT assumptions about patients (some of which are briefly summarized in Figure 4.6), the biosocial theory as it applies to the individual client (described in Chapter 3), the requirements of the client (e.g., consistent attendance at individual and group sessions, homework completion), the DBT hierarchy of treatment targets and how this is used to prioritize problems addressed during sessions, and any important rules (some rules pertain to group, phone coaching, and attendance).

Having described what treatment entails, the therapist then helps the client commit to treatment, using various DBT commitment strategies. These strategies overlap in some cases with those used in motivational interviewing, but—given the gravity of the presenting concerns of complex clients (which are often literally life or death)—tend to be more directive than motivational interviewing. In the case of Mario, given his past history of suicide attempts, current hopelessness, and destabilizing factors such as alcohol use, anger management problems, and interpersonal discord, it would be very important to help him make a strong commitment and develop a solid plan to avoid suicidal behavior. The therapist is likely to be fairly directive about this, as illustrated in the

| Patients in DBT are doing the best they can. |
| Patients in DBT need to do better, try harder, and/or be more motivated to change. |
| Patients cannot fail in DBT. |
| DBT therapists can fail. |
| DBT can fail even when DBT therapists do not. |

Figure 4.6

Selected key dialectical behavior therapy (DBT) assumptions about patients. Data from Linehan (1993a).

example of selling commitment below. We have listed the DBT commitment strategies in Figure 4.7, and we focus next on a couple of key strategies often used in the pretreatment phase: selling commitment and devil's advocate.

Selling commitment involves the therapist conveying a strong rationale for the client to commit to treatment and take suicide off the table in the service of developing a life worth living. Selling commitment often is most effective when the therapist is aware of goals that are important to the client and can link commitment to treatment to those goals. An example of the therapist selling commitment to Mario might include the following:

> OK, Mario, we have to talk about the most important agreement you need to make for this therapy, and that is to stay alive throughout therapy. As it happens, this therapy doesn't work if you're dead. Also, trying to kill yourself or killing yourself will not help you build a life worth living. It also won't help you improve things with your wife or help you to be there for your kids. If you really want to get a handle on your anger problems and start to fix things up with

Selling commitment	Discussing the benefits of committing to DBT
Pros and cons	Helping the client consider the pros and cons of committing to DBT
Devil's advocate	Arguing against commitment (to DBT or desirable behavior change)
Foot in the door/ door in the face	Asking for a smaller change than desired (foot in the door) or asking for a larger change than needed (door in the face)
Freedom to choose/absence of alternatives	Explaining how the client is free to choose not to engage in treatment (e.g., stop attempting suicide), but that there is no other option if she or he wishes to develop a life worth living
Reminding the client of previous commitments	Reminding the client of previous commitments made to the therapist or previous successful commitments (e.g., to get off drugs)
Shaping commitment	Reinforcing successive approximations toward full commitment to treatment

Figure 4.7

Key dialectical behavior therapy commitment strategies. Data from Linehan (1993a).

your wife, you're going to have to jump into therapy with both feet. Hanging on to suicide is sort of like keeping one hand on the edge of the swimming pool during your swimming lessons. You can't really swim. And, you're going to need both arms and legs. So, what I'm asking you is very hard, I know, but I'm asking you to agree to take suicide off the table while we're working together, and to stay alive and give us a chance to build your life back up again.

In dialectical contrast to selling commitment, the therapist using the devil's advocate strategy argues against commitment. Instead of describing how committing to treatment might help Mario manage his anger and improve his relationships, the therapist might voice concerns about how difficult therapy is, how it might be easier to just retain the status quo, and so forth. Often, the devil's advocate strategy magnifies the tension between alternatives (e.g., effectively managing anger vs. keeping things as they are) and elicits arguments from the client in favor of change. The therapist using the devil's advocate strategy with Mario might say the following:

I'm glad to hear that you're willing to come to our sessions and attend group, and it sounds like you're willing to take suicide off the table, which is really important. I'm just wondering, though, why you'd agree to all of this. Therapy is really hard work and can be emotionally painful. You're probably going to have to talk about outbursts you've had at home as well as your alcohol use and deal with the shame that goes along with all of that. You're going to have to try to learn new skills and use them to get through some pretty painful situations without trying to harm yourself. I also think you might find group challenging, based on what you've said about how you don't like listening to other people's problems. If I were you, I might be thinking things are bad right now, but the road to change is also pretty bumpy . . .

Ideally, and often, a client like Mario will argue for the opposite and start to come up with reasons to commit to therapy and change. When this does not occur, and the client agrees with the therapist, all is not lost. The therapist can flexibly move into other strategies, such as helping the client think through the pros and cons to committing to therapy, and so forth. The devil's advocate strategy often is used in the first few sessions of the pretreatment stage of DBT but can be used anytime to help strengthen a client's commitment to change by eliciting self-motivational statements. Usually, by the end of the pretreatment stage, the client has been fully oriented, has committed to treatment, and has begun completing a DBT diary card each week and has started to attend a DBT skills group.

With regard to skills group, some DBT programs also have commitment and orientation sessions with each individual client before they begin, or they conduct such orientation in the client's first group. Generally, we have found that it is most effective (in terms of enhancing commitment and group retention) to at least meet briefly and individually to address individual goals and questions with each client before they begin skills group. Ideally, during these meetings, the therapist will use commitment strategies to secure a strong commitment to skills training. One of us was consulting recently with a DBT team working in corrections in a state system. Several clients were attending and completing their homework only sporadically at best. The suggestion was made that they consider having 20-minute orientation and commitment sessions with each individual client before they start group, and with existing clients who had not had this type of orientation or commitment session. Within about a month, the clinicians had conducted all of these sessions, and they reported that both attendance and homework compliance had improved dramatically. One element of orientation and commitment that they reported was particularly helpful was a focus on how group can help clients achieve important personal goals (e.g., being more connected with others, having fewer restrictions on their freedom in the institution, being able to speak with family members more often, being a good parent and role model).

The most critical commitment that a client can make during the pretreatment stage is to remain alive for the duration of treatment, and this commitment is a major focus of the initial sessions of individual therapy (not group skills training, where the focus is on skills rather than life-threatening behavior). We often explain to new clients that committing to taking suicide off the table is not the same as making a *promise*, and that clients will not be dropped from therapy for having the problems they are seeking help for. Suicide attempts might happen, and if so, we will help the client get back on track, often using chain analyses to figure out what happened and problem-solving to prevent future instances. In our experience, even clients who have difficulty making this commitment at first eventually come around and agree to devote their efforts toward building a life worth living rather than ending their lives. More rarely, despite the therapist pulling out all of the stops, skillfully using commitment strategies and other DBT techniques, a client will not be ready to commit to at least addressing suicide or reducing risk. These unfortunate instances are stressful for the therapist and client alike and put the therapist in a difficult position. When this is the case, the therapist might suggest that this is not the time for the client to engage in DBT, suggest an alternative treatment, provide appropriate referrals, and take steps to adhere to relevant ethical principles to avoid abandoning an at-risk client.

Although this initial orientation and commitment work is the main priority during pretreatment, a DBT therapist is also aware that motivation and commitment may ebb and flow throughout treatment. Therefore, the therapist often returns to these commitment strategies later on in treatment. In this manner, DBT directly targets client motivation to change, rather than considering motivation to be something that clients need to have and sustain independently in order to benefit from treatment.

Primary Stage 1 Strategies

Stage 1 is the most well-defined and studied stage of DBT, and the structure and strategies of Stage 1 treatment often extend into the other stages of DBT. In Stage 1, often spanning the first 6 to 12 months of treatment, the primary aim is to help the client attain behavioral control. Often, complex clients present to treatment with instability in various life domains and have great difficulty tolerating and regulating emotions and self-regulating behavior more broadly. Clients in Stage 1 are often suicidal or regularly self-injure, use drugs or alcohol in a problematic or reckless manner, or engage in various other self-damaging behaviors. Interpersonal discord and instability are common, and some clients struggle to maintain a reasonable degree of psychosocial functioning (e.g., navigating daily living tasks, relationships, occupational or other productive endeavors). Indeed, some research has suggested that the majority of patients with BPD present with psychosocial functioning in the poor range, and that functional impairments sometimes persist for many years (Soloff & Chiappetta, 2017). The primary aim of Stage 1, therefore, is to help the client attain enough behavioral control to function more effectively in different life domains, reduce or eliminate self-damaging behaviors, and establish a strong foundation from which to build a life worth living.

In Stage 1, there is an emphasis on the reduction of problematic behaviors and the building of behavioral skills. The DBT skills training group is the primary means to build behavioral skills, but as mentioned earlier, the primary individual therapist also teaches clients skills as needed to address specific problems (e.g., a client who wants to learn to ask for behavioral changes from their partner without yelling and screaming). Determining what skills or strategies to emphasize requires regular behavioral self-monitoring via the diary card and other tools as well as precise behavioral assessment.

As mentioned earlier, the therapist uses the diary card in conjunction with the individual therapy hierarchy of targets (e.g., life-threatening, therapy-interfering, quality-of-life-interfering, skills deficits, as well as secondary targets) to determine how much time and attention to devote to various topics. If Mario, for example, noted an anger outburst, binge drinking, and an instance of self-injury on his diary card (see Figure 4.8 for an example of some sections of Mario's diary card), the therapist and client would prioritize the self-injury, likely conduct a chain analysis, and then determine what Mario could do differently in a similar situation to avoid harming himself. That's not to say that the binge drinking or anger outburst are unimportant; these quality-of-life issues would also be

Day	Suicide attempt	Self-Injury	Outburst	Alcohol	Anger	Misery
Monday	No	Yes	Yes	6 beers	5	5
Tuesday	No	No	No	None	3	3
Wednesday	No	No	No	None	3	2
Thursday	No	No	Yes	3 beers	4	3
Friday	No	No	Yes	4 beers	4	4
Saturday	No	No	No	1 beer	3	2
Sunday	No	No	No	None	3	2

Figure 4.8

Example section of diary card for Mario. Anger and misery rated on a scale from 0 (*none*) to 5 (*most intense possible*), with ratings corresponding to the *highest peak* anger or misery for that particular day. This example diary card represents only about two thirds of what is normally on a dialectical behavior therapy diary card. Data from Linehan (1993a).

explored if time permits; they may have occurred on the chain of events leading to or following the self-injury. The therapist also might highlight and help Mario see various patterns emerging on the diary card, such as the co-occurrence of drinking and anger outbursts on Monday, Thursday, and Friday, and the 5s for anger and misery on the same day on which self-injury occurred. Over time, the patterns appearing on the diary card would help the therapeutic dyad to better understand Mario's behavior and may generate hypotheses, such as the hypotheses that drinking is either a vulnerability factor for anger outbursts or occurs during or following such outbursts as a way to regulate guilt or shame.

Once key topics are chosen for a particular session (and we generally recommend that therapists try to choose one to three topics given realistic time limitations), the therapist usually collaboratively assesses high priority problem behaviors and helps the client engage in problem-solving to reduce these behaviors or prevent their recurrence. The primary assessment method in Stage 1 individual DBT is the *chain analysis*, used to understand factors occasioning and maintaining target behaviors. Similar to behavioral functional analyses (see Farmer & Chapman, 2016; see also Rizvi, 2019, for a recent book focused entirely on chain analysis in

DBT), a chain analysis is a detailed examination of antecedents, problem behaviors, and consequences, and the various links (thoughts, emotions, physiological sensations, actions, situational factors) between events.

During the chain analysis, the therapist is particularly interested in illuminating the "essence" of the problem contributing to the client's behavior and problem areas. If Mario self-injured after a fight with his wife in which he screamed at her and then felt guilty and ashamed, one hypothesis is that self-injury regulates these emotions or serves as self-punishment (regulating emotions and punishing oneself are common reasons or motivations for self-injury; Brown, Comtois, & Linehan, 2002; Kleindienst et al., 2008, see also Chapman, Gratz, & Brown, 2006). The therapist also would want to know what precipitated Mario's outburst, as his misery and relationship discord will likely continue if he were to continue to yell and scream at his wife. A chain analysis might reveal that the fight started after Mario's wife asked him if he has been looking for job openings, and he felt ashamed about being depressed and unemployed. Let's say that self-directed anger was a secondary reaction to shame, and anger toward his wife for raising the employment issue and prompting all of this misery preceded his outburst. In this case, interventions might aim to systematically solve the problems contributing to shame (by reducing depression and improving his functioning), ways to regulate or communicate his emotions to his wife in the moment, and strategies to avoid yelling and screaming (e.g., distress tolerance skills, taking a time-out) even if he feels strong anger. Other strategies might address the cognitions associated with Mario's shame about unemployment (e.g., "I'm a loser and a failure") and might involve mindfulness (helping Mario observe his thoughts as thoughts, rather than facts), cognitive restructuring, the DBT skill of checking the facts (Linehan, 2015a, 2015b), or various other approaches to ineffective thinking patterns. This interplay of behavioral assessment and treatment continues throughout Stage 1 of DBT, with an emphasis on how the client can attain more behavioral control and replace problematic behavior with effective, skillful behavior.

As mentioned earlier, interventions in individual DBT span the armamentarium of evidence-based CBT and DBT approaches, and a full discussion of these interventions is beyond the scope of this book. In essence, the therapist works with the client to understand the factors maintaining problem behavior and then helps the client change those factors and learn new behavior. There are many ways to do this, but the most common interventions in DBT generally include commitment/ motivational strategies, contingency management, cognitive strategies, skills training, and acceptance and mindfulness approaches. Figure 4.3 shows how a DBT therapist might decide which intervention to use depending on what factor(s) seem to drive a client's problem behavior (see also Chapman & Rosenthal, 2016, for a discussion of this approach). If Mario's anger management difficulties appear to stem primarily from a skill deficit in the ability to recognize anger cues before they become intense, the therapist might help Mario learn the skill of identifying different components of an emotional response (e.g., physiological, cognitive, behavioral). Perhaps Mario is capable of identifying his anger, but his thinking tends to intensify it (e.g., "My partner is being totally unfair and ridiculous asking me to do the dishes after a long day of work!"). In this case, cognitive interventions might help Mario understand and change these thinking patterns, and acceptance or mindfulness might help him recognize thoughts and allow them to come and go. If Mario has the skills to recognize and manage anger, but anger serves an important function (e.g., it gets his partner off his back when he yells), or he is motivated to hold onto anger or resentment, then contingency management strategies (having the partner comply only when Mario doesn't yell) or commitment strategies (helping Mario commit to working on his anger) might be useful. Often, many factors influence a client's behavioral problems; thus, therapy may incorporate several of these types of core intervention strategies, as well as others.

MANAGING OBSTACLES AND CHALLENGES IN DBT

Many obstacles can arise in the treatment of complex clients, and the DBT therapist usually views these obstacles as instances of therapy-interfering behavior (TIB) on the part of the client or therapist. TIB includes any behavior on the part of the client or therapist that (a) makes it difficult for therapy to occur, (b) hampers therapeutic progress or goal attainment, and (c) detracts from an effective therapy relationship (Linehan, 1993a; Chapman & Rosenthal, 2016). In the treatment of complex clients, many TIBs can emerge, such as lateness, absences, last minute cancellations, harsh criticism or hostility directed toward the therapist, frequent requests or attempts to contact the therapist (e.g., overusing phone coaching), verbal or physical aggression toward the therapist or other clients, and so forth. Therapists also sometimes engage in TIB, and the most common therapist TIBs we have observed include lack of preparation, inattentiveness (lack of therapeutic mindfulness), reinforcement of dysfunctional behavior, provision of too much help or support (e.g., therapist is too available by phone, text, or email, and such availability reinforces dysfunctional behavior or precipitates therapist burnout), lack of attentiveness to signs of burnout, and failure to seek consultation when needed, among others. Therapists also sometimes miss or forget sessions, fail to follow through on promises or agreements, and might even let their irritation or frustration get the better of them at times.

When TIB occurs in individual therapy, the primary individual therapist prioritizes and targets TIB according to the DBT hierarchy of treatment targets (where it is second only to life-threatening behavior). Common steps in targeting TIB include (a) highlighting the TIB and providing a rationale for the therapist and client to work on it; (b) assessing the TIB, often using the strategy of chain analysis; (c) collaboratively devising solutions and skills to reduce the likelihood that TIB will occur again and/or to repair any damage caused by the TIB (i.e., in the case of dysfunctional interpersonal behavior that harms the therapy relationship); (d) eliciting a commitment from the client to implement solutions or skills; and (e) troubleshooting (Chapman & Rosenthal, 2016). These steps also are consistent with those used to target other behaviors in DBT (e.g., self-injury).

When the therapist engages in TIB, a modified version of these steps often includes (a) highlighting and acknowledging one's own TIB, (b) explaining how and why it occurred (often after reflecting on it alone or with consultation), (c) modeling how the therapist will use skills to prevent the TIB in the future, and (d) engaging in any appropriate repair activities. When it comes to repair activities, a therapist who was late for a session, for example, might apologize, describe his plan to prevent tardiness in the future, and (if applicable) invoice the client for a reduced fee for the next session or provide an extra-long session next time. DBT therapists addressing their own TIB openly, genuinely, and with humility can model how to solve problems and navigate relationship ruptures (Chapman & Rosenthal, 2016).

Another way that DBT therapists address TIB or potential TIB is to *observe their limits*. Observing limits involves attending to the effect of the client's behavior on the therapist. The therapist using phone coaching, for example, might begin to dread calls from a certain client who is calling several times per week and staying on the phone for longer than the therapist desires. Noticing that the calls are more frequent and time-consuming than desired, along with any related thoughts and emotional reactions (e.g., anxiety, frustration, the thought "I don't want to talk to this person again."), is a critical prerequisite to solving this problem and ensuring that phone coaching gets back on track and works for both parties (Chapman, 2018).

The DBT therapist observing these limits would raise the issue with the client, describing the situation: "I've noticed we've been speaking five or six times per week for over 20 or 30 minutes each time. I'd like to talk about this so that we can make phone coaching work well for both of us." The DBT therapist then describes the effect of the client's behavior on the therapist: "I've noticed that it's hard for me to fit in all of these longer than usual calls, and I think we should talk about how you can get your needs met with fewer and shorter calls." The therapist could then invite the client to discuss possible solutions: "Would you be willing to talk about this?"

Therapists also may observe limits around other client behaviors, such as harsh criticism, hostility, unrelenting suicide crises, last-minute requests to cancel or change appointments, and so forth. Observing limits helps keep the therapy relationship healthy and effective for both parties. Failing to observe limits and marching down the path to burnout is a serious therapist TIB. At times, therapists fail to notice when they need to observe limits, and the DBT consultation team is an invaluable resource in these cases. We have often turned to our team, discovered that we were further down the path to burnout than we thought, and left the meeting with a renewed commitment to observe limits and get therapy back on track.

Other obstacles to DBT sometimes include factors in the client's natural environment that impede progress. Complex clients' living situations sometimes do not promote therapy progress, such as abusive environments or relationships, loved ones who pose interpersonal challenges or stress, consequences from loved ones or the mental health system that serve to reinforce crises or suicidality, and so forth. As mentioned in Chapter 3, when aspects of clients' natural environments serve as barriers to progress, the DBT therapist typically tries to strike an effective balance of *consultation to the client* on how to navigate environmental barriers versus *environmental intervention,* involving the therapist taking steps to change the client's environment. DBT therapists generally err on the side of consultation to the client, as empowering the client with skills to enact positive change is most likely to have persisting benefits. That said, environmental intervention by the treatment provider is sometimes appropriate and effective, such as when the client is in a low-power position and unable to adequately influence the environment (e.g., a teenager trying to influence his parents' disciplinary decisions, a prison inmate, a psychiatric inpatient), the client lacks the skills to influence the environment, or when change is urgently needed to prevent serious harm to the client or others (e.g., in the case of severe imminent suicide risk). The DBT therapist's role in these instances is not to serve as a case manager or go-between but to consult with the environment on how to make changes in the client's best interest. Often, instead of simply trying to enact change in the client's environment, the therapist might seek a synthesis of environmental intervention and consultation to the client.

Remi, for example, was a severely depressed adolescent who refused to go to school and spent most of the day in bed. As he previously had been highly suicidal (having attempted suicide four times in the past), his parents were understandably anxious about the possibility of future suicide attempts. At night, they camped out at Remi's door so they could hear whether he was doing anything to harm himself or going out the window. In the morning, they tried to get him up, but when unsuccessful, often brought him food (breakfast, lunch, and sometimes dinner) in bed. Remi's therapist recognized that the parents may have been reinforcing some of Remi's depressive behavior, but Remi had not yet developed effective skills to communicate what he wanted from his parents, was extremely anxious about asking for help, and was ambivalent about the possible loss of extra support that might ensue if things were to change. Therefore, consulting with Remi about how to independently make requests of his parents was likely to be ineffective. He agreed, however, to have a meeting with his parents and the therapist; during this meeting, the therapist discussed the possible role of social reinforcement in Remi's depression and coached Remi to effectively describe how it affects him when they camp out at his door at night (it seemed like they didn't trust him, and he felt infantilized). In this manner, even in the context of intervening directly in the environment by scheduling a family meeting, the therapist was able to provide some scaffolded consultation to coach Remi to communicate on his own behalf. The therapist helped Remi and his parents devise a reasonable plan involving changes to the contingencies that might have been maintaining Remi's depression. The plan was for the parents not to provide any extra support (or food) when Remi stayed in bed, to support and attend to him more when he got out of bed, to remind him of his crisis plan, and to contact his therapist when they were afraid for his safety (rather than to sleep outside his door).

STANDARD DBT AND "DBT-INFORMED" TREATMENT

DBT is a program of treatment, not a particular intervention or collection of intervention strategies. All of the modes and functions of DBT must be addressed for a program to be considered a DBT program. Often, however, resource limitations or agency policies (i.e., against the use of phone coaching) hamper the provision of standard DBT programs; thus, many programs in various settings (most commonly correctional, outpatient community mental health, and hospital settings, but also including private practice and others) implement only certain components of DBT. Most commonly, programs not offering standard DBT instead offer a DBT skills group but not DBT individual therapy or phone coaching. In other settings, individual clinicians incorporate elements of DBT (e.g., chain analyses) or DBT skills into their everyday practice of individual CBT or other treatments. In addition, in some contexts, such as hospital based programs with varying lengths of stay (e.g., 2 days to a month), standard DBT is nearly impossible, so adaptations must be made to the skills group curriculum and the frequency, duration, and focus of individual therapy sessions; phone coaching often must be replaced with milieu coaching. In our experience training and consulting with agencies providing piecemeal components of DBT, the DBT consultation team often is omitted. In some cases, productivity requirements (e.g., caseloads) do not incorporate time or pay for a weekly meeting, clinicians are not aware that the consultation team is still important even when only one mode of DBT is offered (e.g., group DBT skills training), or clinicians do not have sufficient training or knowledge to navigate these meetings. In our trainings, we often emphasize the key point that DBT programs live or die by their teams. We have observed that programs without a strong, consistent consultation team are much less likely to serve their clients effectively or sustain over the long run than are those that have established such a team.

It is important to consider whether any modifications to the structure or delivery of elements of DBT have sound empirical grounding. The majority of the skills and strategies used in DBT were derived from evidence-based CBT and behavior therapy principles and practices; thus, the incorporation of specific DBT strategies or components likely does not stray from evidence-based practice. Notwithstanding this evidence base, it would be misleading and inaccurate to claim that a program providing only some modes of DBT or particular DBT strategies is providing DBT per se. It would be most accurate to claim that a program offering one or more (but not all) modes of DBT is using a "DBT-informed" approach.

Indeed, it is crucial for clients to know what kind of treatment they are receiving. We have, for example, seen several patients claiming that DBT "didn't work" for them, only to discover that they only attended a DBT skills group or saw an individual clinician who occasionally discussed DBT skills. With the increasing dissemination of DBT and DBT components through training activities, books, and websites devoted to DBT, it is more important than ever for patients to know what treatment they are receiving, and whether that treatment is consistent with what has been manualized and examined in clinical research.

CONCLUSION

DBT includes many modes and types of interventions within a behavioral and dialectical framework. Standard DBT includes individual therapy, group skills training, telephone consultation, and a therapist consultation team. DBT is organized according to four stages, with Stage 1 being the most clearly articulated and commonly used in practice and research. During Stage 1, primary strategies in individual therapy include behavioral assessment (chain analysis) and problem-solving, broadly defined and including the full armamentarium of evidence-based cognitive and behavioral strategies. DBT is best considered a principle-driven treatment that employs protocols in a modular, case-formulation driven manner (Farmer & Chapman, 2016; Persons & Tompkins, 2007). The therapist uses behavioral assessment methods to understand factors maintaining the client's problem areas and collaboratively uses modular interventions (e.g., motivational or commitment strategies, skills training exposure therapy, cognitive strategies) targeting those factors. When difficulties or obstacles arise in therapy, the DBT therapist often views these as TIBs and addresses them collaboratively with the client through chain analysis and other means as well as through appropriately observing therapist limits. It is important to remember that DBT is a program of treatment (a community of therapists treating a community of clients) rather than a specific treatment or intervention.

5

Evaluation: Research on DBT

One of the reasons for the current popularity of dialectical behavior therapy (DBT) is its robust and ever-growing empirical base. Since its inception, a great deal of research has been done that supports the utility of DBT for a range of presenting problems and populations. As a result, many clinical guidelines identify DBT as a recommended treatment for BPD and self-injury (National Health and Medical Research Council, 2013; National Institute for Health and Care Excellence, 2009). In this chapter, we provide a snapshot of the evolving research base on DBT. We focus first on research supporting the efficacy of this treatment. Given how DBT research has proliferated over the past few decades, we also include a comprehensive discussion of evidence for DBT for specific populations and diverse samples. While this comprehensive summary captures the current state of DBT research, this is an ever-changing field with new advances every day.

http://dx.doi.org/10.1037/0000188-005
Dialectical Behavior Therapy, by A. L. Chapman and K. L. Dixon-Gordon

RESEARCH ON THE EFFICACY OF DBT

Most of the initial research focused on standard DBT for clients with BPD and self-injury. *Standard DBT* refers to the typical outpatient models that include individual therapy, group skills training, phone coaching, and consultation team meetings. Although we focus on findings from randomized controlled trials (RCTs) as the most robust evidence for DBT, where such trials do not exist we discuss less rigorous research data.

Standard DBT RCTs Evaluating Treatment Efficacy for BPD

Several RCTs have compared DBT to treatment as usual (TAU). TAU is a common comparison condition given the high-risk nature of the clients often treated in DBT and the related risks associated with putting suicidal clients on a wait-list or in a no-treatment condition. As mentioned in Chapter 2, this volume, the first published RCT on DBT compared DBT with TAU for women with BPD and recurrent self-injury (*N* = 44; Linehan, Armstrong, Suarez, Allmon, & Heard, 1991). Findings indicated that DBT was superior to TAU in reducing frequency and severity of self-injurious behaviors (referred to as *parasuicidal behaviors*, including suicide attempts and nonsuicidal self-injury [NSSI]), number of inpatient psychiatric days, general social functioning, and treatment dropout (Linehan, Armstrong, Suarez, Allmon, & Heard, 1991). There were no significant differences between the conditions in terms of depression, hopelessness, suicidal ideation, or reasons for living, although these outcomes improved in both conditions. In another early RCT of 1 year of DBT for women with BPD (*N* = 58; Verheul et al., 2003), DBT resulted in greater reductions in BPD symptoms and self-injury, and fewer treatment dropouts than TAU. In addition to supporting the efficacy of DBT, these studies also document that DBT can be delivered effectively outside of the treatment developer's lab. Taken together, these findings support the efficacy of standard DBT for the treatment of women with BPD, according to the efficacy criteria set forth by Chambless and Hollon (1998).

Several studies suggest that even 6 months of DBT yields beneficial outcomes. In two RCTs comparing 6 months of DBT with TAU for females with BPD ($N = 73$—Carter, Willcox, Lewin, Conrad, & Bendit, 2010; $N = 20$ veterans—Koons et al., 2001), the DBT arm was not significantly different in terms of self-injury. However, the DBT condition resulted in greater reductions in suicidal ideation, hopelessness, and symptoms (Koons et al., 2001), disability, and quality of life (Carter et al., 2010). Another RCT for men and women with BPD ($N = 90$) found that 6 months of DBT resulted in greater reductions in self-injury, days of hospitalizations, emergency department visits, and psychiatric admissions than TAU (Pasieczny & Connor, 2011).

Taken together, this body of work suggests that DBT outperforms TAU in the community for treatment of self-injurious behaviors and use of crisis services characteristic of BPD. Moreover, findings based on comparisons of DBT with TAU support the *specificity* of DBT, or the extent to which something unique about DBT leads to beneficial outcomes, rather than nonspecific elements of treatment in general (e.g., positive regard, therapeutic rituals, alliance, often considered "common factors"; Wampold, 2015). Nevertheless, these studies may have overestimated the efficacy of the DBT condition, as several other factors differentiated the DBT conditions from the comparison groups. For instance, the provision of DBT by credible experts may have enhanced expectancies regarding treatment. In addition, treatment availability may be limited in TAU, whereas DBT may have more hours of treatment. Further, therapists in the community may have less training and access to consultation or supervision than in research studies. Therefore, while supporting DBT's efficacy and specificity, TAU control comparisons may not be the strongest evidence for specificity, given the differences in the experience and expertise of TAU clinicians as well as the availability and frequency or duration of treatment.

RCTs With More Rigorous Control Conditions

A handful of studies have compared DBT with more rigorous, active treatment control conditions. To control for some of the problems inherent in a TAU condition, researchers compared 1 year of DBT with a comparison condition involving community treatment by experts identified by leaders in the psychiatric/psychological community who had access to expert supervision (Linehan et al., 2006). Clients in this study were females ($N = 101$) with BPD with recent and recurrent self-injurious behaviors. Results demonstrated comparable improvements in depression and NSSI. Further, the DBT arm outperformed treatment by experts in terms of reducing suicide attempts, severity of self-injury, anger, treatment dropouts, and use of crisis services such as psychiatric hospitalization and emergency department visits. These effects were maintained across the 1-year follow-up period. Another RCT compared 1 year of DBT (augmented with psychodynamic case conceptualizations) to client-centered therapy for men and women ($N = 24$) with BPD (Turner, 2000). To minimize differences between conditions in contact hours, DBT skills were provided in individual therapy. The DBT arm resulted in greater reductions in self-injurious behaviors, inpatient days, anger, impulsivity, and depression.

These findings leave open the question of whether DBT offers significant advantages over other bona fide treatments for BPD. One study examining this question used an RCT to examine the efficacy of DBT versus general psychiatric management, designed specifically for BPD (McMain et al., 2009). Males and females ($N = 180$) with BPD and recent, recurrent self-injurious behaviors were assigned to DBT or general psychiatric management. After 1 year of treatment, both conditions had significant reductions in the frequency and severity of NSSI, emergency visits, and hospitalizations, as well as improvements in BPD, depression, anger, and interpersonal functioning. Yet, no differences between conditions emerged. Over a 2-year follow-up, both conditions showed comparable, significant improvements (McMain, Guimond, Streiner, Cardish, & Links, 2012). Another RCT compared DBT with other bona fide therapies for BPD: transference-focused therapy and supportive therapy (Clarkin, Levy, Lenzenweger, & Kernberg, 2007). Although the DBT arm improved in terms of depression, anxiety, suicidal outcomes, and overall functioning, there were few significant differences across the conditions. The only significant difference was that both the DBT and transference-focused therapy surpassed supportive therapy in reducing suicidal outcomes.

In addition, one nonrandomized trial compared DBT with another bona fide treatment. For this trial, clients with BPD ($N = 90$) received 12 months of either DBT or mentalization based therapy in community settings (Barnicot & Crawford, 2018). As this was not an RCT, there were significant differences between the conditions at baseline, with DBT clients being younger and reporting more past self-injury and greater use of emergency health services. Adjusting for these differences, clients in the DBT condition had steeper decreases in self-injury (both suicidal and nonsuicidal) and emotion dysregulation over time. There were no differences between conditions in terms of dropout, health service use, posttraumatic stress, or substance use.

This emerging research base suggests that the outcomes of DBT are at least comparable with those of other specialized treatments for BPD. Further, there is some evidence that DBT may be superior in terms of reducing self-injurious behaviors, at least when examined as an overarching category including both NSSI and suicide attempts. See Figure 5.1 for a summary of recommendations regarding the use of standard DBT.

Meta-Analyses of Standard DBT

The mounting literature evaluating DBT has provided a robust foundation for meta-analyses to synthesize extant evidence. Several meta-analyses evaluated the effectiveness of DBT for BPD. Across eight randomized and eight nonrandomized trials of standard DBT for BPD, a medium-sized effect (.44) was found across outcomes, with a similar sized effect (.37) for reducing self-injurious behaviors (Kliem, Kröger, & Kosfelder, 2010). Focusing on five RCTs of DBT for adults with BPD, another meta-analysis revealed that DBT had a moderate effect size ($g = -.62$) in reducing self-injurious behaviors (Panos, Jackson, Hasan, & Panos, 2014). There were only marginal effects in terms of reducing dropout

Standard DBT is efficacious (with positive results in 2 or more RCTs in multiple research clinics) for clients with BPD in improving:

- Suicidal and self-injurious behaviors
- Anger problems
- Use of crisis services/hospitalizations
- Substance use difficulties

Standard DBT is possibly efficacious for clients with BPD in improving:

- Treatment dropout
- Binge-eating or bulimia nervosa

DBT skills training is efficacious for clients with BPD in improving:

- Psychiatric symptoms
- Emotional outcomes

DBT skills training is possibly efficacious for clients with BPD in improving:

- Suicidal and self-injurious behaviors
- Treatment dropout

Figure 5.1

Considering DBT for BPD?

(risk difference = −.17), and no significant differences in reducing depressive symptoms ($g = -.90$). In a meta-analysis of 28 studies of various treatments for BPD, DBT in particular showed significant and moderate-to-large effects (standardized mean differences −.83 to −.54) relative to TAU in terms of reducing self-injury, anger, and psychiatric symptoms (Stoffers-Winterling et al., 2012). There was no significant difference between DBT and TAU in terms of treatment dropout (risk ratio = 1.25).

Other meta-analyses have examined the effectiveness of DBT in other samples. One meta-analysis, for example, examined third-wave behavioral therapy RCTs, including 13 adaptations of DBT for a range of conditions, including BPD, eating disorders, and depression (Öst, 2008). Among the DBT trials, there was an overall moderate effect size (.58), although relatively larger effect sizes were found when comparing DBT with wait-list controls than comparisons to TAU or active treatments. This review underscored the need to compare DBT to other treatments that offer comparable hours of treatment, given that DBT typically offered more hours of treatment overall. Another meta-analysis evaluated 18 randomized and nonrandomized trials of DBT versus wait-list or TAU that included suicidal outcomes, including mostly BPD samples (DeCou, Comtois, & Landes, 2018). Compared with control conditions, there was a significant effect of DBT on reducing self-injurious behaviors ($d = -.32$) and psychiatric crisis services ($d = -.38$), although there was no significant effect of DBT relative to controls on suicidal ideation ($d = -.23$). Similar findings were found in a meta-analysis of 12 studies of DBT for adolescents, which found that DBT resulted in a large decrease in self-injurious behaviors, and a smaller decrease in depressive symptoms (with a small effect size; Cook & Gorraiz, 2016).

Taken together, the extant literature shows clear superiority of DBT to other treatments in terms of reducing self-injurious behaviors. Yet, as critics note, gaps in the research base warrant caution in interpreting many of the positive outcomes (Reddy & Vijay, 2017). The external validity of findings is always a concern for well-controlled efficacy research, and important differences in client characteristics, therapist training, setting and resource limitations (reducing the viability of standard DBT in some cases), and other variables, should be considered when generalizing the findings of these studies to practice settings. Further, DBT has not consistently shown superiority relative to other BPD-specific structured treatments.

Effectiveness

Despite the promising performance of DBT in many controlled trials, practitioners often wonder about the feasibility of having the same results in real-world settings. In daily clinical practice, the clients are often more variable, and clinicians may have higher caseloads, limited time, fewer resources, and less training. All of these factors can adversely affect outcomes, particularly in a treatment as intensive and comprehensive as DBT. Thus, effectiveness trials examine whether DBT can achieve positive outcomes in more real-world settings.

There is international support for the effectiveness of DBT in real-world clinical settings. In a rigorous effectiveness RCT in the United Kingdom, TAU was compared with DBT provided by the National Health Service for clients ($N = 42$) with cluster B personality disorders (Feigenbaum et al., 2012). Due to the usually high number of dropouts (42%) in DBT in this study, and the fact that statistical analyses focused only on those who completed treatment, these analyses were underpowered and revealed no significant differences between DBT and TAU. Of note, the DBT condition had a significant decrease in clinical severity and suicidal outcomes, whereas this was not true in TAU. Uncontrolled trials likewise show that DBT has positive outcomes in real-world outpatient community mental health settings, including in the United States (Comtois, Elwood, Holdcraft, Smith, & Simpson, 2007), New Zealand (Brassington & Krawitz, 2006), Germany (Stiglmayr et al., 2014), and Sweden (Hjalmarsson, Kåver, Perseius, Cederberg, & Ghaderi, 2008). These studies show that community clinicians can be trained in DBT and have generally positive outcomes, supporting the effectiveness and acceptability of DBT in community settings.

One factor to consider regarding the effectiveness of DBT is whether this treatment reduces public health costs. The clinical problems often targeted in DBT tend to be extraordinarily costly, with complex clients with BPD often seeking repeated care from multiple health care systems. Hospitalization, in particular, is both a common and expensive aspect of the care of suicidal individuals. One RCT of clients ($N = 80$) with BPD showed that DBT resulted in greater reductions in self-injury relative to TAU (Priebe et al., 2012), but the differences in the cost of treatment were nonsignificant. Yet other studies found that DBT resulted in cost savings in the United Kingdom (e.g., $1,059 GBP per client; Amner, 2012) and Ireland (Murphy & Bourke, 2014), largely due to reduced inpatient days (Amner, 2012). Although DBT may prove cost-effective, further research is needed that carefully accounts for all health care costs (Brazier et al., 2006).

Even if DBT is effective, it is important to consider whether this treatment is sustainable. DBT requires substantial clinician training as well as structural changes to standard care provided in community settings (e.g., reduced caseloads, consultation team meetings, weekly group skills training and individual sessions). Some of these changes may be hard to sustain. A review of DBT implementations in the United Kingdom showed that newly implemented DBT community programs run a risk of failure, especially in the second year of the program (Swales, Taylor, & Hibbs, 2012). Despite this potential for failure, findings suggested that, overall, DBT programs are sustainable, with 69% of programs surviving after 8 years. In our experience, successful DBT implementations must proactively address problems that commonly threaten the longevity of programs, including staff turnover, lack of administrative support, limitations in resources (e.g., space, funding, staffing resources), and difficulty maintaining highly trained staff.

ADAPTATIONS OF DBT

Given the resources needed to develop and sustain DBT programs (Carmel, Rose, & Fruzzetti, 2014; National Collaborating Centre for Mental Health, 2009), and the failure of private insurance to consistently provide full coverage for DBT (Swenson, Torrey, & Koerner, 2002), many individuals with BPD are left without access to this treatment. Consequently, many clinicians and researchers have focused on ways to provide briefer adaptations of DBT.

Residential and Inpatient Formats

The often short-term nature of inpatient hospitalization has prompted evaluations of condensed DBT in these settings. These studies have found that clients in brief residential and inpatient programs (Barley et al., 1993), such as 3-month formats (Bohus et al., 2000, 2004; Kröger, Harbeck, Armbrust, & Kliem, 2013; Kröger et al., 2006), show decreases in self-injury frequency and psychiatric symptoms. These improvements were sustained over the 21-month follow-up (Kleindienst et al., 2008). Even briefer inpatient programs (e.g., 5 days—Yen, Johnson, Costello, &

Simpson, 2009; 10 days—Springer, Lohr, Buchtel, & Silk, 1996) resulted in improved psychopathology symptoms in uncontrolled trials, although no differences were found relative to comparison conditions (including a "wellness and living" group) in an RCT (Springer et al., 1996).

Only one RCT has compared DBT-informed residential versus outpatient formats (Sinnaeve, van den Bosch, Hakkaart-van Roijen, & Vansteelandt, 2018). Clients high in BPD features received either 1 year of outpatient DBT or 3 months of residential DBT followed by 6 months of outpatient DBT. Clients in the residential-to-outpatient step-down format had greater quality of life at posttreatment, but the cost of care was significantly higher for these clients, and there were no significant differences in terms of the reduction of BPD symptoms.

The research base on abbreviated DBT programs is too sparse and lacking well-controlled trials to draw firm conclusions about efficacy. Notwithstanding, findings from a systematic review suggested that DBT in inpatient formats is promising and potentially effective (Bloom, Woodward, Susmaras, & Pantalone, 2012). Most of the studies showed evidence of decreased suicidal ideation, self-injurious behaviors, and symptoms of depression and anxiety. In summary, DBT-informed residential and inpatient treatments are promising, but the efficacy, short- and long-term cost effectiveness, and durability of the effects of these programs have yet to be firmly established. Further, the incremental value of inpatient over outpatient DBT programs remains unclear, as does the question of which clients to triage to inpatient versus outpatient forms of DBT. In addition, the variability in duration and format of treatment and populations makes it difficult to generalize across DBT-informed inpatient and residential care.

Stand-Alone DBT Skills

Another promising avenue to enhance the efficiency of DBT is by providing DBT skills training as a stand-alone treatment. Stand-alone DBT skills have been found to be efficacious in several controlled studies (for a review, see Valentine, Bankoff, Poulin, Reidler, & Pantalone, 2015).

RCTs have shown that DBT skills training for clients with BPD is superior to other group treatment in terms of improved depression, anxiety, other psychiatric symptoms (Soler et al., 2009), and lower dropout rates (Soler et al., 2009), although not for self-injury or emergency visits (Soler et al., 2009). One RCT, however, found that 20 weeks of DBT skills training outperformed a wait-list control for suicidal clients with BPD ($N = 84$) in terms of suicide attempts and self-injury through a 32-week follow-up (McMain, Guimond, Barnhart, Habinski, & Streiner, 2017). The DBT condition also showed more improvements in BPD, social adjustment, and other emotional outcomes, although these gains were not maintained at the follow-up. The DBT condition also had nonsignificantly fewer emergency department visits.

Thus, stand-alone DBT skills training is a safe and potentially efficacious intervention for suicidal clients for BPD. Together, these findings suggest that DBT skills training may be superior to wait-list control, but not alternative group treatments, in terms of primary outcomes such as self-injurious behaviors. Despite these promising findings, conclusions are limited by the variability in formats and limited use of control conditions (Valentine et al., 2015).

Abbreviated Outpatient DBT

Controlled trials generally support the utility of abbreviated DBT for BPD. As previously described, several RCTs (Carter et al., 2010; Koons et al., 2001; Pasieczny & Connor, 2011) suggest that 6 months of DBT surpasses TAU in improving symptoms across a number of domains: disability, quality of life, and in one case, self-injurious behaviors (Pasieczny & Connor, 2011). Another RCT compared a 16-week adaptation of DBT for suicidal clients ($N = 108$) with subthreshold BPD and a recent suicide attempt to another bona fide suicide prevention program: collaborative assessment and management of suicidality (CAMS; Andreasson et al., 2016). No significant differences in self-injurious behaviors emerged between conditions. As such, this brief form of DBT was not superior to another established treatment for suicide risk.

Data from uncontrolled trials also suggest that shortened versions of DBT may be useful for BPD. For instance, uncontrolled studies of 6 months of DBT for clients with BPD have demonstrated improvements in depression, self-injury ($N = 20$—Stanley, Brodsky, Nelson, & Dulit, 2007; $N = 50$—Rizvi, Hughes, Hittman, & Vieira Oliveira, 2017), suicidal ideation (Stanley et al., 2007), emotion regulation, symptoms of BPD, and overall adjustment (Rizvi et al., 2017). Despite the brevity of these treatments, effect sizes were comparable with those of other DBT trials ($ds = .68–.91$; Rizvi et al., 2017). With the intention of streamlining treatment provision, another uncontrolled trial study examined the utility of addressing the functions of individual DBT in a group context, alongside standard DBT skills groups (Gutteling, Montagne, Nijs, & van den Bosch, 2012). In this study, women with BPD reported significantly decreased depression, suicidal thoughts, anxiety, and anger.

In conclusion, briefer forms of DBT show promising results, although data are pending regarding whether more DBT may be better. Preliminary data suggest that more DBT may be better, at least for some. At the end of a brief treatment, clients were offered additional DBT as clinically indicated, and garnered further gains (Pasieczny & Connor, 2011; Perroud, Uher, Dieben, Nicastro, & Huguelet, 2010). Thus, longer durations of treatment may provide incremental benefit for some clients. More research is needed comparing briefer to more standard lengths of DBT, as well as the client characteristics that predict who benefits from briefer or longer treatment (McMain et al., 2018).

DIFFERENT SAMPLES AND SYMPTOM DOMAINS

Consider Kara, a cisgender woman in her mid-40s. She described having suffered abuse during childhood and was also assaulted in her 20s. At the time of entering treatment, Kara was financially dependent on her boyfriend, with whom she lived, and she described her relationship as being marked by frequent arguments. She reported frequent anger outbursts, as well as recent nightmares related to her traumas, and was consequently having trouble sleeping. Kara said she managed her stress by hitting herself, binge eating, purging, and excessive use of alcohol. In addition to these difficulties, she expressed a desire for greater financial independence and housing stability. After an initial assessment, Kara's therapist diagnosed Kara with BPD, posttraumatic stress disorder (PTSD), bulimia nervosa, and alcohol use disorder.

Other Disorders

Co-occurring disorders are the norm rather than the exception among complex clients with BPD (Hawton, Houston, Haw, Townsend, & Harriss, 2003; Zanarini et al., 1998), and treatment often must address these other disorders and related problems to help clients improve their lives. Extant research has supported the use of DBT for BPD and related problems, but questions remain regarding the effectiveness of DBT for commonly co-occurring disorders. Accordingly, emerging research has expanded the scope of DBT into areas such as PTSD, eating disorders, depression, and substance use disorders, among other problem areas. See Figure 5.2 for a summary of recommendations regarding modifications of DBT for a range of problems.

DBT modifications are efficacious for

- BPD and co-occurring PTSD
- Binge eating disorder
- Adolescents with self-injurious behaviors

DBT modifications may be useful for

- Depression
- Bipolar disorder
- Emotion dysregulation
- Behavioral dyscontrol in those with intellectual disabilities
- Bulimia nervosa
- ADHD
- Youth with emotional difficulties

Figure 5.2

Considering DBT for another problem?

Co-Occurring PTSD

Among individuals with BPD, more than half present with co-occurring PTSD (Harned, Rizvi, & Linehan, 2010; Zanarini et al., 1998), and the presence of PTSD in BPD is associated with twice the frequency of self-injury (Harned et al., 2010). Although clients with BPD receiving DBT often remit from other co-occurring disorders (overall remission rate = 73.9%), remission rates for PTSD tend to be lower (35%; Harned et al., 2009). Addressing this concern, DBT was augmented with prolonged exposure (PE; Harned, Korslund, Foa, & Linehan, 2012). A small RCT for clients with BPD and PTSD ($N = 26$) found the DBT + PE condition had higher PTSD remission rates (80% vs. 40%) and reduced PTSD symptom severity compared with DBT alone (Harned et al., 2014). Further, a smaller percentage of treatment completers in the DBT + PE condition engaged in self-injury (suicidal behaviors: 17%; NSSI: 67%) compared with the DBT condition (suicidal behaviors: 40%; NSSI: 100%).

Likewise, an adapted version of DBT was tailored to treat childhood sexual abuse-related PTSD (Bohus et al., 2013). This DBT-PTSD adaptation is a 12-week modular residential program that integrates skills to reduce dissociation during standard exposure protocols for PTSD. In an RCT, DBT-PTSD was compared with a wait-list + TAU condition for women with childhood sexual abuse-related PTSD ($N = 74$). Participants in the DBT-PTSD condition reported significantly greater decreases in PTSD symptoms relative to those in the control condition. Together, these studies suggest that adjunctive trauma-focused interventions can feasibly and effectively be combined with DBT, are potentially efficacious for the treatment of co-occurring PTSD and BPD, and may have incremental utility beyond standard DBT.

In the case of Kara, we identified PTSD as an important quality-of-life target. Given that she often impulsively self-harmed or used alcohol when she was distressed, we opted to wait until these behaviors were under adequate control before targeting PTSD. With many of our other clients, however, PTSD symptoms are a common antecedent to self-harm. In these cases, it is even more important to address co-occurring PTSD symptoms as early as possible.

Eating Disorders

Several studies have examined the utility of DBT for eating disorders. Given the emotion regulation focus of DBT and theories that disordered eating behaviors, such as binge eating, are thought to serve as a way to escape aversive emotions (Heatherton & Baumeister, 1991; Wiser & Telch, 1999), researchers have examined DBT for eating disorders. One RCT compared standard DBT to TAU for patients ($N = 21$) with co-occurring eating disorders (50% anorexia nervosa) and substance use disorders (Courbasson, Nishikawa, & Dixon, 2012). DBT had a lower dropout rate, but the high dropout rate in TAU precluded statistical comparisons. DBT was also adapted for binge-eating disorder (BED), including modifying goals to include targets such as binges and mindless eating (Safer, Telch, & Agras, 2001). In RCTs, DBT for BED resulted in greater reductions in eating disorder symptoms than a wait-list control for women ($N = 44$; Telch, Agras, & Linehan, 2001) and reduced dropout from group therapy for men and women ($N = 101$) with BED (Safer, Robinson, & Jo, 2010). Over treatment, DBT-BED also yielded faster declines in binges and higher rates of abstinence (64% vs. 36%), although these differences did not persist over the follow-up year (Safer et al., 2010).

A few RCTs have examined DBT for bulimia nervosa. Findings from RCTs indicated that women with at least one weekly binge/purge episode who received DBT ($N = 31$; Safer et al., 2001) or DBT augmented with appetite focus ($N = 32$; Hill, Craighead, & Safer, 2011) had greater reductions in binge/purge frequency than their counterparts in a wait-list control. Recipients of appetite-focused DBT also showed greater reductions in other disordered eating and depressive symptoms as well as greater increases in positive emotions, although no differences were found in subjective binge frequency or emotion regulation (Hill et al., 2011).

Several uncontrolled trials have examined adaptations of DBT for eating disorders. One small uncontrolled trial found that DBT, with only minimal adaptations, resulted in moderate effect sizes in reducing disordered eating in clients ($N = 8$) with BED or bulimia nervosa and BPD (Chen, Matthews, Allen, Kuo, & Linehan, 2008). Likewise, women with

BPD and co-occurring eating disorders ($N = 24$) showed a significant reduction in symptoms during an inpatient-adapted form of DBT augmented with weight education (Kröger et al., 2010).

An adaptation to DBT, radically open DBT (RO-DBT) was developed to address emotional and behavioral overcontrol more broadly, with one application of RO-DBT being with eating disorders commonly characterized by such overcontrol (anorexia nervosa; Lynch, Hempel, & Dunkley, 2015). Underpinning RO-DBT is the notion that pathological overcontrol, involving social distance, inhibited emotional expression, and pathological perfectionism is a transdiagnostic characteristic that is typical of several clinical problems (e.g., anorexia nervosa, chronic depression, obsessive–compulsive personality disorder, among others). From the RO-DBT perspective, overcontrolled disorders emerge as a result of transactions between a biologically based heightened inhibitory control and sensitivity to threat and a sociodevelopmental context that punishes vulnerability and mistakes and encourages emotional control, resulting in a maladaptive pattern of social avoidance and emotional inhibition.

In an effort to tackle these difficulties, RO-DBT diverges from DBT in several key respects. The therapeutic stance in RO-DBT is less directive, promotes conflict engagement and tolerance, focuses on enhancing the social signaling function of emotions, and seeks to reward authentic expression and self-inquiry. As in DBT, RO-DBT includes individual psychotherapy, skills training groups, phone coaching, and consultation team meetings. An uncontrolled trial examined RO-DBT in an inpatient setting for individuals ($N = 47$) with anorexia nervosa (Lynch et al., 2013). Clients in RO-DBT demonstrated improved body mass, fewer disordered eating symptoms, and less distress. By posttreatment, over 80% of clients were in full or partial remission. More work is needed to validate this approach for anorexia nervosa in controlled trials.

A review of DBT for eating disorders underscores that DBT is a promising approach (Bankoff, Karpel, Forbes, & Pantalone, 2012). Given the heterogeneous nature of the versions of DBT and the populations under study, however, it is unclear whether DBT is efficacious for the treatment of eating disorders. Findings also suggest that eating disorder treatment can be incorporated into standard DBT, as is often the approach with multiproblem clients, where the DBT therapist targets quality-of-life issues when they become high priority. Given the paucity of data on standard DBT for anorexia nervosa, clients with this condition (particularly when medically severe) may require ancillary treatment. In our experience, eating disorder programs often want clients to reduce suicidality and self-injury before entering their programs, or at least have concurrent DBT services targeting life-threatening behaviors. We have on occasion treated suicidal clients so that they can be eligible for eating disorder treatment, but sometimes, the dilemma emerges when the client has medically problematic anorexia. In these cases, ancillary medical or eating disorder-specific care should be arranged.

In the case of Kara, we included disordered eating targets into a standard DBT treatment program. In addition to being a quality-of-life target, chain analyses revealed that bingeing and purging behaviors commonly preceded self-harm for Kara. Therefore, we also included problem solving to reduce disordered eating behaviors as one way of reducing life-threatening behaviors. We harnessed an array of strategies. For instance, Kara monitored binge and purge urges and behaviors on her diary card, and her food intake. We discussed the often counterproductive effects of restriction and purging on weight management and emotional well-being. Kara taped up post-it notes to remind her of alternative skills for managing emotions (including distress tolerance strategies such as ice on her face) in locations where she commonly binged or purged. This standard DBT approach resulted in a decrease in her disordered eating behaviors.

Mood and Anxiety Disorders

Given that DBT was developed to treat the pervasive emotion dysregulation theorized to contribute to many of the problem behaviors in BPD (Linehan, 1993a), researchers have applied DBT for other emotion-related disorders, such as mood and anxiety disorders. One RCT compared DBT plus antidepressants versus medication alone for older adults ($N = 34$) with chronic depression (Lynch, Morse, Mendelson, & Robins, 2003). No significant differences emerged between the conditions, likely due to the small sample size; yet, only the DBT condition resulted in significantly improved coping. Another RCT compared 6 months of RO-DBT to TAU for chronic depression (Lynch et al., 2019). RO-DBT resulted in greater reductions in depression, although this was not sustained over a 6-month follow-up.

A variety of truncated DBT-based group skills training have been examined for emotional symptoms. One RCT compared 12 sessions of DBT skills and self-care psychoeducation with TAU for adults ($N = 26$) with bipolar I or II disorder (Van Dijk, Jeffrey, & Katz, 2013). Recipients of DBT were more likely to be only minimally depressed than the TAU participants and showed greater improvements in mindfulness-based self-efficacy. Another RCT of women ($N = 19$) with chronic depression found that 16 weekly DBT groups outperformed a wait-list control in reducing depression symptoms (Harley, Sprich, Safren, Jacobo, & Fava, 2008). Focusing on clients with anxiety or depressive disorder and reported emotion dysregulation ($N = 44$), an RCT compared 16 weeks of DBT skills with supportive group therapy (Neacsiu, Eberle, Kramer, Wiesmann, & Linehan, 2014). The DBT skills groups were superior to supportive groups in terms of increased skills use, and reduced emotion dysregulation and anxiety, but not depression. In secondary analyses of the RCT comparing DBT to treatment-by-experts for women with BPD and recent self-injurious behaviors ($N = 101$), there were no differences between conditions in remission of co-occurring anxiety or mood disorders (Harned et al., 2009).

Thus, adaptations of DBT may be superior to TAU for bipolar disorder, and at least comparable with other treatments for depression and anxiety. Findings suggest that clinicians trying to decide whether to implement DBT with clients with mood disorders might consider doing so when such clients also present with elevated emotion dysregulation (although findings still need replication) or co-occurring problems, such as suicidality.

Attention-Deficit/Hyperactivity Disorder

Recent conceptualizations of attention-deficit/hyperactivity disorder (ADHD) emphasize its overlap with BPD, both in terms of their co-occurrence and shared symptoms of impulsivity, irritability, and emotion dysregulation (Moukhtarian, Mintah, Moran, & Asherson, 2018). It is therefore perhaps unsurprising that researchers have examined the utility of DBT for ADHD. Two RCTs compared truncated versions of DBT skills-training groups with TAU (Hirvikoski et al., 2011) or with self-guided handouts (Fleming, McMahon, Moran, Peterson, & Dreessen, 2015) for clients with ADHD. DBT was superior to the control conditions in reducing symptoms of executive dysfunction. The idiosyncratic adaptations of DBT do not permit conclusions to be drawn about the efficacy of DBT for ADHD at this time.

Substance Use Disorders

Given the high rate of substance misuse and abuse in BPD (Zanarini et al., 1998), and the documented efficacy of DBT for other out-of-control behaviors, adapting DBT to treat substance use disorders was a natural next step. Although many DBT principles and strategies lend themselves well to treating substance misuse, several key modifications resulted in what is now referred to as DBT-SUD (Dimeff, Rizvi, Brown, & Linehan, 2000; Linehan, 2015a, 2015b). Among other changes, DBT-SUD explicitly incorporates substance use as the top quality-of-life target in the treatment hierarchy (Dimeff & Linehan, 2008). Further, DBT-SUD includes additional attachment strategies to help keep clients with substance use problems in treatment. In addition, DBT-SUD applies the concept of dialectics to goals related to abstinence, formalized as dialectical abstinence. This dialectic acknowledges the importance of permanently stopping use of substances while also acknowledging the likelihood for relapse. In addition, part of accepting the possibility of relapse means viewing relapse as a challenge to overcome, rather than a failure.

In the case of Kara, once her binge-and-purge behaviors had decreased, resulting in a concomitant reduction in self-harm, we prioritized decreasing use of alcohol. Alcohol use was identified as the top quality-of-life-interfering target. After discussing the pros and cons of alcohol use, Kara determined that she would like to abstain from using any alcohol. Given that she was not at the time physically dependent on alcohol, we continued to address this in the context of a standard outpatient DBT program. We worked to minimize contact with environments that might increase cravings or tempt her to use. Then, we focused on building up relationships with friends (including those in group) that reinforced prosocial behaviors. She disappeared from therapy for a week, and could not be reached at home. Based on past relapse behaviors, as a treatment team, we called local hotels and ultimately located Kara. She was voluntarily briefly hospitalized to safely detoxify from alcohol, and we were able to meet with her in the hospital. Kara recommitted to DBT and working towards abstinence. In conjunction with this goal of abstinence, in line with the notion of dialectical abstinence, we also developed a plan to shorten relapses if they were to occur, including keeping credit cards in a different location than her wallet to reduce the likelihood that she would check into a hotel.

The utility of DBT for substance use has some empirical support. Secondary analyses of the Linehan et al. (2006) RCT revealed that the remission rates for substance use disorders were higher in DBT versus the community treatment-by-experts condition (Harned et al., 2009). An earlier RCT compared 1 year of DBT plus replacement medication with TAU for women with BPD and drug dependence (Linehan et al., 1999). Participants in the DBT condition had greater reductions in substance use, as measured by interviews and urinalyses, both over treatment and at the 16-month follow-up. In addition, the DBT condition had lower dropout and greater gains in global and social adjustment at the follow-up than TAU. A comparison of DBT versus comprehensive validation therapy (a treatment solely including the acceptance components of DBT, without skills training) with 12-step for women with BPD and heroin dependence revealed that clients in both treatments showed significantly decreased psychopathology and opiate use, although the DBT condition had greater dropout rates (Linehan et al., 2002). Of interest, clients in the DBT condition were more accurate in their reported opiate use when referenced to urinalysis results, possibly because these clients tracked their drug use on the DBT diary card (Behavioral Research and Therapy Clinics, n.d.). In an open trial, clients ($N = 244$) with alcohol use disorders received 3 months of DBT skills training (Maffei, Cavicchioli, Movalli, Cavallaro, & Fossati, 2018). After treatment, more than 73% of clients achieved abstinence per urinalyses, and clients reported improved emotion dysregulation. In a very preliminary study of three women with BPD with methamphetamine dependence, the two clients who completed 6 months of DBT achieved abstinence (Dimeff et al., 2000).

Although promising, it is important to interpret these findings cautiously. One RCT revealed that DBT was superior to TAU in reducing symptoms of BPD among women ($N = 58$) with BPD, although clients in DBT did not exhibit greater reductions in substance use (van den Bosch, Verheul, Schippers, & van den Brink, 2002). This study, however, did not specifically focus on clients with substance use disorders, nor did it incorporate DBT-SUD strategies. Thus, it is possible that DBT may be less effective for substance use problems if substance use is not explicitly identified as a target for treatment. Clinically, DBT clinicians often prioritize SUDs when (a) SUD problems are related to higher priority targets, such as therapy-interfering or life-threatening behavior; or (b) the client's goal is to reduce problematic use. In practice, therefore, there is variability in terms of when and how SUD problems are targeted in DBT.

Other Samples

The aforementioned literature highlights the problems that DBT helps most, including self-destructive, impulsive, out-of-control behaviors. These problems occur in a number of unique populations, and DBT has been shown to be useful in many of these cases as well.

College Student Samples

Many of the self-destructive behaviors targeted by DBT, such as self-injury, substance use, and disordered eating, are particularly prevalent among college students (M. N. Laska, Pasch, Lust, Story, & Ehlinger, 2009).

Abbreviated formats of standard DBT have been developed to accommodate the time constraints of the semester structure of universities and colleges. A few RCTs have examined forms of DBT for college students. One RCT compared between 7 and 12 months of DBT to TAU supervised by experts for college students ($N = 63$) with a history of self-injury and subthreshold BPD (Pistorello, Fruzzetti, Maclane, Gallop, & Iverson, 2012). DBT resulted in greater reductions in NSSI, suicidal ideation, and depression. In another RCT, treatment-seeking college students ($N = 54$) were randomized to a one-semester DBT skills training group or a positive psychotherapy group (Uliaszek, Rashid, Williams, & Gulamani, 2016). Students receiving DBT had significantly lower dropout and higher attendance than the comparison group. Despite the absence of significant differences in outcomes between conditions, students receiving DBT showed medium to large pre–post effects, whereas the effect sizes were generally small to medium in the comparison condition. Another RCT compared DBT skills training groups with cognitive therapy for Taiwanese college students ($N = 82$) with BPD, depression, and recent suicidal behaviors (Lin et al., 2019). The groups had comparable rates of suicide attempts and reduced depression symptoms at posttreatment and the 6-month follow-up.

A few nonrandomized trials evaluated DBT in college settings. One small nonrandomized trial compared 11-week DBT skills training with TAU for college students ($N = 19$) with Cluster B personality disorder traits (Chugani, Ghali, & Brunner, 2013). The DBT condition showed significantly greater increases in skill use and decreases in maladaptive coping than those in the TAU condition, although no significant differences emerged in emotion regulation difficulties. In an uncontrolled trial, college students with BPD ($N = 17$) completed eight 2-hour DBT group skills training sessions (Meaney-Tavares & Hasking, 2013). Participants reported significant reductions in depression, BPD symptoms, and self-blame, but not anxiety.

Youth Samples

DBT has consistently demonstrated utility for the reduction of self-injury. Given the high prevalence of NSSI among adolescents (Klonsky, 2011), a number of studies in recent years have evaluated the utility of DBT for adolescents. Several modifications were made to DBT to make it more appropriate for adolescents, and the first investigation of this modified DBT for adolescents was a nonrandomized comparison of DBT for adolescents (DBT-A) compared with supportive psychodynamic treatment (Rathus & Miller, 2002; as described in Chapter 2, this volume). The first published RCT compared 19 weeks of DBT for adolescents with recent and recurrent self-injurious behaviors ($N = 77$) versus enhanced usual care (Mehlum et al., 2014). DBT-A was superior to enhanced usual care in terms of reducing self-injurious behaviors, suicidal ideation, and depressive symptoms. Furthermore, DBT-A outperformed the control condition throughout the 1-year follow-up period in reducing self-injury frequency, although for other outcomes the superiority of DBT-A over the control condition did not persist over the follow-up (Mehlum et al., 2016). Furthermore, in a large RCT conducted at three sites (including Linehan's research center at the University of Washington), DBT-A was compared with individual and group supportive therapy for adolescents ($N = 173$) with a past suicide attempt and either recurrent self-injury, suicidal ideation, or emotion dysregulation (McCauley et al., 2018). At posttreatment, participants receiving DBT-A had fewer suicide attempts and instances of self-injury, although these differences became nonsignificant at the 1-year follow-up. Although the conditions were matched for contact hours, the DBT-A condition had greater treatment attendance and retention, such that differences in hours of treatment received may still have affected outcomes.

The health services system in Ireland launched an implementation of 16-week DBT-A (Flynn et al., 2018). Adolescents ($N = 84$) with emotion dysregulation and persistent self-injurious behaviors or chronic suicidal ideation who underwent DBT-A reported a decrease in BPD symptoms, depression, anger, and suicidal ideation, and an increase in DBT skills use. Furthermore, participants exhibited reductions in self-injury frequency and inpatient admissions. Thus, extant findings suggest that DBT for adolescents with self-injury is potentially efficacious and also effective in routine clinical practice. Findings in two studies that DBT outperforms active control treatments during treatment but not generally in the follow-up period suggest that DBT may achieve quicker outcomes for serious behavioral and mental health concerns among adolescents, but that more work is needed to help clients maintain treatment gains.

Precursors to emotion dysregulation and subsequent disorders such as BPD begin to emerge in childhood. For instance, nearly a third of BPD clients report beginning to self-injure, a hallmark of BPD, prior to the age of 12 (Zanarini et al., 2006). As a result, DBT has been adapted for preadolescent children with behavioral and emotion dysregulation (Perepletchikova et al., 2011). An initial examination of this 6-week DBT program for children ($N = 11$) showed that children's reported adaptive coping increased, while their depression symptoms and suicidal ideation decreased. A more recent RCT compared DBT with TAU for children ($N = 43$) with disruptive mood dysregulation disorder (DMDD; Perepletchikova et al., 2017). Children in the DBT condition showed higher rates of DMDD remission than those in TAU as well as better attendance at treatment, and no DBT clients dropped out. Likewise, given that DBT has been useful for bipolar disorder in adults (Van Dijk et al., 2013), researchers conducted an RCT comparing 18 weeks of DBT (individual plus family skills training) with TAU for adolescents ($N = 20$) with bipolar disorder (Goldstein et al., 2015). Adolescents who received DBT reported fewer depressive symptoms and a greater likelihood of improvement in suicidal ideation, although there were no significant group differences in emotion dysregulation or manic symptoms.

Correctional Samples

A review of the literature suggests that DBT is a promising intervention for managing a range of problems seen in correctional contexts (Ivanoff & Marotta, 2019, see also Chapman & Ivanoff, 2018). Many of these programs have implemented DBT, yet these efforts often face logistical challenges, such as providing between-session coaching, conducting consistent individual therapy, or ensuring therapists have access to consultation teams. Further, in part due to ethical and logistical challenges involved in research with incarcerated individuals, only a few controlled trials exist.

The RCTs in correctional contexts evaluated DBT for a range of difficulties. One RCT compared DBT with rational emotive therapy and a control condition for prisoners ($N = 48$) with antisocial personality (Asmand & Valizadeh, 2015). Participants who received DBT reported reductions across a broader number of irrational beliefs than the comparison conditions, but no differences in symptoms were observed. Further, for incarcerated women ($N = 49$) with histories of interpersonal violence, nine sessions of DBT skills training (plus a written trauma component) was superior to a no-contact control in reducing PTSD and mood symptoms (Bradley & Follingstad, 2003). Focusing on specific elements of DBT, an RCT compared the efficacy of 8 weeks of DBT coaching versus case management following 16-week corrections-modified DBT groups (DBT-CM) for inmates ($N = 63$) with impulsive behaviors (Shelton, Sampl, Kesten, Zhang, & Trestman, 2009). Participants in DBT-CM had improved aggression and psychiatric symptoms and fewer disciplinary infractions posttreatment. Although DBT coaching resulted in decreased psychiatric symptoms initially at 6 months, this did not persist 1 year later.

Nonrandomized trials highlight the utility of DBT for reducing behavioral problems in correctional settings. One trial included male forensic clients with BPD ($N = 17$) in a high-security hospital who completed either DBT or TAU (Evershed et al., 2003). The DBT clients showed greater reductions in violence severity and reported anger. Another trial for adolescent girls in juvenile rehabilitation suggested that a DBT-informed approach had promise in reducing behavioral problems and staff use of restrictive consequences (Trupin, Stewart, Beach, & Boesky, 2002). It is worth noting that men with BPD and antisocial personality ($N = 30$) in DBT have shown reduced self-injury, aggression, and criminal offending (Wetterborg et al., 2018).

These studies suggest that DBT may be useful for many problems seen in correctional samples. For instance, DBT may reduce psychiatric symptoms, aggression, criminal behaviors, or staff use of discipline. Yet the small sample sizes coupled with few rigorous trials limits our ability to draw firm conclusions regarding the utility of DBT in these settings.

Veteran Samples

Over 50 Veterans Affairs (VA) health sites in the United States have implemented DBT (Landes et al., 2017), often with modifications to address logistical challenges such as how clinicians could make themselves available for between-session phone coaching (given the standard work hour restrictions in VA). In one uncontrolled study of 12 weeks of DBT-PE for veterans ($N = 33$) with PTSD and BPD symptoms, two thirds of the sample completed treatment (Meyers et al., 2017). Clients reported large decreases in PTSD symptoms and increases in DBT skills. Another evaluation of 4 years of DBT in a VA medical center ($N = 83$) found that 78% of clients completed at least 3 months of treatment, whereas half completed 6 months or more (Spoont, Sayer, Thuras, Erbes, & Winston, 2003). Therapists rated that 60% of clients had some benefit, and 55% of clients reported being very or extremely satisfied with treatment. More work, however, is needed to identify strategies to overcome the structural barriers to implementing standard DBT in VA health care settings (Landes et al., 2017).

Intellectual Disabilities

DBT has also been applied to the treatment of challenging behaviors among individuals with intellectual disabilities and challenging behaviors. An adapted DBT skills system for skills training made the language of DBT materials more accessible for this population (Brown, 2015). In a study of this modified DBT skills system plus standard individual DBT for 40 clients with challenging behaviors and intellectual disabilities, DBT resulted in dramatic reductions in hospitalization (Brown, Brown, & Dibiasio, 2013). A review summarized seven studies that applied DBT adaptations to samples with intellectual and developmental disabilities (McNair, Woodrow, & Hare, 2017). However, ratings of the rigor of the assessments, comparison conditions, and data analysis conclude that there remains promising but still weak or preliminary support for the effectiveness of DBT in this population.

Other Domains of Difficulties

DBT-informed approaches have also been used for other difficulties. For instance, DBT is well-suited to address interpersonal function, which can manifest as serious discord and relational violence. Thus, a brief DBT group skills training and phone coaching was provided to female victims of intimate partner violence in an uncontrolled trial, with promising results (Iverson, Shenk, & Fruzzetti, 2009).

Similarly, the systematic focus on treatment-interfering behaviors and distress tolerance in DBT makes it a natural fit as an ancillary intervention in the treatment of chronic medical conditions. Uncontrolled trials of individual DBT-informed sessions (Hashim, Vadnais, & Miller, 2013) and group skills training (Drossel, Fisher, & Mercer, 2011) have been developed for patients with end-stage kidney disease (Hashim et al., 2013) and caregivers of patients with dementia (Drossel et al., 2011). Results from uncontrolled trials are promising yet inconclusive.

Even after completing DBT, many clients continue to have challenges obtaining and maintaining employment (McMain et al., 2012). As exemplified with Kara, employment can be critical to achieving financial stability and decreasing dependence on problem relationships. With this in mind, Comtois, Kerbrat, Atkins, Harned, and Elwood (2010) developed a follow-up to DBT, titled DBT-Accepting the Challenges of Exiting the System (DBT-ACES). DBT-ACES includes group and individual therapy with contingency management to focus on treatment targets of paid work or school enrollment. An uncontrolled trial showed improved employment or school enrollment (Comtois et al., 2010), and smaller studies have also suggested that DBT is a promising approach for vocational rehabilitation (Koons et al., 2006).

RESEARCH LIMITATIONS

Despite accumulating research supporting the use of DBT for a range of problems, several problems hinder our ability to make clinical recommendations.

Difficulties in Replicating Results

First, although we have consistently seen that DBT is useful for BPD traits and related problems associated with emotional and behavioral dysregulation, including self-injurious behaviors, many of the studies applying DBT to other samples have been underpowered or not replicated. Second, the idiosyncratic modifications to DBT without replication limit our ability to know which modifications are necessary for which populations. Third, we have little knowledge of factors predicting response and dropout in DBT, with a few exceptions. From the studies that exist, we know that less education predicted dropout, and lower inhibitory control predicted decreased self-injury in DBT (Ruocco et al., 2016). The severity of certain psychiatric symptoms was also predicted with response to DBT. Specifically, schizoid personality traits (Perroud et al., 2010) and BPD traits of identity disturbance and frantic efforts to avoid abandonment (Yen et al., 2009) predicted poorer treatment response. Conversely, superior treatment response was associated with narcissistic personality (Perroud et al., 2010) and BPD symptoms of emptiness, relationship instability, and impulsive behaviors (Yen et al., 2009). Fourth, although we know that briefer forms of DBT are useful, additional DBT can also lead to further improvements (Pasieczny & Connor, 2011; Perroud et al., 2010). Thus, additional work is needed to guide us in determining which clients and symptom domains are likely to benefit from which formats of treatment.

Application of DBT to Diverse Samples

Another limitation of the literature base of DBT is the scant work that has DBT examined with diverse samples (McFarr et al., 2014). Culturally sensitive approaches to psychotherapy are those that attempt to define race, culture, and ethnicity; consider characteristics of a particular cultural group; and ensure that a given treatment is responsive to those concerns (Hall, 2001). Despite the growing research base on evidence-based practice in diverse samples (Morales & Norcross, 2010), there remains relatively little research on DBT across cultural and ethnically diverse contexts.

The societal marginalization that can affect individuals with minority sexual and gender identities constitutes an important source of environmental invalidation and may influence the high rates of suicide and self-injury in these populations (Sloan, Berke, & Shipherd, 2017). Indeed, several of our clients who were raised in very conservative regions reported that their experiences of sexual attraction to people of their same gender were among the main antecedents for self-injury and suicidal thoughts. Clinicians have suggested that a dialectical perspective can inform the conceptualization and treatment of such populations (Sloan et al., 2017). Only one study to our knowledge has directly examined whether DBT performs similarly in heterosexual or sexual minority samples (Beard et al., 2017). In this naturalistic uncontrolled study of participants ($N = 441$; 19% lesbian, gay, bisexual, queer, or other sexual minority) undergoing cognitive behavior therapy or DBT, there were no differences in reported symptoms of depression, anxiety, and other problem behaviors. However, bisexual individuals reported more thoughts about self-injurious behaviors and reported poorer perceived care at discharge.

Several uncontrolled trials have evaluated cultural adaptations of DBT. For instance, DBT was adapted to a brief group infused with relevant cultural metaphors for Nepali women (Ramaiya, Fiorillo, Regmi, Robins, & Kohrt, 2017). A pilot of the DBT-Nepali treatment for 10 Nepali women revealed improvements in psychiatric and emotional symptoms and suicidal ideation (Ramaiya et al., 2018). Likewise, DBT-SUD was culturally adapted and integrated into a residential center for Native American/Alaskan Native youth ($N = 229$), yielding improvements in psychiatric outcomes (Beckstead, Lambert, DuBose, & Linehan, 2015).

In the United States, alterations were made to DBT for binge eating to increase amenability for a racially diverse sample. This group-based adaptation (Linking Individuals Being Emotionally Real [LIBER8]) addressed issues such as customs and inconsistent food access (Mazzeo et al., 2013). An RCT compared LIBER8 with weight management for a diverse (42% black) sample of adolescent girls ($N = 45$) with out-of-control eating (Mazzeo et al., 2016). Although both conditions reported decreased eating disorder symptoms, no group differences emerged.

Despite the relative dearth of well-powered trials on the application of DBT to diverse cultural contexts, several case studies illustrate adaptations to increase cultural sensitivity. In one case, the therapist wove in aspects of Chinese culture (such as adding indirect communication strategies to interpersonal effectiveness skills) to DBT for a Chinese international student with an eating disorder (Cheng & Merrick, 2017). The client reported improved symptoms and relational satisfaction. Likewise, DBT skills were adapted for use with a Mexican client in her 40s with depression, anxiety, and suicidal ideation by translating skills to Spanish and incorporating cultural values of family unity and spirituality (Mercado & Hinojosa, 2017). She reported improved symptoms after treatment, which persisted over the 3-month follow-up. Another case study described mixed benefits of embedding DBT in a cultural framework for a suicidal female Navajo adolescent with depression (Kohrt, Lincoln, & Brambila, 2017).

CONCLUSION

Drawing from this extant body of research on DBT, a practical question that clinicians often ask is: Who is DBT for? DBT has proliferated over the past 25 years, having been disseminated in various forms to many countries around the world. The comprehensiveness, flexibility, and commonsense, practical nature of DBT, along with its incorporation of evidence-based CBT principles, has made this treatment appealing to a range of programs serving an even broader range of clients. DBT seems to make sense to many clinicians as a helpful treatment for many problems. Clinician- and consumer-oriented books have addressed the use of DBT elements for various problems, such as anxiety, anger, bipolar disorder, eating disorders, suicidality in adolescents, psychosis, and clients with lower cognitive functioning, among others. In some cases, the evidence for these applications has been minimal or preliminary, and it is important for clinicians to know when, why, and why not to provide DBT to particular types of clients.

DBT is not the treatment for everything. Even after many years of research, the vast majority of well-controlled studies (e.g., RCTs) have examined DBT for BPD and problems (e.g., self-injurious behaviors) falling within a constellation probably best encapsulated as affective–impulsive behavioral problems. The most consistent outcomes for DBT include reductions in harmful behavior (e.g., suicide attempts, and to a lesser extent, NSSI), use of psychiatric health resources, anger and substance use problems, and problems that are broadly related to emotion dysregulation and impulsive, damaging behavior. When we train clinicians, we often emphasize that DBT is not the front-line treatment for certain relatively straightforward clinical syndromes (in the absence of complex or co-occurring disorders), such as major depressive disorder, bipolar disorder, anxiety disorders, posttraumatic stress disorder, and others. Most well-controlled DBT studies have excluded people with bipolar or psychotic disorders, although some recent work has been done in these areas.

Although elements of DBT may be helpful for many of these types of problems, clients should receive treatments with demonstrated efficacy. A client with depression, for example, should receive evidence-based treatment for depression (e.g., CBT, interpersonal therapy) but may benefit from ancillary DBT skills training. In our practice, we recommend standard DBT when a client has a formal diagnosis or significant features of BPD, other clinical problems with co-occurring suicidality, NSSI, and/or substance use problems, or is multidiagnostic with core emotion dysregulation and behavioral dysregulation being core features (e.g., a client with co-occurring depression and serious anger management or alcohol use problems). In addition, although much of the early research on DBT included predominately female samples, a smaller but growing body of evidence suggests that DBT is efficacious with men, and in our experience, men often take to and benefit from DBT just as much as women. Modified DBT has also emerged as a potentially efficacious treatment for PTSD and eating disorders associated with impulsivity, such as binge eating and bulimia nervosa.

6

Process: Primary Change Mechanisms

As discussed in Chapter 4, this volume, a considerable body of research supports the efficacy of dialectical behavior therapy (DBT). Indeed, both the Australian Health and Medical Resource Council and the United Kingdom's National Collaborating Centre for Mental Health have concluded that DBT has the most evidence among current treatments for borderline personality disorder (BPD; National Health and Medical Research Council, 2013; National Institute for Health and Care Excellence, 2009). Comprehensive standard DBT, however, can sometimes be difficult to adopt with fidelity in certain settings. DBT is a comprehensive, relatively long-term (compared with other forms of CBT) treatment requiring considerable implementation resources, such as adequately trained staff, space, time, a team, availability of therapists for between-session phone coaching, and so forth. Knowing which aspects of DBT could be considered the active, essential ingredients would help

http://dx.doi.org/10.1037/0000188-006
Dialectical Behavior Therapy, by A. L. Chapman and K. L. Dixon-Gordon

inform its adoption in various settings, where critical ingredients may be retained even if the full treatment is not feasible. It would also be useful to know what kinds of changes in clients account for the effectiveness of DBT, just as it is helpful to know what beneficial physiological changes result from medical interventions or medications. Knowing this information might help clinicians gear DBT toward the types of changes that lead to beneficial outcomes. In this chapter, we discuss the possible mechanisms of change associated with DBT, including key ingredients of DBT and key changes in the client that might account for beneficial outcomes. Our focus here is broadly on the key treatment elements or client changes that underlie DBT's efficacy. As DBT is based on a bio-social theory of BPD (Crowell, Beauchaine, & Linehan, 2009; Linehan, 1993a) emphasizing the key role of emotion regulation dysfunction in the behavioral problems associated with this disorder, we will primarily consider client-related mechanisms pertaining to emotions and emotion regulation. Within this chapter, we review and summarize some of the research on mechanisms of change in DBT that are related to (a) treatment ingredients and (b) changes in the client. For a more detailed discussion of potential mechanisms associated with specific DBT interventions, please see Lynch, Chapman, Rosenthal, Kuo, & Linehan (2006).

MECHANISMS OF CHANGE IN DBT

The term *mechanisms of change* refers to the processes by which treatment results in beneficial outcomes (Kazdin, 2007). Over the past couple of decades, there has been a strong push to identify these processes, with some key benefits being the ability to (a) streamline and develop efficient treatment that targets core processes underlying psychopathology (with one example being the Unified Protocol for Emotional Disorders; Barlow et al., 2011; Farchione et al., 2012); and (b) measure whether changes are occurring in purported mechanisms and modify theory, case conceptualization, and treatment accordingly. If, for example, one mechanism of change for the treatment of diabetes consists of changes in blood glucose or hormone levels, the physician would want to use a treatment regimen that targets this mechanism and measure changes in the mechanism to determine if the treatment is on target.

As mentioned above, mechanisms of change can be considered on a couple of different levels. At the level of treatment characteristics or ingredients, mechanisms of change relate to the elements of treatment that lead to beneficial outcomes. A comprehensive, cognitive–behavioral treatment such as DBT includes many treatment ingredients (individual therapy, group skills training, phone coaching, consultation team). One key question pertains to which of these elements are necessary and/or sufficient to produce beneficial clinical outcomes. This is a complex question with any treatment, let alone a multifaceted treatment like DBT. There are so many features of the treatment that may be essential or nonessential, and it is possible that no single mode of DBT, but rather the co-occurrence and interplay of the different DBT treatment modes within the broader DBT system, leads to key outcomes. Clinically, we have often observed that suicidal clients benefit greatly from the confluence of individual treatment targeting imminent risk, the therapist's access to cogent advice and support from other team members (both within team meetings and during ad-hoc consultation), and effective coordination between the individual therapist and group skills trainers. For example, we recently saw a client (Andy) who ended his session stating that he wants to quit therapy and kill himself and is unwilling to do anything to reduce his risk. The therapist consulted with a team member, devised a plan to address imminent risk, called Andy to assess his risk of suicide and to intervene as needed, sought support from the team to reduce stress, and asked the skills trainers to reach out to Andy and encourage him to come to his next group session. A suicide plan was averted, Andy continued with treatment, and he and the therapist had a heart-to-heart talk about what needs to change for the client to experience his life as being more worth living. It would be hard to say what the outcomes would have been if Andy were receiving an isolated mode of DBT (e.g., only individual therapy or skills training). The potential for a wide variety of outcomes for complex, multidiagnostic clients also makes it difficult to answer the question of which treatment ingredients are essential. For clients with

BPD, some key outcomes usually include reductions in suicidality, self-injury, use of health resources, anger, substance use, depression, and so forth. Improvements in quality-of-life, social and occupational functioning, and relationships also are often very important, as are client-specific goals. Isolating which treatment elements are necessary for which types of outcomes is a daunting task.

Another level on which to consider mechanisms of change pertains to changes in the client that account for the effects of treatment. In the diabetes example, changes in blood glucose and hormone levels would be considered client-oriented mechanisms. Treatment often consists of insulin injections or medications that moderate blood glucose but may also include directions to modify exercise, diet, and even sleep. The key target remains blood glucose and hormone levels, and perhaps other measures of physical health (given the broad effects of diabetes on cardio-vascular and other difficulties). Understanding client changes that account for outcomes, however, is simpler when a single disorder or syndrome is the focus of treatment. DBT has been applied to many clinical problem areas, and even within particular problem areas (e.g., BPD), the changes in the client resulting from treatment can be complex. One way to simplify and isolate potentially promising client-oriented mechanisms is to return to the theoretical basis for the treatment, which suggests that changes in emotion dysregulation could underlie the effects of DBT.

Clinically, the therapist might observe or measure changes in key mechanisms related to emotion regulation. Over the course of DBT, the therapist might expect to observe changes in Andy's reactivity to emotionally evocative events, which typically involved interpersonal conflict resulting in intense sadness, bitterness, and loneliness. Other changes could include greater use of effective skills to modulate emotions, such as skills to identify sadness and loneliness, cognitive reappraisal of conflict situations (e.g., "Someone being frustrated with me doesn't mean they don't care about me and are going to leave me. We can probably resolve this"). Additional changes could include Andy's ability to tolerate overwhelming emotions, reductions in his fears of being alone, reductions in the time it takes him to return to emotional baseline following intense emotional reactions, and increases in his engagement in effective behavior (e.g., communicate effectively to his close friend) despite strong emotions. Understanding which of these mechanisms will most contribute to improvements in Andy's quality of life would aid the therapist in focusing on the most useful treatment targets, facilitating more rapid and meaningful improvement. A grasp of the most relevant mechanisms of change in DBT is therefore a critical step to optimizing the delivery of this treatment.

MECHANISMS RELATED TO TREATMENT INGREDIENTS

Several potential treatment ingredients may underlie the efficacy of DBT. The research on this topic is limited, however, so we discuss in this section those ingredients that we believe are unique and particularly central to DBT. These include the therapist–client relationship, the structure of the treatment, and interventions encouraging the ongoing use of outpatient therapy and reducing crisis or emergency services.

Therapist–Client Relationship

Akin to many other psychotherapies, the therapeutic relationship plays an important role in DBT. Marsha Linehan (1993) has referred to the therapeutic relationship not only as the "vehicle through which the therapist can effect the therapy, it is also the therapy" (p. 514). Although the therapeutic relationship is not viewed as the *only* critical element of DBT, it is seen as necessary to therapeutic change. There are several unique aspects of DBT that may directly or indirectly enhance the therapeutic relationship. The therapy relationship is characterized by a nonjudgmental style, reciprocity, and warmth, and often involves therapist self-disclosure as a means to model effective coping (e.g., the therapist discussing how using a mindfulness skill helped get them through a frustrating situation) or convey important information about the therapist's ongoing reactions to the client (e.g., the therapist disclosing excitement about the client's progress or disappointment at being yelled at by the client). DBT therapists also balance reciprocity and warmth with an irreverent response style, consisting of unexpected or off-the-wall statements, the strategic use of a matter-of-fact demeanor, humor, and similar tactics. All of this is done from a foundation of compassion. The combination of reciprocity and warmth, irreverence, and radical genuineness (which is a form of validation in DBT) often contributes to the sense that the therapy relationship in DBT is a "real" and genuine, caring relationship between equals. The therapist also provides the client with the opportunity to address therapy relationship issues during phone coaching calls. Furthermore, therapy-interfering behaviors, including those that interfere with the effectiveness of the therapy relationship, are second in priority only to life-threatening behaviors.

Consistent with the importance of the therapy relationship in DBT, research findings have suggested that the therapy alliance is important to outcomes. Indeed, the strength of the working alliance between therapist and client is associated with improvements in DBT (Bedics, Atkins, Harned, & Linehan, 2015; Hirsh, Quilty, Bagby, & McMain, 2012; Turner, 2000). Yet, this alliance does not seem to differentiate DBT from other treatments—there were no differences detected in the strength of the client's reported working alliance in DBT relative to comparison conditions (Bedics et al., 2015; Hirsh et al., 2012; Turner, 2000). There is some indication that the therapeutic relationship may work differently in DBT, compared with other treatments. In one study, clients' views of their therapists as warm and protective predicted greater decreases in self-injury in DBT, but not in nonbehavioral expert psychotherapy (Bedics, Atkins, & Linehan, 2012). In a study mapping specific therapist behaviors to client changes in session, there is indication that greater use of Level Four validation (normalizing the client's behavior, emotions, or thoughts in the context of their learning history or biological dysfunction; Linehan, 1993a, 1997) was associated with an increase in client's negative affect after the therapy session. In contrast, use of greater Level Six validation, radical genuineness, was associated with a decrease in negative affect (Carson-Wong, Hughes, & Rizvi, 2018). How these in-session shifts contribute to long-term improvement in DBT remains unknown. In contrast with other treatments, however, in DBT the therapeutic relationship is not thought to effect change on its own—it is necessary but not sufficient for beneficial outcomes.

Structure of the Treatment

The structure of DBT may partially account for its efficacy. Indeed, experts in the treatment of BPD conclude that all evidence-based specialized treatments for BPD share a structured approach to therapy (Weinberg, Ronningstam, Goldblatt, Schechter, & Maltsberger, 2011). Each mode (i.e., individual, group, consultation team, and phone coaching) of DBT has a certain degree of structure in its flow of activities. For instance, individual therapists structure individual therapy sessions in a consistent but flexible sequence, from diary card review and agenda setting through assessment and problem solving, and finally to a session-ending phase. Likewise, the content of sessions is consistently yet flexibly guided by clients' diary cards and key behavioral targets. Individual therapists also structure therapeutic activities, direct the flow of the session, help clients maintain focus when they veer off course or into unrelated or unproductive topics, and provide additional structure by orienting clients to the rationale and procedures for various therapy interventions and activities. The DBT skills group also has a structured flow of activities. A structured, organized treatment can have a regulating effect for clients who are living chaotic lives or who are emotionally dysregulated. The client knows what to expect and receives practice following a reasonable routine of session activities rather than engaging in mood-dependent behavior, and doing so requires emotion regulation. Andy, for example, often became extremely frustrated with another group member's loud talking, and with the help of skilled group leaders, he learned to use DBT skills to tolerate and regulate his emotions and avoid saying something he would later regret. Having practiced this in group, he eventually found that he was more able to step back, observe, and tolerate frustrating interactions with his loved ones without saying things that just made things worse.

Interventions Enhancing Treatment Engagement
and Reducing Dropout

DBT directly targets behaviors that reduce the effectiveness of therapy, such as poor attendance, homework noncompliance, and dropping out, among others. When clients (or therapists) engage in behaviors that reduce the likelihood that therapy will work, therapists assess and collaboratively seek alternative solutions (see Chapman & Rosenthal, 2016). It is also standard practice for DBT therapists to keep track of clients' urges to quit therapy every session, using the DBT diary card. Attending to urges or thoughts about quitting provides the opportunity to proactively assess and address clients' difficulties with treatment. DBT therapists also view motivation (often referred to as commitment in DBT) as an important treatment target and actively seek to help clients develop and sustain motivation for therapy. These interventions are likely crucial, as it is difficult for complex, suffering clients to sustain the difficult work that accompanies therapy and the building of a life worth living. Findings across several studies have indicated that DBT is associated with considerably lower dropout rates compared with some comparison conditions (Linehan, Armstrong, Suarez, Allmon, & Heard, 1991; 2006; Uliaszek, Rashid, Williams, & Gulamani, 2016). Of note, dropout rates in DBT have been higher (36% and higher) in other studies (Feigenbaum et al., 2012; Linehan et al., 2002). The studies with greater dropout rates tended to be conducted in real-world clinical settings (Feigenbaum et al., 2012), or compared with other treatments that focus on providing clients with support and validation (Linehan et al., 2002). Attending sessions more consistently and remaining in therapy until its natural conclusion would seem to create the opportunity for better outcomes, particularly in the treatment of complex, multiproblem clients, where the trajectory of change often resembles a bumpy road, with episodic improvements and setbacks. For meaningful and long-term improvement to occur, both the client and the therapist often need to stay the course through these ups and downs. Findings from some research has suggested that DBT's approach to targeting treatment engagement may influence outcomes. One study of adolescents with a history of recurrent self-injurious behaviors, for example, found that the number of treatment contacts partially accounted for the relationship between receiving DBT (relative to care as usual) and reduced suicidality (Mehlum et al., 2014).

The structure of DBT also includes consultation teams for therapists, and in so doing, may indirectly enhance client engagement in treatment by supporting therapists. Therapists on DBT consultation teams are encouraged to prioritize problems with therapy-interfering behavior and therapy attendance when they seek consultation and support from their colleagues. Other team members often help the therapist assess, problem solve, and troubleshoot these difficulties. Accordingly, in one effectiveness study, therapist participation in consultation team meetings was associated with higher client retention (Stiglmayr et al., 2014).

Interventions to Reduce the Use of Crisis Services

It is also possible that it is not what DBT adds but what it reduces that contributes to its efficacy. DBT therapists actively work with clients to de-escalate crises and develop safety plans to reduce the need for hospitalizations and use of crisis services. Some of this work occurs in individual therapy sessions, and some of it occurs during phone coaching, where therapists are available to coach clients in skills to avert or manage crises. In essence, DBT therapists engage in efforts to keep clients in outpatient treatment who might otherwise frequently visit the emergency department or end up in inpatient hospital units.

Averting hospitalization can have a couple of key potential benefits. First, most crisis and hospital services for suicidal clients with BPD run the risk of inadvertently reinforcing suicidality. Clients receive more care and more urgent attention when they are suicidal than when they are not. Curtailing this pattern would be expected to reduce suicidal crises and behavior. Second, while hospitalization may provide relief from the stress of daily life in the short term, in the long term, hospitalizations may present barriers to occupational functioning, increase the likelihood of financial hardship, and harm relationships. Thus, reducing engagement with crisis and hospital services may improve client functioning, as clients are able to stay "in the game" so to speak, use new skills, maintain meaningful pursuits, and learn how to function despite considerable emotional distress. Findings have indicated that DBT is associated with decreased use of psychiatric crisis services in treatment, compared with treatment as usual (Coyle, Shaver, & Linehan, 2018), and that this decrease in the use of crisis services accounted for the association between DBT and reduced risk of suicide over a follow-up period.

Andy, for example, presented to the emergency room approximately 25 times in the year before he began treatment. When he was admitted to hospital, he remained largely miserable but still found it relieving to temporarily withdraw from his normal work and home responsibilities. Although he received some treatment in hospital, and his mood usually improved over the course of a few days, upon release he quickly became overwhelmed with everyday life. Andy and his therapist worked hard to help him use skills instead of harming himself or visiting the hospital, and although it was harder to "stay in the game," in the long run, he began to learn to recognize and regulate his emotions during conflict at home and when he was overwhelmed at work. As a result, he felt more capable and hopeful that things could change, and he had fewer serious suicidal thoughts.

Skills Training

Based on the skills-deficit model, it is reasonable to consider whether skills training contributes to the efficacy of DBT. In an effort to evaluate the importance of the skills training component of DBT, a component analysis of DBT randomized clients to receive either DBT skills training and case management (DBT-S), DBT individual therapy (DBT-I) and an activities group (a group involving psychoeducation and shared activities, such as movies, etc.), or standard DBT that includes both skills training and individual therapy (Linehan et al., 2015). All of these conditions resulted in comparable improvements in frequency and severity of suicide attempts, ideation, and suicide-related use of crisis services. Clients in standard DBT and DBT-S showed greater improvements in nonsuicidal self-injury and depression compared with clients in the DBT-I condition. In addition, clients in standard DBT had half the treatment dropout rate of DBT-I and were less likely to use crisis services or be hospitalized during the follow-up year. A much earlier nonrandomized study evaluated standard DBT versus skills group only (Harley, Baity, Blais, & Jacobo, 2007). Clients who received DBT skills alone showed significant improvement in symptoms of BPD, depression, and suicidal ideation. Of note, however, a higher proportion of clients with individual therapists outside of the hospital where the study took place dropped out of the skills group. These findings suggest that DBT skills training may be a critical element of what makes DBT efficacious, but individual therapy may be important to keeping clients in treatment.

Yet, the question remains as to which skills are most important. Mindfulness is considered a core skill in DBT. Mindfulness may target problematic emotions in several ways (Gratz & Tull, 2010). First, mindfulness may serve as attentional training, promoting attentional control and reducing attentional biases characteristic of psychopathology that amplify or prolong emotional responses. There is evidence that mindfulness interventions promote sustained attention (Chambers, Lo, & Allen, 2008) and increase neural activation in regions associated with attentional control (Goldin & Gross, 2010). Second, mindfulness of one's emotions may constitute exposure to emotions, resulting in inhibitory learning (Craske, Treanor, Conway, Zbozinek, & Vervliet, 2014; Gratz & Tull, 2010), whereby clients learn that emotional states (e.g., sadness) are not associated with unfortunate events or experiences (e.g., being punished or chastised, being out of control). Findings have suggested that mindfulness training is associated with down-regulation of brain regions linked to emotional experiencing, including the amygdala (Taylor et al., 2011). Third, mindfulness decreases repetitive thought patterns, such as worry and rumination, which in turn reduces the intensity of emotional responding (van der Velden et al., 2015). Fourth, mindfulness may help clients learn how to experience and reflect on strong emotional states without acting on them. Indeed, some findings have shown that mindfulness training improves neural substrates associated with emotional control (Hölzel et al., 2013).

Emerging findings also support the importance of mindfulness practice in DBT. To evaluate the importance of mindfulness training in particular, two separate nonrandomized trials compared the effect of eight sessions of DBT mindfulness skills training adjunctive to general psychiatric management to general psychiatric management alone for clients with BPD (Feliu-Soler et al., 2014; Soler et al., 2012). Results revealed that the more time clients spent each week practicing mindfulness, the greater their improvement in reported mindfulness, symptoms of general psychopathology (Soler et al., 2012), symptoms of depression (Feliu-Soler et al., 2014; Soler et al., 2012), and self-reported emotional reactivity (Feliu-Soler et al., 2014).

Given the centrality of emotion regulation problems and emotion dysregulation to the biosocial theory of BPD, DBT emotion regulation skills training also may serve as a critical ingredient. According to the biosocial theory, emotion dysregulation either directly or indirectly contributes to many of the problems seen among clients in DBT (Crowell et al., 2009; Linehan, 1993a). Such emotion dysregulation can be seen in the emotional lability and inappropriate anger characteristic of BPD. In addition, many of the self-destructive and impulsive behaviors occurring among individuals with BPD can be conceptualized as efforts to avoid or escape emotional distress (Chapman, Gratz, & Brown, 2006; Weiss, Tull, Viana, Anestis, & Gratz, 2012). Furthermore, many of the social difficulties seen in BPD are emotion-dependent or exacerbated by stress (Dixon-Gordon, Chapman, Lovasz, & Walters, 2011). Thus, most of the interventions and strategies within DBT purportedly aim to reduce emotion dysregulation.

To our knowledge, only a few fairly preliminary studies have examined whether DBT emotion regulation skills specifically improve emotion regulation. In one such study, an alternating design examined the effects of teaching the skill of opposite action to emotion urges versus acting consistent with emotion urges among 16 individuals with BPD

(Sauer-Zavala, Wilner, Cassiello-Robbins, Saraff, & Pagan, 2019). In this study, participants came to six sessions; in half of these sessions, participants were instructed to act opposite to emotion urges, and consistent with urges in the other half of the sessions. Participants were randomly assigned to one specific emotion (e.g., anxiety, sadness, anger, shame/guilt) that was elicited in all sessions for that participant. Participants generally showed greater decreases in emotional intensity when acting opposite to urges in the sadness and guilt/shame conditions. Likewise, exposure to shame scripts plus opposite action to shame resulted in reduced shame for five women with BPD (Rizvi & Linehan, 2005). In another study, 19 clients with BPD were randomized to receive 6 weeks of DBT emotion regulation skills training, DBT interpersonal effectiveness skills training, or an active control group (Dixon-Gordon, Chapman, & Turner, 2015). Findings suggested greater improvement in reported self-injury and mindfulness in the emotion regulation condition compared to the other conditions. The preliminary nature of this study, however, suggests that replication of these results would be necessary before conclusions can be drawn regarding the importance of emotion regulation skills in particular.

MECHANISMS RELATED TO CHANGES IN THE CLIENT

Several potential changes in the client may account for the efficacy of DBT. Theoretically, in DBT, clients learn a variety of skills that ameliorate preexisting skills deficits. In turn, these skills should allow them to be more aware and in charge of their attention, notice and effectively manage emotional reactions, navigate interpersonal situations, and curb impulses to engage in problematic behaviors (Linehan, 1993a, 1993b, 2015b). By reducing emotional reactivity, clients are able to avoid problems that tend to occur in the presence of unregulated, intense emotions, such as impulsive behaviors and interpersonal problems. Although there is scant empirical basis on exactly what client processes are most important in driving treatment change in DBT, several studies indirectly highlight some of the processes involved.

Improvements in Capabilities (Skills)

One type of change in clients that could account for the positive outcomes of DBT is improvement in their repertoire of adaptive skills; some research has supported this possibility. In one study, among clients with BPD who completed a year of DBT, increases in reported days using skills (across mindfulness, distress tolerance, emotion regulation, and interpersonal effectiveness) predicted decreased likelihood of dropout and decreases in self-injurious behaviors (Barnicot, Gonzalez, McCabe, & Priebe, 2016). In another study of clients (85% women) with BPD, reported skills use on DBT diary cards among clients with BPD undergoing DBT was associated with reductions in BPD symptoms (Stepp, Epler, Jahng, & Trull, 2008). Furthermore, in a larger randomized trial comparing DBT with comparison treatments for women with BPD, increased reported use of adaptive skills was associated with reduced self-injurious behaviors and depression in the DBT condition (Neacsiu, Rizvi, & Linehan, 2010). Likewise, a similar pattern was found in a trial comparing DBT skills training to a supportive therapy comparison group for clients with emotion dysregulation and an emotional disorder, such as depression or anxiety (Neacsiu, Eberle, Kramer, Wiesmann, & Linehan, 2014). Increases in reported use of adaptive skills correlated with greater improvements in emotion dysregulation and anxiety seen in the DBT condition. These findings suggest that clinicians practicing DBT or teaching DBT skills should emphasize the importance of skills practice.

Beyond skill use and development more broadly, increases in mindfulness and attentional control may at least partially account for the effects of DBT. Indeed, many of the components of DBT directly or indirectly aim to increase awareness. For instance, mindfulness is the most frequently taught skill in group, with mindfulness exercises serving as the opening for each group, and mindfulness skills interleaved with all the other skills modules. As noted above, in RCTs comparing DBT mindfulness skills training plus general psychiatric management to general psychiatric management alone, the amount of time clients spent practicing mindfulness predicted improvements in reported mindfulness and other outcomes (Soler et al., 2012). Furthermore, the number of minutes of mindfulness practice was also associated with reduced symptoms of psychopathology and depression. Clients with BPD who underwent intensive DBT followed by 10 months of standard DBT also showed increases in reported mindfulness (Perroud, Nicastro, Jermann, & Huguelet, 2012). Furthermore, among the many DBT skills, clients report using mindfulness skills (along with distress tolerance skills) the most, across the course of DBT (Lindenboim, Comtois, & Linehan, 2007).

Andy, for example, reported that the mindfulness skill of stepping back and observing stressful situations and overwhelming emotions was critical. Instead of reacting urgently and impulsively in the moment, Andy learned to step back, observe the signs that his distress was increasing, notice urges to engage in problem behaviors (for him, these included yelling, drinking, self-harming, or planning a suicide attempt), and take the time to figure out what skills to use to manage or tolerate his emotions. Mindfulness, for Andy, was the doorway to other skills that replaced his problem behaviors and improved his life in the long run.

Improvements in Emotion Regulation

In DBT, reduced emotional reactivity and enhanced emotion regulation are important DBT targets and may constitute mechanisms of change; emerging research supports these processes in DBT. Studies have investigated reductions in emotion dysregulation in several ways, including self-report measures of emotion regulation strategies and difficulties, laboratory assessment of emotional reactivity to particular stimuli, and neuroimaging studies examining changes in patterns of brain functioning. Compared to a cognitive therapy comparison condition, DBT skills training resulted in greater decreases in reported use of emotional suppression and increased use of acceptance-based emotion regulation strategies (Lin et al., 2019). Findings of studies using self-report measures of emotion regulation problems (e.g., the Difficulties in Emotion Regulation Scale [DERS]; Gratz & Roemer, 2004) have suggested that DBT reduces difficulties in emotion regulation, that such reductions may account for the effects of DBT on behavior (e.g., substance use; Axelrod, Perepletchikova,

Holtzman, & Sinha, 2011), and that DBT or DBT components may reduce laboratory-measured reactivity to emotional stimuli (Dixon-Gordon, Weiss, et al., 2015; Goodman et al., 2014).

Research using neuroimaging methods has indicated that DBT might result in changes in functioning in brain areas associated with emotions and emotion regulation. A few studies to date have examined changes in neural activity from pretreatment to post-DBT. One pilot study (Schnell & Herpertz, 2007) examined the effects of 12 weeks of DBT inpatient treatment on the reactivity of clients with BPD ($n = 9$) to standardized negative images. A comparison group of healthy controls ($n = 5$) not undergoing treatment also was included. Compared with their pretreatment reactivity to negative images, BPD clients showed reduced activity in the anterior cingulate cortex, and temporal and posterior cingulate cortices. Clients who responded most to treatment in this study also showed a reduced left amygdala response. In the Goodman et al. (2014) study previously mentioned, BPD clients underwent 12 months of comprehensive, standard DBT and showed decreased activity in left amygdala responses from pre- to post-treatment, whereas untreated healthy controls did not show this difference. Further, change in amygdala activity was positively associated with changes in scores on the DERS, a self-report measure of emotion regulation difficulties (Goodman et al., 2014). In another study, BPD clients who underwent brief 12-week residential DBT showed decreased activity in brain regions associated with emotion regulation (e.g., supramarginal gyrus, anterior cingulate) when asked to distract from emotional images (Winter et al., 2017) or reappraise emotional images (Schmitt, Winter, Niedtfeld, Herpertz, & Schmahl, 2016). Furthermore, in this research, clients who showed particular benefit from DBT had reductions in anterior cingulate activity (Winter et al., 2017).

The only study to our knowledge that has compared DBT with another treatment condition in terms of brain functioning examined changes in amygdala response to pain in clients assigned to DBT ($n = 28$) versus treatment as usual ($n = 15$; Niedtfeld et al., 2017). Before treatment, BPD clients showed a tendency toward amygdala deactivation in response to physical pain, suggesting that pain regulated emotional responding. Following treatment, this tendency was reduced in DBT clients but not in those receiving TAU. This finding suggests that treatment might reduce the link between self-injury and the automatic down-regulation of emotional arousal, thus attenuating an important negative reinforcer considered to maintain self-injury for many people (Chapman et al., 2006; Nock & Prinstein, 2004).

Improvements in Other Domains

Research is limited as to whether other skills training domains, such as interpersonal effectiveness and distress tolerance, may also be mechanisms of change in DBT. For instance, improvements in interpersonal functioning have been proposed as an alternative mechanism in the treatment of BPD (Markowitz, Skodol, & Bleiberg, 2006). In addition, given that reductions in self-injurious behaviors is one of the most robust effects of DBT, it is possible that gaining alternative methods of coping with acute distress is one of the means by which DBT works. Thus, additional work is warranted to evaluate other candidate mechanisms of change in DBT.

OBSTACLES TO UNCOVERING MECHANISMS OF CHANGE

To date, very few studies have attempted to investigate DBT's theorized change mechanisms. It is important for studies of potential mechanisms to examine what about the effectiveness of DBT is due to its specific ingredients, rather than more general characteristics of being in therapy or research, such as attention, expectations for change, experimenter demand, and factors common to many treatments such as the therapeutic relationship (Olatunji & Lohr, 2004). Although emerging research provides some support for considering these factors as mechanisms of change, including their theoretical plausibility and associations between the treatment, candidate mechanism, and outcomes, this is not sufficient to identify these factors as mechanisms (Nock, 2007). To truly establish that a variable is a key treatment ingredient, participants must be randomly assigned to various treatment ingredients. To determine whether changes in the client serve as key mechanisms, multiple measurements over time must be collected both for the putative mechanism and the outcome variable in order to establish that the mechanism causes subsequent change, rather than the other way around (Kazdin, 2007). Furthermore, it is important to consider a range of potential mechanisms to evaluate which element or combinations of elements are responsible for contribution to change in DBT.

PRACTICAL AND CLINICAL IMPLICATIONS AND OBSERVATIONS

Although much of the theorizing about DBT mechanisms remains speculative and based on preliminary research, there are some practical implications of the possible candidate mechanisms described above. Clearly, it goes without saying that clinicians must conduct DBT on a foundation consisting of a strong therapy alliance, but it is also important to remember that the therapy alliance is necessary but not considered sufficient for beneficial outcomes. In terms of the process of delivering treatment, ensuring that DBT is delivered in a structured manner with fidelity to the DBT manual should (a) help clinicians most closely match what they are doing to the versions of DBT examined in research, and (b) enhance or maintain the effects of treatment. It is easy to veer off schedule, go off script, paint outside the lines, and so forth, with complex, challenging clients, but the foundational structure of DBT should be considered high priority. Therapists who tend to drift from this structure should seek help from their DBT consultation teams in getting back on track with this potentially critical feature of treatment.

The possibility that skills training and skills practice are crucial to the success of DBT suggests that skills training should be considered a critical mode of treatment. Further, the marriage of individual DBT and group skills training (combined with the DBT consultation team) appears to enhance client retention in therapy. It is quite possible that the diligence of individual DBT therapists in conducting chain analyses on therapy absences and monitoring and targeting desires to quit therapy and so forth, along with team support in targeting therapy interfering behaviors, help to enhance retention. Programs that only offer group skills training should consider ways to coordinate care and take steps to reduce dropout. When we have seen "group only" clients, we have sometimes spent more time supporting their attendance, coaching them in skills to get the most out of group, and helping them stay on track with homework.

As skills practice and acquisition could at least partly account for the effects of DBT, beyond including and emphasizing skills training in DBT programs, clinicians might remain vigilant to clients' practice of skills, both through structured homework assignments and ad-hoc practice in everyday life. Clients often have difficulty sustaining homework and skills practice, and yet, staying on track may be critical if they wish to reach their goals. We have seen many clients who have continued to thrive following DBT, and almost uniformly, they have said that they continue to practice their skills when opportunities arise in everyday life, and that they still seek guidance on skills from their manuals or worksheets.

Additionally, while we do not know which skills are truly critical for outcomes in DBT (and this likely depends greatly on the characteristics and circumstances of individual clients), improvements in mindfulness and emotion regulation are good possible candidate mechanisms (and may also enhance other outcomes, e.g., interpersonal functioning), both theoretically and in terms of emerging research findings. Both mindfulness and emotion regulation already receive substantial emphasis in DBT, and clinicians might consider looking for additional opportunities to encourage regular mindfulness practice (which is not a requirement in DBT as it is in some other treatments, e.g., mindfulness-based cognitive therapy; Segal, Williams, & Teasdale, 2002; Teasdale et al., 2000). In our groups, we sometimes assign a standing homework assignment of a couple of minutes per day of purposeful mindfulness practice, increasing the amount of practice (e.g., up to 5 minutes by the end of 6 months) as the group continues. Such mindfulness practice could occur formally through sitting meditation or through mindfully engaging in everyday activities (e.g., walking, reading, eating, engaging in self-care activities).

In terms of emotion regulation, throughout treatment, and not just during the structured ER module in group, opportunities arise to help clients identify, label, experience, and effectively regulate their emotions. Clinicians should be particularly attuned to these opportunities when, for example, a client presents with strong emotional reactions during a therapy session or a phone coaching call. Typically, in DBT, these instances are viewed as excellent opportunities to coach clients in effective emotion regulation and help them generalize what they are learning in therapy to difficult situations in everyday life.

CONCLUSION

Although DBT is generally regarded as an efficacious treatment for BPD (Kliem, Kröger, & Kosfelder, 2010) and is also useful for a range of other conditions (Öst, 2008), less is known about *how* DBT exerts these changes. These mechanisms of change can be thought of as specific ingredients in DBT that produce change, and specific processes that change within the client that result in improvement in treatment. The preliminary research in this area highlights several key ingredients in DBT that may contribute to its efficacy. First, the focus on a strong therapeutic relationship may be one factor that contributes to gains in treatment. Second, several structural elements of DBT may also be important ingredients for what makes DBT effective. For instance, the flexible but consistent structure of sessions, consistent focus on targets according to the treatment hierarchy, among other elements, may offer stability in the context of the otherwise often volatile lives of clients undergoing DBT. Third, DBT contains several strategies and elements that enhance treatment engagement, including monitoring urges to quit treatment, directly targeting therapy-interfering behaviors, and supporting therapists to maintain an effective stance to treatment. Fourth, DBT works with clients to reduce use of crisis services through many strategies, including providing clients with new skills to tolerate distress, and phone coaching to support implementing strategies to de-escalate crises. Fifth, teaching DBT skills may be especially important. Yet, less is known about which specific skills are most important. Data suggest that mindfulness and emotion regulation skills, such as opposite action, may be especially important skills.

Other work has highlighted important processes that may shift within the client and thereby contribute to improvements in DBT. First, learning new skills may be an important change that occurs within a client. Second, clients may improve mindfulness and attentional control in DBT, which in turn could account for improvements in DBT. Third, clients may benefit from DBT by virtue of its effects on attenuating emotional reactivity. Although research on mechanisms of change in DBT is in its infancy, this remains an important direction for future work. Additional research will be important to clarify which treatment ingredients map onto specific change processes. Ultimately, this field has the potential to help streamline and optimize the delivery of DBT.

7

Summary

Dialectical behavior therapy (DBT) is a comprehensive, cognitive behavior therapy originally developed to help highly suicidal, complex clients build lives that are worth living. Through the trials and tribulations of treatment development, Dr. Marsha Linehan tailored elements of the theory and treatment to the complex challenges of clients with borderline personality disorder (BPD). In terms of theory, DBT is based on a combination of theoretical elements specifying the nature of reality (dialectics and Zen practice), the causes and maintaining factors for human behavior (behavioral theory), and the transactional processes underlying the development of particular clinical problems (the biosocial developmental theory of BPD).

As a comprehensive treatment, DBT aims to address both client and therapist capacities and motivation, generalize what the client learns in therapy to everyday life, and structure the client's treatment and natural

http://dx.doi.org/10.1037/0000188-007
Dialectical Behavior Therapy, by A. L. Chapman and K. L. Dixon-Gordon

environment in a manner that promotes progress. To accomplish these aims, DBT includes four primary modes of treatment: individual therapy, telephone consultation, group skills training, and a therapist consultation team. DBT also occurs in stages, with the pretreatment stage focusing on continued assessment, orientation, and commitment to treatment, Stage 1 addressing out-of-control behavior, Stage 2 often addressing emotional experiencing, Stage 3 targeting everyday problems in living, and Stage 4 addressing issues that are more existential, such as meaning, fulfillment, freedom, and the client's capacity for joy.

The duration of DBT varies depending on clinical setting and client problem areas. In many research studies, the duration of DBT for children, adolescents, and adults often has been set at somewhere between 6 and 12 months. In clinical settings, when there is flexibility to tailor the treatment length to the client's presenting concerns, DBT (or at least, certain modes of DBT, such as individual therapy) may last anywhere from a few months to a few years. Typically, DBT is a voluntary, outpatient treatment, but it has been adapted for use in residential treatment, inpatient psychiatric, and correctional settings.

Additionally, DBT is a program of treatment, rather than a specific protocol or package of interventions, and the DBT consultation team forms the backbone of a DBT program. Team members take responsibility for the motivation, skills, and well-being of fellow clinicians and all of the clients seen on the team. In this way, DBT is a community of therapists helping a community of clients learn how to build lives that are worth living.

In this final chapter, we return to the case example of "Mandy" from Chapter 1 to illustrate some of the key principles and elements of DBT and then address important future directions.

MANDY'S TREATMENT

As mentioned in Chapter 1, at intake Mandy had recently withdrawn from all of her college courses and made a suicide attempt resulting in hospitalization. She first saw her clinician, "Anne," about a week after hospital discharge. The beginning of treatment for Mandy, consisting of the pretreatment stage of DBT, took about four sessions. During these sessions, Anne's primary aims were to conduct continued assessment, orient Mandy to treatment, and elicit a commitment to DBT. She had a lot to accomplish. In terms of continued assessment, Anne needed to understand the factors that typically precipitate suicide attempts so that she and Mandy could devise a reasonable crisis plan. She also aimed to gather more relevant information on Mandy's history, current functioning, and patterns of problem behaviors, such as self-injury and drinking. Clarifying Mandy's specific goals for treatment and her broader goals (e.g., what would characterize a life worth living for her) was necessary to provide a compass for treatment. In terms of orientation, Anne aimed to familiarize Mandy with some key aspects of DBT, including the biosocial theory; the different modes of DBT and how they work; the target hierarchy and structure of individual therapy; when, how, and why to call for phone coaching; the structure and focus of the DBT skills group and how the skills taught in this group will help Mandy achieve her goals; and practical considerations, such as how to complete a diary card. Finally, Anne had to ensure that Mandy was committed to DBT, with the most crucial commitment being to remain alive so that Mandy could benefit from treatment. What follows is a brief excerpt of Anne addressing the agreement or commitment to stay alive.

Therapist: So, over the last couple of sessions, we've talked a lot about DBT, what you're in for, and how this treatment might help you. As we're getting ready to get started, I want to spend a few minutes talking about the most important agreement we need to make.

Client: What is that?

Therapist: Well, as it turns out, treatment won't work if you're dead. Also, if you're dead, you can't build a life that's worth living, and you won't be able to become a social worker, mend fences with your family, and so on. Are we agreed on that?

Client: Yeah, I guess that's true! I hadn't really thought of it that way.

Therapist: I understand; a lot of people don't. What this means is that, for this treatment to work, you have to make a wholehearted commitment to see it through. That means taking suicide off the table and staying alive.

Client: I see what you mean, but that seems really hard. I mean, you know what happened just before I came in here. I had that blowup with my boyfriend and failed a midterm, and it dawned on me that things are just never going to work out for me. I'm not in that mind-set right now, but I can't promise I won't be in the future. If there was just one more disaster, I just don't think I could handle it, and I don't want to make any promises that I can't keep.

Therapist: That makes sense, and I'm not asking for a promise. It's more of a commitment to work on building a life worth living. You might have times when you think everything is hopeless and pointless. You might have thoughts of suicide, and it might be hard not to act on those thoughts. When that happens, we'll have a plan, and I'll be here to help you through it. I'm not asking for a promise. What I'm asking is for you to turn toward life. To do that, you have to close and lock the suicide door, turn away from it, and walk around with me to find other doors out of misery and into the life you want.

Mandy ultimately agreed to take suicide off the table and embarked on an 18-month course of DBT. She attended individual therapy once a week for 18 months, completed two 6-month cycles of skills group, and periodically made use of phone coaching. In the beginning of Stage 1, following the DBT hierarchy of targets (within which life-threatening behavior was the top of the list), Anne helped Mandy reduce and eliminate self-injury and reduce suicide risk. To do so, Anne and Mandy collaboratively engaged in chain analyses whenever high suicide urges or self-injury appeared on Mandy's diary card, and this practice helped them discover that alcohol use and having long stretches of unstructured time alone were key vulnerability factor for self-injury and suicidal behavior. She rarely cut herself, for example, when she hadn't been drinking or when she hadn't been alone for a prolonged period. Also, important prompting events included certain types of interactions with her family (particularly if Mandy perceived that family members disapproved of her decision to take a leave from school or were frustrated with her for asking for support), being alone and without options to socialize on a Friday night. Mandy also reported that flare-ups in romantic relationships were often prompting events for her self-injury in the past, but that she was avoiding such relationships for the time being. Many of these factors that elevated risk of self-injury were also involved in previous suicide attempts.

On the basis of this conceptualization of Mandy's behavior, Mandy and Anne decided to work on reducing alcohol use, improving Mandy's communication with her family and using skills to cope with feelings of sadness or shame following conversations with her family, structuring her time and tolerating loneliness. They also emphasized Mandy's use of emotion regulation and distress tolerance skills, as self-injury (and suicide attempts) often functioned to down-regulate overwhelming emotions, particularly sadness and shame. It became clear that, despite having life-threatening behavior at the top of the priority list, therapy often must concurrently address important quality of life problems (e.g., interpersonal problems, alcohol use) that contribute to Mandy's misery. Therapists such as Anne must directly target risk for self-injury and suicide while not focusing the entire therapy on life-threatening behavior, or clients like Mandy may not get the help they need to solve the problems in life that are contributing to their misery.

During the beginning few months of therapy, Mandy was in a dip in her everyday functioning, and this was reflected in some therapy-interfering behaviors (TIBs) that required attention. Mandy was often late for sessions, called the day before to ask if she really needed to attend, expressed doubt that therapy could help her (she spent a lot of time in session verbalizing hopeless thoughts), and failed to do her group homework. Anne directly addressed these TIBs, emphasizing to Mandy that her challenges sustaining the work of therapy and organizing herself to come to sessions presented opportunities to work on problems that impeded important life goals as well. Mandy wanted to return to school and work toward her social work degree and engage in some part-time volunteer work, and the same behavioral problems interfering with therapy also hampered her pursuit of these important goals. Further, when Mandy fell into a pattern of making numerous statements that things were hopeless, they completed brief chain analyses of hopeless talking in session. Mandy and Anne discovered that hopeless thoughts and statements often functioned to roadblock problem solving and help Mandy avoid the painful emotions that arose when she tried to work on her problems. As a result, Mandy and Anne agreed that when hopeless thoughts arose, Mandy would first practice mindfulness of her current emotional experience, just noticing it as it came and went, and then turn her mind back to her problems and how to chip away at them.

Skills group was a challenging but valuable experience for Mandy. At times, she felt so anxious or sad that she had difficulty focusing, became frustrated with other group members, had the urge to leave, or did not do her homework. When Mandy had difficulty remaining in group, the group leader and coleader sometimes took her aside during break and coached her on skills to tolerate her emotions and the frustrations arising during group. On one occasion, Mandy expressed suicidal thoughts at the end of group, and the group leader briefly assessed her suicide risk and had her call Anne for phone coaching, as the individual therapist's role is to provide such coaching and targeting of life-threatening behavior. Generally, however, Mandy found group increasingly helpful over time, began to practice mindfulness on a regular basis, and found the skills of opposite action and DEAR MAN (from the interpersonal effectiveness module; Linehan, 2015a, 2015b) particularly helpful with her family. When she felt hurt and angry about an interaction with a family member, she would first gently avoid that person (one of the steps in opposite action for anger; Linehan, 2015b), assess how intense her emotions were, determine skills that might help her tolerate or regulate these emotions, and then come up with a plan to talk with the family member later on. At that point, she often would practice a DEAR MAN script with Anne and then approach the family member and express how she felt when, for example, she was criticized about her mental health problems. Although these situations did not always proceed smoothly, over time she found that her family members listened to her and respected her wishes, and she started to feel closer to them.

About 4 months into treatment, when Mandy had stopped self-injuring and suicidal urges had reduced, Mandy also started to work on barriers to her functional goals (e.g., school, career). She and Anne incorporated principles from behavioral activation treatment into a schedule of structured activities, in order to help Mandy get used to structuring her time and to reduce risk of depressive relapse. As Mandy got used to a busier schedule, she started to plan how she would manage school and volunteer work. She started with the volunteer work for a couple of months and then registered for another semester at college. By around the 10-month mark in therapy, Mandy had been at school for a couple of months, successfully got through midterms, and had started dating one of her classmates. Although she still was prone to intense episodes of dysphoria, had to work hard to resist binge drinking during social events, and was very sensitive to perceived criticism or rejection, she found herself able to step back from her emotions and urges and use skills effectively much of the time.

At 12 months, Mandy graduated from her second cycle of DBT skills group and decided to continue to work with Anne for another 6 months. Anne had told Mandy in the beginning of therapy that they would probably evaluate how things were going every 3 to 6 months, and if she was continuing to benefit and improve, therapy might continue. This contingency in DBT—that the client receives more therapy if they are benefitting—counters the more common contingency in community and hospital settings whereby the client receives more care and help when they are suicidal. At the end of therapy, Mandy had largely met most of her goals. Although she by no means considered herself "cured" and still had to work hard to counter old behavioral patterns, she felt she had the tools to continue to move along the path toward a life worth living.

CONCLUSION AND FUTURE DIRECTIONS

The illustration of a course of DBT with Mandy is fairly consistent with how DBT often proceeds with complex clients. There often are bumps in the road and TIBs to work on, and progress can be episodic and inconsistent (Linehan, 1993a). Although many clients do well and meet their therapy goals, the vulnerabilities accompanying BPD and other complex disorders may persist well beyond the termination of therapy. Indeed, findings have suggested that over half of suicidal individuals with BPD often continue to display functional deficits for several years after treatment (Soloff & Chiappetta, 2017).

In terms of future directions, a few key questions need to be answered to move the field forward and improve the care of complex clients. One key question pertains to who does not respond to treatment. Some findings have suggested that among clients with BPD, age does not predict treatment outcome; higher severity of BPD symptoms and self-injury may actually predict greater change in these outcomes; and those with PTSD may fare more poorly in treatment (Barnicot & Priebe, 2013). As mentioned earlier, promising work has been done to incorporate the treatment of PTSD into Stage 1 of DBT (Harned, Korslund, & Linehan, 2014). Future work might continue to optimize the efficiency and effectiveness of evidence-based PTSD treatment for relevant clients.

Another question has to do with how we can improve the functioning of complex clients with BPD. At least with suicidal clients with BPD, much of the initial work in DBT involves stabilization, the reduction of suicidal, self-injuring, and other problematic behaviors, and the building of skills. In our experience, much of the therapeutic change occurs within the first 6 months or so, plateauing somewhat after that, with clients continuing to report more subtle improvements in their daily lives. It is possible that the broad-based measures used to gauge functional improvements in the research are missing these subtle behavioral changes that often show up in the client's in-session self-report or on diary cards. At the same time, we likely need to get better at improving clients' functioning.

Notwithstanding, perhaps DBT could be conceptualized as one step on a much longer path to recovery. Another way to think about this is that we do not necessarily have to be good at everything in DBT! In our experience, clinicians in community mental health settings sometimes report frustration with what little they can accomplish with DBT clients. Caseloads are high, it is difficult to sustain regular, weekly individual therapy sessions, and some agencies prohibit phone coaching. In the context of these limitations, clinicians often report that they simply do not have enough time to work on sustainable changes in functioning. We have often advised these clinicians to set realistic goals for DBT. DBT is very good at reducing problematic behavior (particularly life-threatening behavior), especially in the first several months of therapy. Further, reductions in life-threatening behaviors tend to persist for at least a year beyond therapy, and changes in mental health symptoms often also tend to persist. A realistic goal for DBT, therefore, may be to help clients reach a baseline level of symptoms and problems, from which they can continue to improve their lives, either with continued DBT, other types of treatment, natural supports, or a combination of all of the above.

As reviewed in Chapter 6, the jury is still out regarding how and why DBT works. Several exciting lines of research have suggested that skills training and practice may be essential, and that DBT may result in important changes in the brain, but we are still unsure exactly (a) what the essential ingredients of DBT are, and (b) which changes in the client account for the effects of DBT. As we begin to piece this puzzle together, findings should shed light on ways to make DBT more efficient and effective. We should be able to emphasize key ingredients of the treatment and interventions that target important changes in the client, ultimately making DBT leaner, meaner, and more easily disseminated and implemented in a variety of practice settings. At the same time, reducing the treatment down to a few key elements and trying to make therapy as targeted and efficient as possible should be balanced with the goal of providing comprehensive care that results in lasting changes in the lives of complex clients. Over time, we hope that a confluence of information from the front lines, efficacy studies, research on mechanisms (and predictors) of change, and other research, will continue to make us better at helping clients build lives worth living.

Glossary of Key Terms

ACCEPT NATURAL CHANGE   One tenet of the dialectical philosophy underlying DBT is that reality is constantly changing. It can be effective, therefore, for therapists to accept the natural changes that come about in the lives, thoughts, emotions, and actions of their clients.

ACCEPTANCE   Acknowledging, allowing, and confronting reality as it is without resisting, denying, or trying to change reality.

ACTIVE PASSIVITY   A secondary treatment target in DBT. Active passivity is apparent when a client takes a passive approach to solving their own problems but an active approach to recruiting others to help solve them.

ANTECEDENT   An event preceding a behavior.

APPARENT COMPETENCE   A secondary treatment target in DBT. Apparent competence describes the phenomenon whereby a client appears much more skillful, capable, and competent than they are, and/or displays high competence in some contexts but not others.

BEHAVIOR   Any action, thought, emotional, or other response (physiological).

BEHAVIORAL THEORY   Broadly, this describes a collection of theoretical perspectives that have in common the tenet that contextual factors are important determinants and maintaining factors for behavior.

BIOSOCIAL THEORY   The theory that specific person–environment transactions contribute to the development of borderline personality disorder and other clinical problems.

BORDERLINE PERSONALITY DISORDER (BPD)   A serious psychiatric disorder characterized by instability in emotions, cognition, behavior, identity, and interpersonal relationships, with impulsivity, emotion dysregulation, and interpersonal problems considered central to the disorder.

CHAIN ANALYSIS   Also referred to as a functional analysis in other behavioral approaches, a chain analysis is a method of assessing the factors that preceded and followed a specific instance of a behavior (e.g., an act of self-injury occurring a couple of days ago) that is targeted to decrease or increase in therapy.

COGNITIVE BEHAVIOR THERAPY (CBT)   A collection of interventions based on the theory that cognition, emotion, behavior, and context all transact to produce and maintain clinical problems, often consisting of a combination of cognitive interventions, training in coping skills, behavior modification strategies, and exposure therapy, among others.

CONSEQUENCE   An event occurring following a specific behavior and contingent on the occurrence of that behavior.

CONSULTATION TEAM   A team of DBT therapists that meets regularly (usually weekly) with the aim of maintaining and improving therapist skill and motivation.

CONSULTATION TO THE CLIENT   The principle that it can be effective to help clients learn skills to navigate their natural or treatment environments.

COPING AHEAD   A skill in the emotion regulation module of DBT involving the anticipation of an upcoming stressor and structured in vivo or imaginal practice in skills and strategies to cope with the upcoming stressor.

DEVIL'S ADVOCATE   A commitment and dialectical strategy that involves arguing against a desired change or behavior (e.g., stopping self-injury, committing to treatment), based on the assumption that clients will often respond by arguing in favor of the desired behavior or change.

DIALECTICAL ABSTINENCE   In DBT for substance use disorders (DBT-SUD), the notion that, on the one hand, clients actively work toward abstinence, and on the other hand, clients accept that lapses are often a part of recovery. This approach allows clients to work towards recovery, acknowledge and guard against the possibility of lapses, and recover nonjudgmentally from lapses should they occur.

DIALECTICAL BEHAVIOR THERAPY (DBT)   A comprehensive, cognitive behavior treatment program that addresses five key functions (improving client motivation, improving client capabilities, generalizing client skills and capabilities to relevant situations, structuring the client's treatment and natural environments, and maintaining and improving therapist skills and motivation) through four primary treatment modes (individual therapy, skills training, phone coaching, and a therapist consultation team). DBT is based on dialectical theory, Zen practice and principles, behavioral theory, and a biosocial theory of the origins and maintaining factors for relevant clinical problem areas (e.g., borderline personality disorder, suicidal behavior). The treatment emphasizes the role of emotion dysregulation in the development and maintenance of clinical problems and focuses on improving emotion regulation as a key treatment aim. DBT progresses through a pretreatment stage and four additional stages, with Stage 1 (focused on attaining behavioral control) being the stage most commonly implemented in practice and examined in research.

DIALECTICAL BEHAVIOR THERAPY FOR ADOLESCENTS (DBT-A)   A form of DBT, modified to include skills and dialectical dilemmas specific to adolescents. DBT-A also includes multifamily skills training groups to provide family members with DBT skills training alongside the adolescent clients.

DIALECTICAL DILEMMAS   Polarized behavioral patterns occurring in therapy or in a client's everyday life that are often missed during the initial assessment. These patterns involve the client oscillating between extremes and include active passivity versus apparent competence, emotion vulnerability versus self-invalidation, and unrelenting crisis versus inhibited grieving.

DIALECTICAL PHILOSOPHY   The worldview that reality consists of polar opposites (e.g., thesis vs. antithesis, positive vs. negative charge, acceptance vs. change), that tension exists between these opposites because each pole is incomplete on its own, and that change in reality continually occurs through the balance and synthesis of opposing forces.

DIALECTICAL STRATEGIES   Strategies used in DBT to promote therapeutic change by magnifying tension and helping clients work toward balancing and synthesizing polarized perspectives or behaviors.

DIARY CARD   A self-monitoring tool used in DBT to organize and prioritize session-by-session therapy targets. Typically, the client completes the diary card weekly, reporting on various treatment targets (e.g., self-injury and suicidal urges and actions; substance use; emotional states, such as misery and joy; and the client's use of various skills).

DISTRESS TOLERANCE   The ability to withstand emotional distress without engaging in behavior to avoid or escape it.

EMOTION DYSREGULATION   A deficit in the implicit (e.g., through physiological homeostatic mechanisms) or explicit (e.g., through effortful emotion regulation) regulation of the emotion system that hampers an individual's ability to engage in effective or goal- or value-oriented behavior. Emotion dysregulation often manifests as excessively intense or labile emotional responses or dysfunctional behaviors occurring in the context of emotional responses.

EMOTION REGULATION   The process by which people identify and modify their emotional experience, expression, or emotion-related actions.

EMOTION VULNERABILITY   One of the primary biological factors considered to contribute to the development of BPD, emotion vulnerability involves a combination of a low threshold for emotional activation (emotional sensitivity), intense emotional responses (emotional reactivity), and a slow recovery or normalization of emotional responding (slow return to baseline).

ENTERING THE PARADOX   A dialectical strategy whereby the therapist comments on a paradox (e.g., clients need to remove the option of suicide to build a life worth living and need to build a life worth living to remove the option of suicide) without trying to resolve it for the client.

ENVIRONMENTAL INTERVENTION   The therapist taking active steps to help the client modify their natural or treatment environment. An example would be a therapist telling parents how to best interact with their son or daughter, or informing psychiatric inpatient unit staff about effective ways to care for a client.

FIVE FUNCTIONS OF COMPREHENSIVE TREATMENT   Improving client motivation, improving client capabilities, generalizing client skills and capabilities to relevant situations, structuring the client's treatment and natural environments, and maintaining and improving therapist skills and motivation.

GENERAL PSYCHIATRIC MANAGEMENT   An evidence-based treatment model of BPD that is intended to be a first-line treatment that can be implemented by clinicians without expertise in BPD.

GROUP DBT SKILLS TRAINING   One of the four treatment modes of DBT, typically consisting of a 1.5- to 2.5-hour (shorter groups being more common with youth, and longer groups with adults) weekly group session structured like a class and involving the teaching of core DBT skills in the areas of mindfulness, emotion regulation, distress tolerance, and emotion regulation.

INDIVIDUAL THERAPY   One of the four treatment modes of DBT, typically consisting of weekly sessions with the client's primary individual therapist, involving the reviewing of the client's diary card, the organization of an agenda based on the DBT treatment hierarchy (and the client's ongoing goals and problem areas), and core DBT and CBT assessment and treatment strategies.

INFORMAL EXPOSURE   Exposure-based interventions occurring ad hoc during a therapy session and involving the therapist presenting or maintaining the presence of a cue eliciting emotions in the client, helping the client maintain attention to the cue and related emotional experiences, blocking the client's avoidance of the cue or related emotions, and (at times) assessing changes in the client's emotional experience throughout the intervention.

INHIBITED GRIEVING   A secondary treatment target in DBT. Inhibited grieving involves the client's efforts to avoid, escape, suppress, or not experience particular emotional states, commonly sadness or grief but also including other emotions (e.g., shame, embarrassment, fear, anger).

INTERNAL REINFORCEMENT   Changes in emotional, cognitive, or physiological states contingent on the occurrence of a particular behavior that increase the likelihood that the behavior will occur again under similar circumstances.

INTERPERSONAL EFFECTIVENESS   A module taught during skills training in DBT, consisting of skills to help clients identify their goals in interpersonal situations; determine when, how intensely, and whether to make a request or say no to another person's request; and make requests or discuss issues with other people while maintaining or enhancing the relationship.

INVALIDATING ENVIRONMENT   One of the primary environmental factors considered to contribute to the development of BPD, consisting of (a) indiscriminate rejection of the child's communication of thoughts or emotions, (b) oversimplification of the ease of coping or problem-solving, and (c) intermittent reinforcement of emotional or behavioral escalation. The invalidating environment may also be characterized by abuse or neglect.

IRREVERENT STYLE   A therapeutic style in DBT, often consisting of the therapist being overly matter-of-fact about topics that many people might consider outrageous, using humor, making unexpected or off-the-wall statements, or commenting on implications of the client's behavior that the client had not considered, among other strategies. An irreverent style often is used to help the client attend to the present moment, become unstuck from rigid patterns of behaving or thinking, or consider issues from another perspective.

MAKING LEMONADE OUT OF LEMONS   A dialectical strategy involving the therapist highlighting the opportunity or positive elements in a challenging situation.

MECHANISMS OF CHANGE   The processes by which treatment results in beneficial outcomes. Mechanisms of change often are divided into (a) essential ingredients within the treatment and (b) processes that change within the client.

MINDFULNESS   The act of attending to one's present experience.

MISSING LINKS ANALYSIS   An abbreviated form of chain analysis often used during group or individual sessions when the target behavior consists of an absence of behavior, such as an absence of homework completion. The therapist inquires about factors that might have impeded the desired behavior, including whether the client (a) did not understand what was required (e.g., the homework assignment), (b) was unwilling to engage in the desired behavior, (c) did not remember to engage in the desired behavior, or (d) experienced other impeding factors.

MOVEMENT, SPEED, AND FLOW   A dialectical strategy involving the therapist using many different treatment strategies, varying the tempo and intensity of their manner during the session, alternating rapidly among different therapy strategies, and expressing positions or opinions wholeheartedly.

PARASUICIDAL BEHAVIORS   A term that historically referred to a range of intentionally self-injurious behaviors, including suicide attempts as well as self-injurious behaviors that cause tissue damage without any suicidal intent (i.e., nonsuicidal self-injury [NSSI]). Currently, this term is rarely used, with researchers referring more often to suicidal behaviors or NSSI separately, or self-injurious behaviors as an umbrella term.

PERSON VARIABLE   An individual's learning history, personality, temperament, or biological characteristics.

PHONE COACHING   One of the four treatment modes of DBT, commonly involving the therapist's availability to provide coaching and guidance in the client's use of skills in between sessions, with the aim of helping the client generalize what they are learning in therapy to everyday life.

PROBLEM-SOLVING   The use of core DBT or CBT strategies (e.g., motivational or commitment strategies, skills training, contingent management, behavior modification) to address clinical problem areas. Additionally, problem-solving refers to the use of specific, structured skills or steps, often consisting of (a) identifying and describing the problem, (b) checking the facts, (c) identifying goals, (d) brainstorming possible solutions, (e) evaluating the pros and cons of viable solutions, (f) implementing solutions, and (g) evaluating outcomes.

RADICAL ACCEPTANCE   A skill taught during the distress tolerance module of DBT, consisting of the complete acceptance of reality as it is, without resisting, denying, avoiding or escaping such reality.

RADICAL GENUINENESS   One form of validation (Level 6) in DBT that involves treating the client as a human being and an equal. This involves the therapist acting genuinely, in an ordinary, sometimes spontaneous, yet professional manner.

RADICALLY OPEN DBT (RO-DBT)   A treatment that was initially an adaptation of DBT intended to target pathological emotional and behavioral overcontrol, which involves social distance, inhibited emotional expressions, and pathological perfectionism. These difficulties are seen in a number of psychiatric disorders, including anorexia nervosa, chronic depression, and obsessive–compulsive personality disorder.

RANDOMIZED CONTROLLED TRIAL (RCT)   A type of experiment in which clients are randomly assigned to receive one or more treatments (e.g., DBT, medication) or to be in one or more control conditions (e.g., an alternative treatment, wait-list control, placebo, or no treatment), with random assignment theoretically ensuring that differences in outcomes between the different treatments are causally related to treatment effects rather than differences in the clients assigned to the treatment conditions.

RECIPROCAL STYLE   A therapeutic style in DBT, often consisting of the therapist being responsive to the client's concerns and wishes, attending to the client's in-session behaviors or emotional expression, expressing warmth, maintaining a nonjudgmental therapeutic stance, making appropriate use of self-disclosure, and maintaining an appropriate power balance.

SELF-INVALIDATION   See invalidating environment. Engagement in these or other forms of invalidation toward oneself in a manner that conveys that one's emotions, thoughts, or behaviors are unreasonable, pathological, or not understandable. Also, a secondary target in DBT.

SELLING COMMITMENT   A commitment strategy in DBT involving the therapist conveying the advantages of the client's commitment to treatment or behavior change.

THERAPY-INTERFERING BEHAVIOR (TIB)   Any behavior on the part of the client, therapist, or treatment team that prevents the occurrence of treatment, interferes with the client's pursuit of therapy goals, or hampers the therapy relationship.

TREATMENT AS USUAL (TAU)   A comparison condition in many clinical studies that involves the clients receiving standard care in whatever setting they are currently in, whether that is community-based outpatient care or other treatment options in residential settings.

UNRELENTING CRISIS   A secondary target in DBT whereby the client appears to experience intensely stressful events with an unusual frequency and duration.

VALIDATION   One of the core strategies for communicating acceptance in DBT. Validation conveys to the client an acknowledgement that their behavior, thoughts, or emotions are understandable. There are seven distinct types of validation in DBT:

- actively attending to the client;
- accurately reflecting what the client has said;
- labeling the client's unverbalized experiences;
- normalizing the client's behavior, thoughts, or emotions in terms of the client's past learning history or biological dysfunction;
- normalizing the client's behavior, thoughts, or emotions in terms of the client's current circumstances;

- interacting in a radically genuine manner (see radical genuineness); and
- communicating the therapist's belief in the client's capacity to change, improve, or attain their goals.

ZEN PRACTICE   Most commonly, the practice of *zazen* (sitting meditation) during which the practitioner attends to the experience of the present moment, either with a specific focus (e.g., the sensations of breathing) or a broad focus (e.g., an open mind, attentive to all of the sensations and experiences of sitting). Zen practice may include walking meditation and or any other deliberate practice that involves maintaining alertness and awareness of the nature of self or reality.

Suggested Readings
and Resources

SUGGESTED READINGS

Brown, J. F. (2015). *The emotion regulation skills system for cognitively challenged clients: A DBT-informed approach*. New York, NY: Guilford Press.

Chapman, A. L. (2018). *Phone coaching in dialectical behavior therapy*. New York, NY: Guilford Press.

Chapman, A. L., & Rosenthal, M. Z. (2016). *Managing therapy-interfering behavior: Strategies from dialectical behavior therapy*. Washington, DC: American Psychological Association.

Dimeff, L. A., & Koerner, K. (2007). *Dialectical behavior therapy in clinical practice: Applications across disorders and settings*. New York, NY: Guilford Press.

Farmer, R. F., & Chapman, A. L. (2016). *Behavioral interventions in cognitive behavior therapy: Practical guidance for putting theory into action* (2nd ed.). Washington, DC: American Psychological Association.

Gross, J. J. (2015). *Handbook of emotion regulation* (2nd ed.). New York, NY: Guilford Press.

Koerner, K. (2011). *Doing dialectical behavior therapy: A practical guide*. New York, NY: Guilford Press.

Linehan, M. M. (1993). *Cognitive–behavioral treatment of borderline personality disorder*. New York, NY: Guilford Press.

Linehan, M. M. (1993). *Skills training manual for treating borderline personality disorder*. New York, NY: Guilford Press.

Linehan, M. M. (1997). Validation and psychotherapy. In A. Bohart & L. S. Greenberg (Eds.), *Empathy reconsidered: New directions in psychotherapy* (pp. 353–392). Washington, DC: American Psychological Association.

Linehan, M. M. (2011). Dialectical behavior therapy and telephone coaching. *Cognitive and Behavioral Practice, 18,* 207–208. http://dx.doi.org/10.1016/j.cbpra.2010.06.003

Linehan, M. M. (2015). *DBT skills training handouts and worksheets.* New York, NY: Guilford Press.

Linehan, M. M. (2015). *DBT skills training manual* (2nd ed.). New York, NY: Guilford Press.

Lynch, T. R. (2018). *Radically open dialectical behavior therapy: Theory and practice for treating disorders of overcontrol.* Oakland, CA: Context Press.

Lynch, T. R. (2018). *The skills training manual for radically open dialectical behavior therapy: A clinician's guide for treating disorders of overcontrol.* Oakland, CA: Context Press.

Lynch, T. R., Chapman, A. L., Rosenthal, M. Z., Kuo, J. K., & Linehan, M. M. (2006). Mechanisms of change in dialectical behavior therapy: Theoretical and empirical observations. *Journal of Clinical Psychology, 62,* 459–480. http://dx.doi.org/10.1002/jclp.20243

Manning, S. Y. (2011). Common errors made by therapists providing telephone consultation in dialectical behavior therapy. *Cognitive and Behavioral Practice, 18,* 178–185.

Mazza, J., Dexter-Mazza, E. T., Miller, A. L., Rathus, J. H., & Murphy, H. E. (2016). *DBT skills in schools: Skills training for emotional problem solving for adolescents (DBT STEPS-A).* New York, NY: Guilford Press.

Miller, A. L., Rathus, J. H., & Linehan, M. M. (2006). *Dialectical behavior therapy with suicidal adolescents.* New York, NY: Guilford Press.

Nhat Hanh, T. (1999). *The miracle of mindfulness: An introduction to the practice of meditation.* Boston, MA: Beacon Press.

Pryor, K. (1984). *Don't shoot the dog.* New York, NY: Simon & Schuster.

Rathus, J. H., & Miller, A. L. (2014). *DBT skills manual for adolescents.* New York, NY: Guilford Press.

Rizvi, S. L. (2019). *Chain analysis in dialectical behavior therapy.* New York, NY: Guilford Press.

Suzuki, S. (2011). *Zen mind, beginner's mind.* Boston, MA: Shambhala.

Swales, M. A. (2019). *The Oxford handbook of dialectical behaviour therapy.* Oxford, England: Oxford University Press.

Swenson, C. R. (2018). *DBT principles in action: Acceptance, change, and dialectics.* New York, NY: Guilford Press.

Valentine, S. E., Bankoff, S. M., Poulin, R. M., Reidler, E. B., & Pantalone, D. W. (2015). The use of dialectical behavior therapy skills training as stand-alone treatment: A systematic review of the treatment outcome literature. *Journal of Clinical Psychology, 71,* 1–20. http://dx.doi.org/10.1002/jclp.22114

WEB RESOURCES

Behavioral Tech, LLC: https://behavioraltech.org/

British Isles DBT Training: https://www.dbt-training.co.uk

DBT Centre of Vancouver: http://dbtvancouver.com/

Evidence-Based Treatment Centers of Seattle: http://ebtseattle.com

International Society for the Improvement and Teaching of Dialectical Behavior Therapy: http://isitdbt.net/

The Linehan Institute: https://linehaninstitute.org

National Education Alliance for Borderline Personality Disorder: https://www. borderlinepersonalitydisorder.org/

Portland DBT Institute: https://www.pdbti.org

Practice Ground: https://www.practiceground.org

Radically Open (Radically Open Dialectical Behavior Therapy [RO DBT]): https://www.radicallyopen.net/about-ro-dbt/

Tara4BPD (TARA: Treatment and Research Advancements for Borderline Personality Disorder): http://www.tara4bpd.org/

University of Washington, Behavioral Research and Therapy Clinics: http:// depts.washington.edu/uwbrtc/

VIDEO RESOURCES

American Psychological Association (Producer). (2008). *Dialectical behavior therapy for adolescents with multiple problems* [DVD]. Available from https:// www.apa.org/pubs/videos/4310809

American Psychological Association (Producer). (2014). *Dialectical behavior therapy* [Video file]. Available from https://www.apa.org/pubs/videos/4310914

Behavioral Tech [Streaming videos]: https://behavioraltech.org/training/ streaming/

References

Abramowitz, J. S., Deacon, B. J., & Whiteside, S. P. H. (2011). *Exposure therapy for anxiety: Principles and practice.* New York, NY: Guilford Press.

American Psychiatric Association. (2013). *Diagnostic and statistical manual of mental disorders* (5th ed.). Arlington, VA: Author.

American Psychological Association. (2017). *Multicultural guidelines: An ecological approach to context, identity, and intersectionality.* Retrieved from http://www.apa.org/about/policy/multicultural-guidelines.pdf

Amner, K. (2012). The effect of DBT provision in reducing the cost of adults displaying the symptoms of BPD. *British Journal of Psychotherapy, 28,* 336–352. http://dx.doi.org/10.1111/j.1752-0118.2012.01286.x

Andreasson, K., Krogh, J., Wenneberg, C., Jessen, H. K. L., Krakauer, K., Gluud, C., . . . Nordentoft, M. (2016). Effectiveness of dialectical behavior therapy versus collaborative assessment and management of suicidality treatment for reduction of self-harm in adults with borderline personality traits and disorder—A randomized observer-blinded clinical trial. *Depression and Anxiety, 33,* 520–530. http://dx.doi.org/10.1002/da.22472

Asmand, P., & Valizadeh, R. (2015). The effectiveness of dialectical behavior therapy and rational emotional therapy in irrational believes treatment, depression prisoners who have antisocial personality disorder. *Journal of Preventative Medicine and Holistic Health, 1,* 27–33. Retrieved from https://pdfs.semanticscholar.org/9a4e/6f7438e1f458f91a64a7c4340cb48d9f69ae.pdf

Axelrod, S. R., Perepletchikova, F., Holtzman, K., & Sinha, R. (2011). Emotion regulation and substance use frequency in women with substance dependence and borderline personality disorder receiving dialectical behavior therapy. *The American Journal of Drug and Alcohol Abuse, 37,* 37–42. http://dx.doi.org/10.3109/00952990.2010.535582

Bankoff, S. M., Karpel, M. G., Forbes, H. E., & Pantalone, D. W. (2012). A systematic review of dialectical behavior therapy for the treatment of eating disorders. *Eating Disorders: The Journal of Treatment & Prevention, 20,* 196–215. http://dx.doi.org/10.1080/10640266.2012.668478

Barley, W. D., Buie, S. E., Peterson, E. W., Hollingsworth, A. S., Griva, M., Hickerson, S. C., . . . Bailey, B. J. (1993). Development of an inpatient cognitive-behavioral treatment program for borderline personality disorder. *Journal of Personality Disorders, 7,* 232–240. http://dx.doi.org/10.1521/pedi.1993.7.3.232

Barlow, D. H., Ellard, K. K., Fairholme, C. P., Farchione, T. J., Boisseau, C. L., Allen, L. B., & Ehrenreich-May, J. (2011). *The unified protocol for transdiagnostic treatment of emotional disorders: Client workbook.* New York, NY: Oxford University Press.

Barnicot, K., & Crawford, M. (2018). Dialectical behavior therapy v. mentalisation-based therapy for borderline personality disorder. *Psychological Medicine, 49,* 2060–2068. http://dx.doi.org/10.1017/S0033291718002878

Barnicot, K., Gonzalez, R., McCabe, R., & Priebe, S. (2016). Skills use and common treatment processes in dialectical behaviour therapy for borderline personality disorder. *Journal of Behavior Therapy and Experimental Psychiatry, 52,* 147–156. http://dx.doi.org/10.1016/j.jbtep.2016.04.006

Barnicot, K., & Priebe, S. (2013). Post-traumatic stress disorder and the outcome of dialectical behaviour therapy for borderline personality disorder. *Personality and Mental Health, 7,* 181–190. http://dx.doi.org/10.1002/pmh.1227

Beard, C., Kirakosian, N., Silverman, A. L., Winer, J. P., Wadsworth, L. P., & Björgvinsson, T. (2017). Comparing treatment response between LGBQ and heterosexual individuals attending a CBT- and DBT-skills-based partial hospital. *Journal of Consulting and Clinical Psychology, 85,* 1171–1181. http://dx.doi.org/10.1037/ccp0000251

Beauchaine, T. P. (2015). Future directions in emotion dysregulation and youth psychopathology. *Journal of Clinical Child & Adolescent Psychology, 44,* 875–896. http://dx.doi.org/10.1080/15374416.2015.1038827

Beauchaine, T. P., Hinshaw, S. P., & Bridge, J. A. (2019). Nonsuicidal self-injury and suicidal behaviors in girls: The case for targeted prevention in pre-adolescence. *Clinical Psychological Science, 7,* 643–667. http://dx.doi.org/10.1177/2167702618818474

Beckstead, D. J., Lambert, M. J., DuBose, A. P., & Linehan, M. (2015). Dialectical behavior therapy with American Indian/Alaska Native adolescents diagnosed with substance use disorders: Combining an evidence based treatment with cultural, traditional, and spiritual beliefs. *Addictive Behaviors, 51,* 84–87. http://dx.doi.org/10.1016/j.addbeh.2015.07.018

Bedics, J. D., Atkins, D. C., Harned, M. S., & Linehan, M. M. (2015). The therapeutic alliance as a predictor of outcome in dialectical behavior therapy versus nonbehavioral psychotherapy by experts for borderline personality disorder. *Psychotherapy, 52*, 67–77. http://dx.doi.org/10.1037/a0038457

Bedics, J. D., Atkins, D. C., & Linehan, M. M. (2012). Treatment differences in the therapeutic relationship and introject during a 2-year randomized controlled trial of dialectical behavior therapy versus non-behavioral psychotherapy experts for borderline personality disorder. *Journal of Consulting and Clinical Psychology, 80*, 66–77. http://dx.doi.org/10.1037/a0026113

Behavioral Research and Therapy Clinics. (n.d.). *NIMH S-DBT diary card.* Retrieved from http://depts.washington.edu/uwbrtc/wp-content/uploads/NIMH4-S-DBT-Diary-Cards-with-Instructions.pdf

Biskin, R. S. (2015). The lifetime course of borderline personality disorder. *Canadian Journal of Psychiatry, 60*, 303–308. http://dx.doi.org/10.1177/070674371506000702

Bloom, J. M., Woodward, E. N., Susmaras, T., & Pantalone, D. W. (2012). Use of dialectical behavior therapy in inpatient treatment of borderline personality disorder: A systematic review. *Psychiatric Services, 63*, 881–888. http://dx.doi.org/10.1176/appi.ps.201100311

Bohus, M., Dyer, A. S., Priebe, K., Krüger, A., Kleindienst, N., Schmahl, C., . . . Steil, R. (2013). Dialectical behaviour therapy for post-traumatic stress disorder after childhood sexual abuse in patients with and without borderline personality disorder: A randomised controlled trial. *Psychotherapy and Psychosomatics, 82*, 221–233. http://dx.doi.org/10.1159/000348451

Bohus, M., Haaf, B., Simms, T., Limberger, M. F., Schmahl, C., Unckel, C., . . . Linehan, M. M. (2004). Effectiveness of inpatient dialectical behavioral therapy for borderline personality disorder: A controlled trial. *Behaviour Research and Therapy, 42*, 487–499. http://dx.doi.org/10.1016/S0005-7967(03)00174-8

Bohus, M., Haaf, B., Stiglmayr, C., Pohl, U., Böhme, R., & Linehan, M. (2000). Evaluation of inpatient dialectical-behavioral therapy for borderline personality disorder—A prospective study. *Behaviour Research and Therapy, 38*, 875–887. http://dx.doi.org/10.1016/S0005-7967(99)00103-5

Bopp, M. J., & Weeks, G. R. (1984). Dialectical metatheory in family therapy. *Family Process, 23*, 49–61. http://dx.doi.org/10.1111/j.1545-5300.1984.00049.x

Bradley, R. G., & Follingstad, D. R. (2003). Group therapy for incarcerated women who experienced interpersonal violence: A pilot study. *Journal of Traumatic Stress, 16*, 337–340. http://dx.doi.org/10.1023/A:1024409817437

Brassington, J., & Krawitz, R. (2006). Australasian dialectical behaviour therapy pilot outcome study: Effectiveness, utility and feasibility. *Australasian Psychiatry, 14*, 313–318. http://dx.doi.org/10.1080/j.1440-1665.2006.02285.x

Brazier, J., Tumur, I., Holmes, M., Ferriter, M., Parry, G., Dent-Brown, K., & Paisley, S. (2006). Psychological therapies including dialectical behaviour therapy for borderline personality disorder: A systematic review and preliminary economic evaluation. *Health Technology Assessment, 10*(35). http://dx.doi.org/10.3310/hta10350

Brown, J. F. (2015). *The emotion regulation skills system for cognitively challenged clients: A DBT-informed approach.* New York, NY: Guilford Press.

Brown, J. F., Brown, M. Z., & Dibiasio, P. (2013). Treating individuals with intellectual disabilities and challenging behaviors with adapted dialectical behavior therapy. *Journal of Mental Health Research in Intellectual Disabilities, 6,* 280–303. http://dx.doi.org/10.1080/19315864.2012.700684

Brown, M. Z., Comtois, K. A., & Linehan, M. M. (2002). Reasons for suicide attempts and nonsuicidal self-injury in women with borderline personality disorder. *Journal of Abnormal Psychology, 111,* 198–202. http://dx.doi.org/10.1037/0021-843X.111.1.198

Carmel, A., Rose, M., & Fruzzetti, A. E. (2014). Barriers and solutions to implementing dialectical behavior therapy in a public behavioral health system. *Administration and Policy in Mental Health and Mental Health Research Services, 41,* 608–614. http://dx.doi.org/10.1007/s10488-013-0504-6

Carpenter, R. W., & Trull, T. J. (2013). Components of emotion dysregulation in borderline personality disorder: A review. *Current Psychiatry Reports, 15,* 335. http://dx.doi.org/10.1007/s11920-012-0335-2

Carson-Wong, A., Hughes, C. D., & Rizvi, S. L. (2018). The effect of therapist use of validation strategies on change in client emotion in individual dbt treatment sessions. *Personality Disorders: Theory, Research, and Treatment, 9,* 165–171. http://dx.doi.org/10.1037/per0000229

Carter, G. L., Willcox, C. H., Lewin, T. J., Conrad, A. M., & Bendit, N. (2010). Hunter DBT project: Randomized controlled trial of dialectical behaviour therapy in women with borderline personality disorder. *Australian and New Zealand Journal of Psychiatry, 44,* 162–173. http://dx.doi.org/10.3109/00048670903393621

Chambers, R., Lo, B. C. Y., & Allen, N. B. (2008). The impact of intensive mindfulness training on attentional control, cognitive style, and affect. *Cognitive Therapy and Research, 32,* 303–322. http://dx.doi.org/10.1007/s10608-007-9119-0

Chambless, D. L., & Hollon, S. D. (1998). Defining empirically supported therapies. *Journal of Consulting and Clinical Psychology, 66,* 7–18. http://dx.doi.org/10.1037/0022-006X.66.1.7

Chapman, A. L. (2018). *Phone coaching in dialectical behavior therapy.* New York, NY: Guilford Press.

Chapman, A. L. (2019). Borderline personality disorder and emotion dysregulation. *Development and Psychopathology. 31*, pp. 1143–1156 http://dx.doi.org/10.1017/S0954579419000658

Chapman, A. L., & Cellucci, T. (2007). The role of antisocial and borderline personality features in substance dependence among incarcerated females. *Addictive Behaviors, 3*, 1131–1145. http://dx.doi.org/10.1016/j.addbeh.2006.08.001

Chapman, A. L., Gratz, K. L., & Brown, M. Z. (2006). Solving the puzzle of deliberate self-harm: The experiential avoidance model. *Behaviour Research and Therapy, 44*, 371–394. http://dx.doi.org/10.1016/j.brat.2005.03.005

Chapman, A. L., & Ivanoff, A. (2018). Forensic issues in borderline personality disorder. In B. Stanley & A. New (Eds.), *Primer on borderline personality disorder* (pp. 403–420). New York, NY: Oxford University Press.

Chapman, A. L., & Rosenthal, M. Z. (2016). *Managing therapy-interfering behavior: Strategies from dialectical behavior therapy.* Washington, DC: American Psychological Association. http://dx.doi.org/10.1037/14752-000

Chapman, A. L., Specht, M. W., & Cellucci, T. (2005). Borderline personality disorder and deliberate self-harm: Does experiential avoidance play a role? *Suicide & Life-Threatening Behavior, 35*, 388–399. http://dx.doi.org/10.1521/suli.2005.35.4.388

Chen, E. Y., Matthews, L., Allen, C., Kuo, J. R., & Linehan, M. M. (2008). Dialectical behavior therapy for clients with binge-eating disorder or bulimia nervosa and borderline personality disorder. *International Journal of Eating Disorders, 41*, 505–512. http://dx.doi.org/10.1002/eat.20522

Cheng, P. H., & Merrick, E. (2017). Cultural adaptation of dialectical behavior therapy for a Chinese international student with eating disorder and depression. *Clinical Case Studies, 16*, 42–57. http://dx.doi.org/10.1177/1534650116668269

Chugani, C. D., Ghali, M. N., & Brunner, J. (2013). Effectiveness of short term dialectical behavior therapy skills training in college students with Cluster B personality disorders. *Journal of College Student Psychotherapy, 27*, 323–336. http://dx.doi.org/10.1080/87568225.2013.824337

Clarkin, J. F., Levy, K. N., Lenzenweger, M. F., & Kernberg, O. F. (2007). Evaluating three treatments for borderline personality disorder: A multiwave study. *The American Journal of Psychiatry, 164*, 922–928. http://dx.doi.org/10.1176/ajp.2007.164.6.922

Comtois, K. A., Elwood, L., Holdcraft, L. C., Smith, W. R., & Simpson, T. L. (2007). Effectiveness of dialectical behavior therapy in a community mental health center. *Cognitive and Behavioral Practice, 14,* 406–414. http://dx.doi.org/ 10.1016/j.cbpra.2006.04.023

Comtois, K. A., Kerbrat, A. H., Atkins, D. C., Harned, M. S., & Elwood, L. (2010). Recovery from disability for individuals with borderline personality disorder: A feasibility trial of DBT-ACES. *Psychiatric Services, 61,* 1106–1111. http://dx.doi.org/10.1176/ps.2010.61.11.1106

Cook, N. E., & Gorraiz, M. (2016). Dialectical behavior therapy for nonsuicidal self-injury and depression among adolescents: Preliminary meta-analytic evidence. *Child and Adolescent Mental Health, 21,* 81–89. http://dx.doi.org/ 10.1111/camh.12112

Courbasson, C., Nishikawa, Y., & Dixon, L. (2012). Outcome of dialectical behaviour therapy for concurrent eating and substance use disorders. *Clinical Psychology & Psychotherapy, 19,* 434–449. http://dx.doi.org/10.1002/cpp.748

Coyle, T. N., Shaver, J. A., & Linehan, M. M. (2018). On the potential for iatrogenic effects of psychiatric crisis services: The example of dialectical behavior therapy for adult women with borderline personality disorder. *Journal of Consulting and Clinical Psychology, 86,* 116–124. http://dx.doi.org/10.1037/ ccp0000275

Craske, M. G., Treanor, M., Conway, C. C., Zbozinek, T., & Vervliet, B. (2014). Maximizing exposure therapy: An inhibitory learning approach. *Behaviour Research and Therapy, 58,* 10–23. http://dx.doi.org/10.1016/j.brat.2014.04.006

Crowell, S. E., Beauchaine, T. P., & Linehan, M. M. (2009). A biosocial developmental model of borderline personality: Elaborating and extending Linehan's theory. *Psychological Bulletin, 135,* 495–510. http://dx.doi.org/10.1037/ a0015616

Crowell, S. E., Kaufman, E. A., & Beauchaine, T. P. (2014). A biosocial model of BPD: Theory and empirical evidence. In C. Sharp & J. L. Tackett (Eds.), *Handbook of borderline personality disorder in children and adolescents* (pp. 143–157). http://dx.doi.org/10.1007/978-1-4939-0591-1_11

DeCou, C. R., Comtois, K. A., & Landes, S. J. (2018). Dialectical behavior therapy is effective for the treatment of suicidal behavior: A meta-analysis. *Behavior Therapy, 50,* 60–72. http://dx.doi.org/10.1016/j.beth.2018.03.009

Dimeff, L. A., & Linehan, M. M. (2008). Dialectical behavior therapy for substance abusers. *Addiction Science & Clinical Practice, 4,* 39–47. http://dx.doi.org/ 10.1151/ascp084239

Dimeff, L. A., Rizvi, S. L., Brown, M., & Linehan, M. M. (2000). Dialectical behavior therapy for substance abuse: A pilot application to methamphetamine-dependent women with borderline personality disorder. *Cognitive and Behavioral Practice, 7,* 457–468. http://dx.doi.org/10.1016/S1077-7229(00) 80057-7

Dixon-Gordon, K. L., Chapman, A. L., Lovasz, N., & Walters, K. (2011). Too upset to think: The interplay of borderline personality features, negative emotions, and social problem solving in the laboratory. *Personality Disorders: Theory, Research, and Treatment, 2,* 243–260. http://dx.doi.org/10.1037/a0021799

Dixon-Gordon, K. L., Chapman, A. L., & Turner, B. J. (2015). A preliminary pilot study comparing dialectical behavior therapy emotion regulation skills with interpersonal effectiveness skills and a control group treatment. *Journal of Experimental Psychopathology, 6,* 369–388. http://dx.doi.org/10.5127/jep.041714

Dixon-Gordon, K. L., Turner, B. J., Rosenthal, M. Z., & Chapman, A. L. (2017). Emotion regulation in borderline personality disorder: An experimental investigation of the effects of instructed acceptance and suppression. *Behavior Therapy, 48,* 750–764. http://dx.doi.org/10.1016/j.beth.2017.03.001

Dixon-Gordon, K. L., Weiss, N. H., Tull, M. T., DiLillo, D., Messman-Moore, T. L., & Gratz, K. L. (2015). Characterizing emotional dysfunction in borderline personality, major depression, and their co-occurrence. *Comprehensive Psychiatry, 62,* 187–203. http://dx.doi.org/10.1016/j.comppsych.2015.07.014

Doering, S., Hörz, S., Rentrop, M., Fischer-Kern, M., Schuster, P., Benecke, C., . . . Buchheim, P. (2010). Transference-focused psychotherapy v. treatment by community psychotherapists for borderline personality disorder: Randomised controlled trial. *The British Journal of Psychiatry, 196,* 389–395. http://dx.doi.org/10.1192/bjp.bp.109.070177

Drossel, C., Fisher, J. E., & Mercer, V. (2011). A DBT skills training group for family caregivers of persons with dementia. *Behavior Therapy, 42,* 109–119. http://dx.doi.org/10.1016/j.beth.2010.06.001

Ekman, P. (1992). An argument for basic emotions. *Cognition and Emotion, 6,* 169–200. http://dx.doi.org/10.1080/02699939208411068

Evershed, S., Tennant, A., Boomer, D., Rees, A., Barkham, M., & Watson, A. (2003). Practice-based outcomes of dialectical behaviour therapy (DBT) targeting anger and violence, with male forensic patients: A pragmatic and non-contemporaneous comparison. *Criminal Behaviour and Mental Health, 13,* 198–213. http://dx.doi.org/10.1002/cbm.542

Farchione, T. J., Fairholme, C. P., Ellard, K. K., Boisseau, C. L., Thompson-Hollands, J., Carl, J. R., . . . Barlow, D. H. (2012). Unified protocol for transdiagnostic treatment of emotional disorders: A randomized controlled trial. *Behavior Therapy, 43,* 666–678. http://dx.doi.org/10.1016/j.beth.2012.01.001

Farmer, R. F., & Chapman, A. L. (2016). *Behavioral interventions in cognitive behavior therapy: Practical guidance for putting theory into action* (2nd ed.). Washington, DC: American Psychological Association.

Feigenbaum, J. D., Fonagy, P., Pilling, S., Jones, A., Wildgoose, A., & Bebbington, P. E. (2012). A real-world study of the effectiveness of DBT in the UK National Health Service. *British Journal of Clinical Psychology*, *51*, 121–141. http://dx.doi.org/10.1111/j.2044-8260.2011.02017.x

Feliu-Soler, A., Pascual, J. C., Borràs, X., Portella, M. J., Martín-Blanco, A., Armario, A., . . . Soler, J. (2014). Effects of dialectical behaviour therapy-mindfulness training on emotional reactivity in borderline personality disorder: Preliminary results. *Clinical Psychology & Psychotherapy*, *21*, 363–370. http://dx.doi.org/10.1002/cpp.1837

Fleming, A. P., McMahon, R. J., Moran, L. R., Peterson, A. P., & Dreessen, A. (2015). Pilot randomized controlled trial of dialectical behavior therapy group skills training for ADHD among college students. *Journal of Attention Disorders*, *19*, 260–271. http://dx.doi.org/10.1177/1087054714535951

Flynn, D., Kells, M., Joyce, M., Corcoran, P., Hurley, J., Gillespie, C., . . . Arensman, E. (2018). Multisite implementation and evaluation of 12-month standard dialectical behavior therapy in a public community setting. *Journal of Personality Disorders*. Advance online publication. http://dx.doi.org/10.1521/pedi_2018_32_402

Fox, R., & Cooper, M. (1998). The effects of suicide on the private practitioner: A professional and personal perspective. *Clinical Social Work Journal*, *26*, 143–157. http://dx.doi.org/10.1023/A:1022866917611

Frew, J., & Spiegler, M. (2012). *Contemporary psychotherapies for a diverse world* (1st rev. ed.). New York, NY: Routledge

Giesen-Bloo, J., van Dyck, R., Spinhoven, P., van Tilburg, W., Dirksen, C. D., van Asselt, T., . . . Arntz, A. (2006). Outpatient psychotherapy for borderline personality disorder: Randomized trial of schema-focused therapy vs. transference-focused psychotherapy. *Archives of General Psychiatry*, *63*, 649–658. http://dx.doi.org/10.1001/archpsyc.63.6.649

Goldfried, M. R., & Davison, G. C. (1976). *Clinical behavior therapy.* New York, NY: Holt Rinehart and Winston.

Goldin, P. R., & Gross, J. J. (2010). Effects of mindfulness-based stress reduction (MBSR) on emotion regulation in social anxiety disorder. *Emotion*, *10*, 83–91. http://dx.doi.org/10.1037/a0018441

Goldstein, T. R., Fersch-Podrat, R. K., Rivera, M., Axelson, D. A., Merranko, J., Yu, H., . . . Birmaher, B. (2015). Dialectical behavior therapy for adolescents with bipolar disorder: Results from a pilot randomized trial. *Journal of Child and Adolescent Psychopharmacology*, *25*, 140–149. http://dx.doi.org/10.1089/cap.2013.0145

Goodman, M., Carpenter, D., Tang, C. Y., Goldstein, K. E., Avedon, J., Fernandez, N., . . . Hazlett, E. A. (2014). Dialectical behavior therapy alters emotion regulation and amygdala activity in patients with borderline personality disorder. *Journal of Psychiatric Research, 57,* 108–116. http://dx.doi.org/10.1016/j.jpsychires.2014.06.020

Gratz, K. L., & Roemer, L. (2004). Multidimensional assessment of emotion regulation and dysregulation: Development, factor structure, and initial validation of the Difficulties in Emotion Regulation Scale. *Journal of Psychopathology and Behavioral Assessment, 26,* 41–54. http://dx.doi.org/10.1023/B:JOBA.0000007455.08539.94

Gratz, K. L., & Tull, M. T. (2010). Emotion regulation as a mechanism of change in acceptance-and mindfulness-based treatments. In R. A. Baer (Ed.), *Assessing mindfulness and acceptance: Illuminating the processes of change* (pp. 107–133). Oakland, CA: New Harbinger.

Gross, J. J. (1998). The emerging field of emotion regulation: An integrative review. *Review of General Psychology, 2,* 271–299. http://dx.doi.org/10.1037/1089-2680.2.3.271

Gross, J. J. (2015). *Handbook of emotion regulation* (2nd ed.). New York, NY: Guilford Press.

Gunderson, J. G., & Links, P. (2014). *Handbook of good psychiatric management for borderline personality disorder.* Washington, DC: American Psychiatric Publishing.

Gunderson J. G., Stout, R. L., McGlashan, T. H., Shea, M. T., Morey, L.C, Grilo, C. M., . . . Skodol, A. E. (2011). Ten-year course of borderline personality disorder: Psychopathology and function from the Collaborative Longitudinal Personality Disorders study. *Archives of General Psychiatry, 68,* 827–837. http://dx.doi.org/10.1001/archgenpsychiatry.2011.37

Gutteling, B. M., Montagne, B., Nijs, M., & van den Bosch, L. M. C. (2012). Dialectical behavior therapy: Is outpatient group psychotherapy an effective alternative to individual psychotherapy?: Preliminary conclusions. *Comprehensive Psychiatry, 53,* 1161–1168. http://dx.doi.org/10.1016/j.comppsych.2012.03.017

Haley, J. (1997). *Leaving home: The therapy of disturbed young people.* New York, NY: Routledge.

Hall, G. C. N. (2001). Psychotherapy research with ethnic minorities: Empirical, ethical, and conceptual issues. *Journal of Consulting and Clinical Psychology, 69,* 502–510. http://dx.doi.org/10.1037/0022-006X.69.3.502

Harley, R. M., Baity, M. R., Blais, M. A., & Jacobo, M. C. (2007). Use of dialectical behavior therapy skills training for borderline personality disorder in a naturalistic setting. *Psychotherapy Research, 17,* 351–358. http://dx.doi.org/ 10.1080/10503300600830710

Harley, R., Sprich, S., Safren, S., Jacobo, M., & Fava, M. (2008). Adaptation of dialectical behavior therapy skills training group for treatment-resistant depression. *The Journal of Nervous and Mental Disease, 196,* 136–143. http:// dx.doi.org/10.1097/NMD.0b013e318162aa3f

Harned, M. S., Chapman, A. L., Dexter-Mazza, E. T., Murray, A., Comtois, K. A., & Linehan, M. M. (2009). Treating co-occurring Axis I disorders in recurrently suicidal women with borderline personality disorder: A 2-year randomized trial of dialectical behavior therapy versus community treatment by experts. *Personality Disorders: Theory, Research, and Treatment, S*(1), 35–45.

Harned, M. S., Korslund, K. E., Foa, E. B., & Linehan, M. M. (2012). Treating PTSD in suicidal and self-injuring women with borderline personality disorder: Development and preliminary evaluation of a dialectical behavior therapy prolonged exposure protocol. *Behaviour Research and Therapy, 50,* 381–386. http://dx.doi.org/10.1016/j.brat.2012.02.011

Harned, M. S., Korslund, K. E., & Linehan, M. M. (2014). A pilot randomized controlled trial of dialectical behavior therapy with and without the dialectical behavior therapy prolonged exposure protocol for suicidal and self-injuring women with borderline personality disorder and PTSD. *Behaviour Research and Therapy, 55,* 7–17. http://dx.doi.org/10.1016/j.brat.2014.01.008

Harned, M. S., Rizvi, S. L., & Linehan, M. M. (2010). Impact of co-occurring posttraumatic stress disorder on suicidal women with borderline personality disorder. *The American Journal of Psychiatry, 167,* 1210–1217. http://dx.doi.org/ 10.1176/appi.ajp.2010.09081213

Hashim, B. L., Vadnais, M., & Miller, A. L. (2013). Improving adherence in adolescent chronic kidney disease: A dialectical behavior therapy (DBT) feasibility trial. *Clinical Practice in Pediatric Psychology, 1,* 369–379. http:// dx.doi.org/10.1037/cpp0000024

Hawton, K., Houston, K., Haw, C., Townsend, E., & Harriss, L. (2003). Comorbidity of Axis I and Axis II disorders in patients who attempted suicide. *The American Journal of Psychiatry, 160,* 1494–1500. http://dx.doi.org/10.1176/ appi.ajp.160.8.1494

Hayes, S. C., Strosahl, K. D., & Wilson, K. G. (1999). *Acceptance and commitment therapy: An experiential approach to behavior change.* New York, NY: Guilford Press.

Heatherton, T. F., & Baumeister, R. F. (1991). Binge eating as escape from self-awareness. *Psychological Bulletin, 110,* 86–108. http://dx.doi.org/10.1037/ 0033-2909.110.1.86

Hill, D. M., Craighead, L. W., & Safer, D. L. (2011). Appetite-focused dialectical behavior therapy for the treatment of binge eating with purging: A preliminary trial. *International Journal of Eating Disorders, 44*, 249–261. http://dx.doi.org/10.1002/eat.20812

Hirsh, J. B., Quilty, L. C., Bagby, R. M., & McMain, S. F. (2012). The relationship between agreeableness and the development of the working alliance in patients with borderline personality disorder. *Journal of Personality Disorders, 26*, 616–627. http://dx.doi.org/10.1521/pedi.2012.26.4.616

Hirvikoski, T., Waaler, E., Alfredsson, J., Pihlgren, C., Holmström, A., Johnson, A., . . . Nordström, A. L. (2011). Reduced ADHD symptoms in adults with ADHD after structured skills training group: Results from a randomized controlled trial. *Behaviour Research and Therapy, 49*, 175–185. http://dx.doi.org/10.1016/j.brat.2011.01.001

Hjalmarsson, E., Kåver, A., Perseius, K.-I., Cederberg, K., & Ghaderi, A. (2008). Dialectical behavior therapy for borderline personality disorder among adolescents and young adults: Pilot study, extending the research findings in new settings and cultures. *Clinical Psychologist, 12*, 18–29. http://dx.doi.org/10.1080/13284200802069035

Hofmann, S. G. (2007). Cognitive factors that maintain social anxiety disorder: A comprehensive model and its treatment implications. *Cognitive Behaviour Therapy, 36*, 193–209. http://dx.doi.org/10.1080/16506070701421313

Hölzel, B. K., Hoge, E. A., Greve, D. N., Gard, T., Creswell, J. D., Brown, K. W., . . . Lazar, S. W. (2013). Neural mechanisms of symptom improvements in generalized anxiety disorder following mindfulness training. *NeuroImage. Clinical, 2*, 448–458. http://dx.doi.org/10.1016/j.nicl.2013.03.011

Hope, N. H., & Chapman, A. L. (2019). Difficulties regulating emotions mediates the associations of parental psychological control and emotion invalidation with borderline personality features. *Personality Disorders: Theory, Research, and Treatment, 10*, 267–274. http://dx.doi.org/10.1037/per0000316

Ivanoff, A., & Marotta, P. L. (2019). DBT in forensic settings. In M. A. Swales (Ed.), *Oxford handbook of dialectical behavior therapy* (Vol. 1, pp. 615–645). Oxford, England: Oxford University Press.

Iverson, K. M., Shenk, C., & Fruzzetti, A. E. (2009). Dialectical behavior therapy for women victims of domestic abuse: A pilot study. *Professional Psychology: Research and Practice, 40*, 242–248. http://dx.doi.org/10.1037/a0013476

Kaminstein, D. S. (1987). Toward a dialectical metatheory for psychotherapy. *Journal of Contemporary Psychotherapy, 17*, 87–101. http://dx.doi.org/10.1007/BF00946279

Kazdin, A. E. (2007). Mediators and mechanisms of change in psychotherapy research. *Annual Review of Clinical Psychology, 3,* 1–27. http://dx.doi.org/10.1146/annurev.clinpsy.3.022806.091432

Kernberg, O. F. (1984). *Severe personality disorders: Psychotherapeutic strategies.* New Haven, CT: Yale University Press.

Kleindienst, N., Limberger, M. F., Schmahl, C., Steil, R., Ebner-Priemer, U. W., & Bohus, M. (2008). Do improvements after inpatient dialectical behavioral therapy persist in the long term?: A naturalistic follow-up in patients with borderline personality disorder. *Journal of Nervous and Mental Disease, 196,* 847–851. http://dx.doi.org/10.1097/NMD.0b013e31818b481d

Kliem, S., Kröger, C., & Kosfelder, J. (2010). Dialectical behavior therapy for borderline personality disorder: A meta-analysis using mixed-effects modeling. *Journal of Consulting and Clinical Psychology, 78,* 936–951. http://dx.doi.org/10.1037/a0021015

Klonsky, E. D. (2011). Non-suicidal self-injury in United States adults: Prevalence, sociodemographics, topography and functions. *Psychological Medicine, 41,* 1981–1986. http://dx.doi.org/10.1017/S0033291710002497

Kohrt, B. K., Lincoln, T. M., & Brambila, A. D. (2017). Embedding DBT skills training within a transactional-ecological framework to reduce suicidality in a Navajo adolescent female. *Clinical Case Studies, 16,* 76–92. http://dx.doi.org/10.1177/1534650116668271

Koons, C. R., Chapman, A. L., Betts, B. B., O'Rourke, B., Morse, N., & Robins, C. J. (2006). Dialectical behavior therapy adapted for the vocational rehabilitation of significantly disabled mentally ill adults. *Cognitive and Behavioral Practice, 13,* 146–156. http://dx.doi.org/10.1016/j.cbpra.2005.04.003

Koons, C. R., Robins, C. J., Tweed, J. L., Lynch, T. R., Gonzalez, A. M. Morse, J. Q., . . . Bastian, L. A. (2001). Efficacy of dialectical behavior therapy in women veterans with borderline personality disorder. *Behavior Therapy, 32,* 371–390. http://dx.doi.org/10.1016/S0005-7894(01)80009-5

Kröger, C., Harbeck, S., Armbrust, M., & Kliem, S. (2013). Effectiveness, response, and dropout of dialectical behavior therapy for borderline personality disorder in an inpatient setting. *Behaviour Research and Therapy, 51,* 411–416. http://dx.doi.org/10.1016/j.brat.2013.04.008

Kröger, C., Schweiger, U., Sipos, V., Arnold, R., Kahl, K. G., Schunert, T., . . . Reinecker, H. (2006). Effectiveness of dialectical behaviour therapy for borderline personality disorder in an inpatient setting. *Behaviour Research and Therapy, 44,* 1211–1217. http://dx.doi.org/10.1016/j.brat.2005.08.012

Kröger, C., Schweiger, U., Sipos, V., Kliem, S., Arnold, R., Schunert, T., & Reinecker, H. (2010). Dialectical behavior therapy and an added cognitive behavioral treatment module for eating disorders in women with borderline personality disorder and anorexia nervosa or bulimia nervosa who failed to respond to previous treatments: An open trial with a 15-month follow-up. *Journal of Behavior Therapy and Experimental Psychiatry, 41,* 381–388. http://dx.doi.org/10.1016/j.jbtep.2010.04.001

Landes, S. J., Rodriguez, A. L., Smith, B. N., Matthieu, M. M., Trent, L. R., Kemp, J., & Thompson, C. (2017). Barriers, facilitators, and benefits of implementation of dialectical behavior therapy in routine care: Results from a national program evaluation survey in the Veterans Health Administration. *Translational Behavioral Medicine, 7,* 832–844. http://dx.doi.org/10.1007/s13142-017-0465-5

Laska, K. M., & Wampold, B. E. (2014). Ten things to remember about common factor theory. *Psychotherapy, 51,* 519–524. http://dx.doi.org/10.1037/a0038245

Laska, M. N., Pasch, K. E., Lust, K., Story, M., & Ehlinger, E. (2009). Latent class analysis of lifestyle characteristics and health risk behaviors among college youth. *Prevention Science, 10,* 376–386. http://dx.doi.org/10.1007/s11121-009-0140-2

Levenson, R. W. (1994). Human emotions: A functional view. In P. Ekman & R. J. Davidson (Eds.), *The nature of emotion* (pp. 123–126). New York, NY: Oxford University Press.

Lewis, G., & Appleby, L. (1988). Personality disorder: The patients psychiatrists dislike. *The British Journal of Psychiatry, 153,* 44–49. http://dx.doi.org/10.1192/bjp.153.1.44

Lin, T. J., Ko, H. C., Wu, J. Y., Oei, T. P., Lane, H. Y., & Chen, C. H. (2019). The effectiveness of dialectical behavior therapy skills training group vs. cognitive therapy group on reducing depression and suicide attempts for borderline personality disorder in Taiwan. *Archives of Suicide Research, 23,* 82–99. http://dx.doi.org/10.1080/13811118.2018.1436104

Lindenboim, N., Comtois, K. A., & Linehan, M. M. (2007). Skills practice in dialectical behavior therapy for suicidal women meeting criteria for borderline personality disorder. *Cognitive and Behavioral Practice, 14,* 147–156. http://dx.doi.org/10.1016/j.cbpra.2006.10.004

Linehan, M. M. (1987a). Dialectical behavioral therapy: A cognitive behavioral approach to parasuicide. *Journal of Personality Disorders, 1,* 328–333. http://dx.doi.org/10.1521/pedi.1987.1.4.328

Linehan, M. M. (1987b). Dialectical behavior therapy for borderline personality disorder: Theory and method. *Bulletin of the Menninger Clinic, 51,* 261–276.

Linehan, M. M. (1993a). *Cognitive-behavioral treatment of borderline personality disorder.* New York, NY: Guilford Press.

Linehan, M. M. (1993b). *Skills training manual for treating borderline personality disorder*. New York, NY: Guilford Press.

Linehan, M. M. (1997). Validation and psychotherapy. In A. Bohart & L. S. Greenberg (Eds.), *Empathy reconsidered: New directions in psychotherapy* (pp. 353–392). Washington, DC: American Psychological Association. http://dx.doi.org/10.1037/10226-016

Linehan, M. M. (2015a). *DBT skills training handouts and worksheets*. New York, NY: Guilford Press.

Linehan, M. M. (2015b). *DBT skills training manual* (2nd ed.). New York, NY: Guilford Press.

Linehan, M. M., Armstrong, H. E., Suarez, A., Allmon, D., & Heard, H. L. (1991). Cognitive-behavioral treatment of chronically parasuicidal borderline patients. *Archives of General Psychiatry, 48*, 1060–1064. http://dx.doi.org/10.1001/archpsyc.1991.01810360024003

Linehan, M. M., Comtois, K. A., Murray, A. M., Brown, M. Z., Gallop, R. J., Heard, H. L., . . . Lindenboim, N. (2006). Two-year randomized controlled trial and follow-up of dialectical behavior therapy vs. therapy by experts for suicidal behaviors and borderline personality disorder. *Archives of General Psychiatry, 63*, 757–766. http://dx.doi.org/10.1001/archpsyc.63.7.757

Linehan, M. M., Dimeff, L. A., Reynolds, S. K., Comtois, K. A., Welch, S. S., Heagerty, P., & Kivlahan, D. R. (2002). Dialectical behavior therapy versus comprehensive validation therapy plus 12-step for the treatment of opioid dependent women meeting criteria for borderline personality disorder. *Drug and Alcohol Dependence, 67*, 13–26. http://dx.doi.org/10.1016/S0376-8716(02)00011-X

Linehan, M. M., & Heard, H. L. (1993). Impact of treatment accessibility on clinical course of parasuicidal patient—Reply [to R. E. Hoffman]. *Archives of General Psychiatry, 50*, 157–158. http://dx.doi.org/10.1001/archpsyc.1993.01820140083011

Linehan, M. M., Heard, H. L., & Armstrong, H. E. (1993). Naturalistic follow-up of a behavioral treatment for chronically parasuicidal borderline patients. *Archives of General Psychiatry, 50*, 971–974. http://dx.doi.org/10.1001/archpsyc.1993.01820240055007

Linehan, M. M., Korslund, K. E., Harned, M. S., Gallop, R. J., Lungu, A., Neacsiu, A. D., . . . Murray-Gregory, A. M. (2015). Dialectical behavior therapy for high suicide risk in individuals with borderline personality disorder: A randomized clinical trial and component analysis. *JAMA Psychiatry, 72*, 475–482. http://dx.doi.org/10.1001/jamapsychiatry.2014.3039

Linehan, M. M., Schmidt, H., III, Dimeff, L. A., Craft, J. C., Kanter, J., & Comtois, K. A. (1999). Dialectical behavior therapy for patients with borderline personality disorder and drug-dependence. *The American Journal on Addictions, 8*, 279–292. http://dx.doi.org/10.1080/105504999305686

Linehan, M. M., Tutek, D. A., Heard, H. L., & Armstrong, H. E. (1994). Interpersonal outcome of cognitive behavioral treatment for chronically suicidal borderline patients. *The American Journal of Psychiatry, 151*, 1771–1776. http://dx.doi.org/10.1176/ajp.151.12.1771

Links, P. S., Ross, J., & Gunderson, J. G. (2015). Promoting good psychiatric management for patients with borderline personality disorder. *Journal of Clinical Psychology, 71*, 753–763. http://dx.doi.org/10.1002/jclp.22203

Lynch, T. R. (2018). *Radically open dialectical behavior therapy: Theory and practice for treating disorders of overcontrol.* Reno, NV: Context Press/New Harbinger.

Lynch, T. R., Chapman, A. L., Rosenthal, M. Z., Kuo, J. K., & Linehan, M. M. (2006). Mechanisms of change in dialectical behavior therapy: Theoretical and empirical observations. *Journal of Clinical Psychology, 62*, 459–480. http://dx.doi.org/10.1002/jclp.20243

Lynch, T. R., Cheavens, J. S., Cukrowicz, K. C., Thorp, S. R., Bronner, L., & Beyer, J. (2007). Treatment of older adults with co-morbid personality disorder and depression: A dialectical behavior therapy approach. *International Journal of Geriatric Psychiatry, 22*, 131–143. http://dx.doi.org/10.1002/gps.1703

Lynch, T. R., Gray, K. L. H., Hempel, R. J., Titley, M., Chen, E. Y., & O'Mahen, H. A. (2013). Radically open-dialectical behavior therapy for adult anorexia nervosa: Feasibility and outcomes from an inpatient program. *BMC Psychiatry, 13*, 293. http://dx.doi.org/10.1186/1471-244X-13-293

Lynch, T. R., Hempel, R. J., & Dunkley, C. (2015). Radically open-dialectical behavior therapy for disorders of over-control: Signaling matters. *The American Journal of Psychotherapy, 69*, 141–162. http://dx.doi.org/10.1176/appi.psychotherapy.2015.69.2.141

Lynch, T. R., Hempel, R. J., Whalley, B., Byford, S., Chamba, R., Clarke, P., . . . Russell, I. T. (2018). Radically open dialectical behaviour therapy for refractory depression: The RefraMED RCT. *Efficacy & Mechanism Evaluation, 5*(7). http://dx.doi.org/10.3310/eme05070

Lynch, T. R., Hempel, R. J., Whalley, B., Byford, S., Chamba, R., Clarke, P., . . . Russell, I. T. (2019). Refractory depression—Mechanisms and efficacy of radically open dialectical behaviour therapy (RefraMED): Findings of a randomised trial on benefits and harms. *The British Journal of Psychiatry*, 1–9. Advance online publication. http://dx.doi.org/10.1192/bjp.2019.53

Lynch, T. R., Morse, J. Q., Mendelson, T., & Robins, C. J. (2003). Dialectical behavior therapy for depressed older adults: A randomized pilot study. *The American Journal of Geriatric Psychiatry, 11*, 33–45. http://dx.doi.org/10.1097/00019442-200301000-00006

Maffei, C., Cavicchioli, M., Movalli, M., Cavallaro, R., & Fossati, A. (2018). Dialectical behavior therapy skills training in alcohol dependence treatment:

Findings based on an open trial. *Substance Use & Misuse, 53,* 2368–2385. http://dx.doi.org/10.1080/10826084.2018.1480035

Markowitz, J. C., Skodol, A. E., & Bleiberg, K. (2006). Interpersonal psychotherapy for borderline personality disorder: Possible mechanisms of change. *Journal of Clinical Psychology, 62,* 431–444. http://dx.doi.org/10.1002/jclp.20242

Marx, K., & Engels, F. (1970). *Selected works.* London, England: Lawrence & Wishart.

Mazzeo, S. E., Kelly, N. R., Stern, M., Palmberg, A. A., Belgrave, F. Z., Tanofsky-Kraff, M., . . . Bulik, C. M. (2013). LIBER8 design and methods: An integrative intervention for loss of control eating among African American and White adolescent girls. *Contemporary Clinical Trials, 34,* 174–185. http://dx.doi.org/10.1016/j.cct.2012.10.012

Mazzeo, S. E., Lydecker, J., Harney, M., Palmberg, A. A., Kelly, N. R., Gow, R. W., . . . Stern, M. (2016). Development and preliminary effectiveness of an innovative treatment for binge eating in racially diverse adolescent girls. *Eating Behaviors, 22,* 199–205. http://dx.doi.org/10.1016/j.eatbeh.2016.06.014

McCauley, E., Berk, M. S., Asarnow, J. R., Adrian, M., Cohen, J., Korslund, K., . . . Linehan, M. M. (2018). Efficacy of dialectical behavior therapy for adolescents at high risk for suicide: A randomized clinical trial. *JAMA Psychiatry, 75,* 777–785. http://dx.doi.org/10.1001/jamapsychiatry.2018.1109

McFarr, L., Gaona, L., Barr, N., Ramirez, U., Henriquez, S., Farias, A., & Flores, D. (2014). Cultural considerations in dialectical behavior therapy. In A. Masuda (Ed.) *Mindfulness and acceptance in multicultural competency* (pp. 75–92). Reno, NV: Context Press.

McMain, S. F., Chapman, A. L., Kuo, J. R., Guimond, T., Streiner, D. L., Dixon-Gordon, K. L., . . . Hoch, J. S. (2018). The effectiveness of 6 versus 12-months of dialectical behaviour therapy for borderline personality disorder: The feasibility of a shorter treatment and evaluating responses (FASTER) trial protocol. *BMC Psychiatry, 18,* 230. http://dx.doi.org/10.1186/s12888-018-1802-z

McMain, S. F., Guimond, T., Barnhart, R., Habinski, L., & Streiner, D. L. (2017). A randomized trial of brief dialectical behaviour therapy skills training in suicidal patients suffering from borderline disorder. *Acta Psychiatrica Scandinavica, 135,* 138–148. http://dx.doi.org/10.1111/acps.12664

McMain, S. F., Guimond, T., Streiner, D. L., Cardish, R. J., & Links, P. S. (2012). Dialectical behavior therapy compared with general psychiatric management for borderline personality disorder: Clinical outcomes and functioning over a 2-year follow-up. *The American Journal of Psychiatry, 169,* 650–661. http://dx.doi.org/10.1176/appi.ajp.2012.11091416

McMain, S. F., Links, P. S., Gnam, W. H., Guimond, T., Cardish, R. J., Korman, L., & Streiner, D. L. (2009). A randomized trial of dialectical behavior therapy versus general psychiatric management for borderline personality disorder. *The American Journal of Psychiatry, 166,* 1365–1374. http://dx.doi.org/10.1176/appi.ajp.2009.09010039

McNair, L., Woodrow, C., & Hare, D. (2017). Dialectical behavior therapy [DBT] with people with intellectual disabilities: A systematic review and narrative analysis. *Journal of Applied Research in Intellectual Disabilities, 30,* 787–804. http://dx.doi.org/10.1111/jar.12277

Meaney-Tavares, R., & Hasking, P. (2013). Coping and regulating emotions: A pilot study of a modified dialectical behavior therapy delivered in a college counseling service. *Journal of American College Health, 61,* 303–309. http://dx.doi.org/10.1080/07448481.2013.791827

Mehlum, L., Ramberg, M., Tørmoen, A. J., Haga, E., Diep, L. M., Stanley, B. H., . . . Grøholt, B. (2016). Dialectical behavior therapy compared with enhanced usual care for adolescents with repeated suicidal and self-harming behavior: Outcomes over a one-year follow-up. *Journal of the American Academy of Child & Adolescent Psychiatry, 55,* 295–300. http://dx.doi.org/10.1016/j.jaac.2016.01.005

Mehlum, L., Tørmoen, A. J., Ramberg, M., Haga, E., Diep, L. M., Laberg, S., . . . Grøholt, B. (2014). Dialectical behavior therapy for adolescents with repeated suicidal and self-harming behavior: A randomized trial. *Journal of the American Academy of Child & Adolescent Psychiatry, 53,* 1082–1091. http://dx.doi.org/10.1016/j.jaac.2014.07.003

Mercado, A., & Hinojosa, Y. (2017). Culturally adapted dialectical behavior therapy in an underserved community mental health setting: A latina adult case study. *Practice Innovations, 2,* 80–93. http://dx.doi.org/10.1037/pri0000045

Meyers, L., Voller, E. K., McCallum, E. B., Thuras, P., Shallcross, S., Velasquez, T., & Meis, L. (2017). Treating veterans with PTSD and borderline personality symptoms in a 12-week intensive outpatient setting: Findings from a pilot program. *Journal of Traumatic Stress, 30,* 178–181. http://dx.doi.org/10.1002/jts.22174

Miller, A. L., Rathus, J. H., & Linehan, M. M. (2017). *Dialectical behavior therapy with suicidal adolescents.* New York, NY: Guilford Press.

Morales, E., & Norcross, J. C. (2010). Evidence-based practices with ethnic minorities: Strange bedfellows no more. *Journal of Clinical Psychology, 66,* 821–829. http://dx.doi.org/10.1002/jclp.20712

Moukhtarian, T. R., Mintah, R. S., Moran, P., & Asherson, P. (2018). Emotion dysregulation in attention-deficit/hyperactivity disorder and borderline personality disorder. *Borderline Personality Disorder and Emotion Dysregulation,* *5*, 9. http://dx.doi.org/10.1186/s40479-018-0086-8

Murphy, A. M., & Bourke, J. (2014). Economic evaluation of dialectical behavior therapy (DBT) amongst those with borderline personality disorder (BPD) who engage in self-harm in Ireland. *Value in Health, 17,* A463. http://dx.doi.org/ 10.1016/j.jval.2014.08.1288

National Collaborating Centre for Mental Health. (2009). *Borderline personality disorder: Treatment and management.* Leicester, England: British Psychological Society.

National Health and Medical Research Council. (2013). *Clinical practice guideline for the management of borderline personality disorder.* Canberra, Australia: Author.

National Institute for Health and Care Excellence. (2009). *Borderline personality disorder: Recognition and management.* Clinical Guideline [CG78]. Retrieved from https://www.nice.org.uk/guidance/CG78/chapter/introduction

Neacsiu, A. D., Eberle, J. W., Kramer, R., Wiesmann, T., & Linehan, M. M. (2014). Dialectical behavior therapy skills for transdiagnostic emotion dysregulation: A pilot randomized controlled trial. *Behaviour Research and Therapy, 59,* 40–51. http://dx.doi.org/10.1016/j.brat.2014.05.005

Neacsiu, A. D., Rizvi, S. L., & Linehan, M. M. (2010). Dialectical behavior therapy skills use as a mediator and outcome of treatment for borderline personality disorder. *Behaviour Research and Therapy, 48,* 832–839. http://dx.doi.org/ 10.1016/j.brat.2010.05.017

Niedtfeld, I., Schmitt, R., Winter, D., Bohus, M., Schmahl, C., & Herpertz, S. C. (2017). Pain-mediated affect regulation is reduced after dialectical behavior therapy in borderline personality disorder: A longitudinal fMRI study. *Social Cognitive and Affective Neuroscience, 12,* 739–747. http://dx.doi.org/10.1093/ scan/nsw183

Nock, M. K. (2007). Conceptual and design essentials for evaluating mechanisms of change. *Alcoholism, Clinical & Experimental Research, 31*(Suppl.), 4s–12s. http://dx.doi.org/10.1111/j.1530-0277.2007.00488.x

Nock, M. K., & Prinstein, M. J. (2004). A functional approach to the assessment of self-mutilative behavior. *Journal of Consulting and Clinical Psychology, 72,* 885–890. http://dx.doi.org/10.1037/0022-006X.72.5.885

Norcross, J. C., & Prochaska, J. O. (2003). *Systems of psychotherapy: A transtheoretical analysis.* Pacific Grove, CA: Brooks/Cole.

Olatunji, B. O., & Lohr, J. M. (2004–2005). Nonspecific factors and the efficacy of psychosocial treatments for anger. *Scientific Review of Mental Health Practice: Objective Investigations of Controversial and Unorthodox Claims in*

Clinical Psychology, Psychiatry, and Social Work, 3(2), 3–18. Retrieved from https://pdfs.semanticscholar.org/b9db/2b35b60ff019c958d482f0c187f4dcfc46f4.pdf

Öst, L. G. (2008). Efficacy of the third wave of behavioral therapies: A systematic review and meta-analysis. *Behaviour Research and Therapy, 46*, 296–321. http://dx.doi.org/10.1016/j.brat.2007.12.005

Panos, P. T., Jackson, J. W., Hasan, O., & Panos, A. (2014). Meta-analysis and systematic review assessing the efficacy of dialectical behavior therapy (DBT). *Research on Social Work Practice, 24*, 213–223. http://dx.doi.org/10.1177/1049731513503047

Pasieczny, N., & Connor, J. (2011). The effectiveness of dialectical behaviour therapy in routine public mental health settings: An Australian controlled trial. *Behaviour Research and Therapy, 49*, 4–10. http://dx.doi.org/10.1016/j.brat.2010.09.006

Patterson, C. M., & Newman, J. P. (1993). Reflectivity and learning from aversive events: Toward a psychological mechanism for the syndromes of disinhibition. *Psychological Review, 100*, 716–736. http://dx.doi.org/10.1037/0033-295x.100.4.716

Patterson, G. R., DeBaryshe, B D., & Ramsey, E. (1989). A developmental perspective on antisocial behavior. *American Psychologist, 44*, 329–335. http://dx.doi.org/10.1037/0003-066X.44.2.329

Perepletchikova, F., Axelrod, S., Kaufman, J., Rounsaville, B., Douglas-Palumberi, H., & Miller, A. (2011). Adapting dialectical behaviour therapy for children: Towards a new research agenda for paediatric suicidal and non-suicidal self-injurious behaviours. *Child and Adolescent Mental Health, 16*, 116–121. http://dx.doi.org/10.1111/j.1475-3588.2010.00583.x

Perepletchikova, F., Nathanson, D., Axelrod, S. R., Merrill, C., Walker, A., Grossman, M., . . . Walkup, J. (2017). Randomized clinical trial of dialectical behavior therapy for preadolescent children with disruptive mood dysregulation disorder: Feasibility and outcomes. *Journal of the American Academy of Child & Adolescent Psychiatry, 56*, 832–840. http://dx.doi.org/10.1016/j.jaac.2017.07.789

Perroud, N., Nicastro, R., Jermann, F., & Huguelet, P. (2012). Mindfulness skills in borderline personality disorder patients during dialectical behavior therapy: Preliminary results. *International Journal of Psychiatry in Clinical Practice, 16*, 189–196. http://dx.doi.org/10.3109/13651501.2012.674531

Perroud, N., Uher, R., Dieben, K., Nicastro, R., & Huguelet, P. (2010). Predictors of response and drop-out during intensive dialectical behavior therapy. *Journal of Personality Disorders, 24*, 634–650. http://dx.doi.org/10.1521/pedi.2010.24.5.634

Persons, J. B., & Tompkins, M. A. (2007). Cognitive-behavioral case formulation. In T. D. Eells (Ed.), *Handbook of psychotherapy case formulation* (2nd ed., pp. 290–316). New York, NY: Guilford Press.

Pistorello, J., Fruzzetti, A. E., Maclane, C., Gallop, R., & Iverson, K. M. (2012). Dialectical behavior therapy (DBT) applied to college students: A randomized clinical trial. *Journal of Consulting and Clinical Psychology, 80*, 982–994. http://dx.doi.org/10.1037/a0029096

Priebe, S., Bhatti, N., Barnicot, K., Bremner, S., Gaglia, A., Katsakou, C., . . . Zinkler, M. (2012). Effectiveness and cost-effectiveness of dialectical behaviour therapy for self-harming patients with personality disorder: A pragmatic randomised controlled trial. *Psychotherapy and Psychosomatics, 81*, 356–365. http://dx.doi.org/10.1159/000338897

Ramaiya, M. K., Fiorillo, D., Regmi, U., Robins, C. J., & Kohrt, B. A. (2017). A cultural adaptation of dialectical behavior therapy in Nepal. *Cognitive and Behavioral Practice, 24*, 428–444. http://dx.doi.org/10.1016/j.cbpra.2016.12.005

Ramaiya, M. K., McLean, C., Regmi, U., Fiorillo, D., Robins, C. J., & Kohrt, B. A. (2018). A dialectical behavior therapy skills intervention for women with suicidal behaviors in rural Nepal: A single-case experimental design series. *Journal of Clinical Psychology, 74*, 1071–1091. http://dx.doi.org/10.1002/jclp.22588

Rathus, J. H., & Miller, A. L. (2000). DBT for adolescents: Dialectical dilemmas and secondary treatment targets. *Cognitive and Behavioral Practice, 7*, 425–434. http://dx.doi.org/10.1016/S1077-7229(00)80054-1

Rathus, J. H., & Miller, A. L. (2002). Dialectical behavior therapy adapted for suicidal adolescents. *Suicide & Life-Threatening Behavior, 32*, 146–157. http://dx.doi.org/10.1521/suli.32.2.146.24399

Rathus, J. H., & Miller, A. L. (2014). *DBT skills manual for adolescents.* New York, NY: Guilford Press.

Reddy, M. S., & Vijay, M. S. (2017). Empirical reality of dialectical behavioral therapy in borderline personality. *Indian Journal of Psychological Medicine, 39*, 105–108. http://dx.doi.org/10.4103/IJPSYM.IJPSYM_132_17

Rizvi, S. L. (2019). *Chain analysis in dialectical behavior therapy.* New York, NY: Guilford Press.

Rizvi, S. L., Hughes, C. D., Hittman, A. D., & Vieira Oliveira, P. (2017). Can trainees effectively deliver dialectical behavior therapy for individuals with borderline personality disorder? Outcomes from a training clinic. *Journal of Clinical Psychology, 73*, 1599–1611. http://dx.doi.org/10.1002/jclp.22467

Rizvi, S. L., & Linehan, M. M. (2005). The treatment of maladaptive shame in borderline personality disorder: A pilot study of "opposite action."

Cognitive and Behavioral Practice, 12, 437–447. http://dx.doi.org/10.1016/S1077-7229(05)80071-9

Ross, C. A., & Goldner, E. M. (2009). Stigma, negative attitudes and discrimination towards mental illness within the nursing profession: A review of the literature. *Journal of Psychiatric and Mental Health Nursing, 16*, 558–567. http://dx.doi.org/10.1111/j.1365-2850.2009.01399.x

Ruocco, A. C., Rodrigo, A. H., McMain, S. F., Page-Gould, E., Ayaz, H., & Links, P. S. (2016). Predicting treatment outcomes from prefrontal cortex activation for self-harming patients with borderline personality disorder: A preliminary study. *Frontiers in Human Neuroscience, 10*, 220. http://dx.doi.org/10.3389/fnhum.2016.00220

Safer, D. L. Robinson, A. H., & Jo, B. (2010). Outcome from a randomized controlled trial of group therapy for binge eating disorder: Comparing dialectical behavior therapy adapted for binge eating to an active comparison group therapy. *Behavior Therapy, 41*, 106–120. http://dx.doi.org/10.1016/j.beth.2009.01.006

Safer, D. L., Telch, C. F., & Agras, W. S. (2001). Dialectical behavior therapy for bulimia nervosa. *The American Journal of Psychiatry, 158*, 632–634. http://dx.doi.org/10.1176/appi.ajp.158.4.632

Santangelo, P. S., Bohus, M., & Ebner-Priemer, U. W. (2014). Ecological momentary assessment in borderline personality disorder: A review of recent findings and methodological challenges. *Journal of Personality Disorders, 28*, 1–22. http://dx.doi.org/10.1521/pedi_2012_26_067

Sauer-Zavala, S., Wilner, J. G., Cassiello-Robbins, C., Saraff, P., & Pagan, D. (2019). Isolating the effect of opposite action in borderline personality disorder: A laboratory-based alternating treatment design. *Behaviour Research and Therapy, 117*, 1–8. http://dx.doi.org/10.1016/j.brat.2018.10.006

Sayrs, J. H. R., & Linehan, M. M. (2019). *DBT teams: Development and practice.* New York, NY: Guilford Press.

Schmitt, R., Winter, D., Niedtfeld, I., Herpertz, S. C., & Schmahl, C. (2016). Effects of psychotherapy on neuronal correlates of reappraisal in female patients with borderline personality disorder. *Biological Psychiatry, 1*, 548–557. http://dx.doi.org/10.1016/j.bpsc.2016.07.003

Schnell, K., & Herpertz, S. C. (2007). Effects of dialectic-behavioral-therapy on the neural correlates of affective hyperarousal in borderline personality disorder. *Journal of Psychiatric Research, 41*, 837–847. http://dx.doi.org/10.1016/j.jpsychires.2006.08.011

Segal, Z. V., Williams, J. M. G., & Teasdale, J. D. (2002). *Mindfulness-based cognitive therapy for depression: A new approach to preventing relapse.* New York, NY: Guilford Press.

Shearin, E. N., & Linehan, M. M. (1992). Patient–therapist ratings and relationship to progress in dialectical behavior therapy for borderline personality disorder. *Behavior Therapy, 23*, 730–741. http://dx.doi.org/10.1016/S0005-7894(05)80232-1

Shelton, D., Sampl, S., Kesten, K. L., Zhang, W., & Trestman, R. L. (2009). Treatment of impulsive aggression in correctional settings. *Behavioral Sciences & the Law, 27*, 787–800. http://dx.doi.org/10.1002/bsl.889

Sheppard, M., Layden, B. K., Turner, B. J., Chapman, A. L. (2016). Dialectical behavior therapy in forensic contexts. *The Behavior Therapist, 39*, 181–183.

Sinnaeve, R., van den Bosch, L. M. C., Hakkaart-van Roijen, L., & Vansteelandt, K. (2018). Effectiveness of step-down versus outpatient dialectical behaviour therapy for patients with severe levels of borderline personality disorder: A pragmatic randomized controlled trial. *Borderline Personality Disorder and Emotion Dysregulation, 5*, 12. http://dx.doi.org/10.1186/s40479-018-0089-5

Skodol, A. E., Gunderson, J. G., Pfohl, B., Widiger, T. A., Livesley, W. J., & Siever, L. J. (2002). The borderline diagnosis I: Psychopathology, comorbidity, and personality structure. *Biological Psychiatry, 51*, 936–950. http://dx.doi.org/10.1016/S0006-3223(02)01324-0

Sloan, C. A., Berke, D. S., & Shipherd, J. C. (2017). Utilizing a dialectical framework to inform conceptualization and treatment of clinical distress in transgender individuals. *Professional Psychology, Research and Practice, 48*, 301–309. http://dx.doi.org/10.1037/pro0000146

Soler, J., Pascual, J. C., Tiana, T., Cebrià, A., Barrachina, J., Campins, M. J., . . . Pérez, V. (2009). Dialectical behaviour therapy skills training compared to standard group therapy in borderline personality disorder: A 3-month randomised controlled clinical trial. *Behaviour Research and Therapy, 47*, 353–358. http://dx.doi.org/10.1016/j.brat.2009.01.013

Soler, J., Valdepérez, A., Feliu-Soler, A., Pascual, J. C., Portella, M. J., Martín-Blanco, A., . . . Pérez, V. (2012). Effects of the dialectical behavioral therapy–mindfulness module on attention in patients with borderline personality disorder. *Behaviour Research and Therapy, 50*, 150–157. http://dx.doi.org/10.1016/j.brat.2011.12.002

Soloff, P. H., & Chiappetta, L. (2017). Suicidal behavior and psychosocial outcome in borderline personality disorder at 8-year follow-up. *Journal of Personality Disorders, 31*, 774–789. http://dx.doi.org/10.1521/pedi_2017_31_280

Spoont, M. R., Sayer, N. A., Thuras, P., Erbes, C., & Winston, E. (2003). Practical psychotherapy: Adaptation of dialectical behavior therapy by a VA medical center. *Psychiatric Services, 54*, 627–629. http://dx.doi.org/10.1176/appi.ps.54.5.627

Springer, T., Lohr, N. E., Buchtel, H. A., & Silk, K. R. (1996). A preliminary report of short-term cognitive-behavioral group therapy for inpatients with personality disorders. *The Journal of Psychotherapy Practice and Research, 5*, 57–71. Retrieved from https://www.ncbi.nlm.nih.gov/pmc/articles/PMC3330405/pdf/57.pdf

Staats, A. W. (1975). *Social behaviorism.* Oxford, England: Dorsey.

Staats, A. W. (1995). Paradigmatic behaviorism and paradigmatic behavior therapy. In W. T. O'Donohue & L. Krasner (Eds.), *Theories of behavior therapy: Exploring behavior change* (p. 659–693). Washington, DC: American Psychological Association. http://dx.doi.org/10.1037/10169-047

Stanley, B., Brodsky, B., Nelson, J. D., & Dulit, R. (2007). Brief dialectical behavior therapy (DBT-B) for suicidal behavior and non-suicidal self injury. *Archives of Suicide Research, 11*, 337–341. http://dx.doi.org/10.1080/13811110701542069

Stepp, S. D., Epler, A. J., Jahng, S., & Trull, T. J. (2008). The effect of dialectical behavior therapy skills use on borderline personality disorder features. *Journal of Personality Disorders, 22*, 549–563. http://dx.doi.org/10.1521/pedi.2008.22.6.549

Stiglmayr, C., Stecher-Mohr, J., Wagner, T., Meißner, J., Spretz, D., Steffens, C., . . . Renneberg, B. (2014). Effectiveness of dialectic behavioral therapy in routine outpatient care: The Berlin Borderline Study. *Borderline Personality Disorder and Emotion Dysregulation, 1*, 20. http://dx.doi.org/10.1186/2051-6673-1-20

Stoffers-Winterling, J. M., Völlm, B. A., Rucker, G., Timmer, A., Huband, N., & Lieb, K. (2012). Psychological therapies for people with borderline personality disorder. *Cochrane Database of Systematic Reviews.* http://dx.doi.org/10.1002/14651858.CD005652.pub2

Suzuki, S. (1970). *Zen mind, beginner's mind.* New York, NY: Weatherhill.

Suzuki, S. (2011). *Zen mind, beginner's mind* (40th anniv. ed.). Boston, MA: Shambhala.

Swales, M. A., Taylor, B., & Hibbs, R. A. B. (2012). Implementing dialectical behaviour therapy: Programme survival in routine healthcare settings. *Journal of Mental Health, 21*, 548–555. http://dx.doi.org/10.3109/09638237.2012.689435

Swenson, C. R., Torrey, W. C., & Koerner, K. (2002). Implementing dialectical behavior therapy. *Psychiatric Services, 53*, 171–178. http://dx.doi.org/10.1176/appi.ps.53.2.171

Taylor, V. A., Grant, J., Daneault, V., Scavone, G., Breton, E., Roffe-Vidal, S., . . . Beauregard, M. (2011). Impact of mindfulness on the neural responses to emotional pictures in experienced and beginner meditators. *NeuroImage, 57*, 1524–1533. http://dx.doi.org/10.1016/j.neuroimage.2011.06.001

Teasdale, J. D., Segal, Z. V., Williams, J. M. G., Ridgeway, V. A., Soulsby, J. M., & Lau, M. A. (2000). Prevention of relapse/recurrence in major depression by mindfulness-based cognitive therapy. *Journal of Consulting and Clinical Psychology, 68*, 615–623. http://dx.doi.org/10.1037/0022-006X.68.4.615

Telch, C. F., Agras, W. S., & Linehan, M. M. (2001). Dialectical behavior therapy for binge eating disorder. *Journal of Consulting and Clinical Psychology, 69,* 1061–1065. http://dx.doi.org/10.1037/0022-006X.69.6.1061

Thompson, R. A. (1994). Emotion regulation: A theme in search of definition. *Monographs of the Society for Research in Child Development, 59,* 25–52. http://dx.doi.org/10.1111/j.1540-5834.1994.tb01276.x/abstract

Trull, T. J., Tomko, R. L., Brown, W. C., & Scheiderer, E. M. (2010). Borderline personality disorder in 3-D: Dimensions, symptoms, and measurement challenges. *Social and Personality Psychology Compass, 4,* 1057–1069. http://dx.doi.org/10.1111/j.1751-9004.2010.00312.x

Trupin, E. W., Stewart, D. G., Beach, B., & Boesky, L. (2002). Effectiveness of a dialectical behavior therapy program for incarcerated female juvenile offenders. *Child and Adolescent Mental Health, 7,* 121–127. http://dx.doi.org/10.1111/1475-3588.00022

Turner, R. M. (2000). Naturalistic evaluation of dialectical behavior therapy-oriented treatment for borderline personality disorder. *Cognitive and Behavioral Practice, 7,* 413–419. http://dx.doi.org/10.1016/S1077-7229(00)80052-8

Uliaszek, A. A., Rashid, T., Williams, G. E., & Gulamani, T. (2016). Group therapy for university students: A randomized control trial of dialectical behavior therapy and positive psychotherapy. *Behaviour Research and Therapy, 77,* 78–85. http://dx.doi.org/10.1016/j.brat.2015.12.003

Valentine, S. E., Bankoff, S. M., Poulin, R. M., Reidler, E. B., & Pantalone, D. W. (2015). The use of dialectical behavior therapy skills training as stand-alone treatment: A systematic review of the treatment outcome literature. *Journal of Clinical Psychology, 71,* 1–20. http://dx.doi.org/10.1002/jclp.22114

van den Bosch, L. M. C., Verheul, R., Schippers, G. M., & van den Brink, W. (2002). Dialectical behavior therapy of borderline patients with and without substance use problems. Implementation and long-term effects. *Addictive Behaviors, 27,* 911–923. http://dx.doi.org/10.1016/S0306-4603(02)00293-9

van der Velden, A. M., Kuyken, W., Wattar, U., Crane, C., Pallesen, K. J., Dahlgaard, J., ... Piet, J. (2015). A systematic review of mechanisms of change in mindfulness-based cognitive therapy in the treatment of recurrent major depressive disorder. *Clinical Psychology Review, 37,* 26–39. http://dx.doi.org/10.1016/j.cpr.2015.02.001

VandenBos, G. R. (Ed.). (2015). *APA dictionary of psychology* (2nd ed.). Washington, DC: American Psychological Association. http://dx.doi.org/10.1037/14646-000

Van Dijk, S., Jeffrey, J., & Katz, M. R. (2013). A randomized, controlled, pilot study of dialectical behavior therapy skills in a psychoeducational group for individuals with bipolar disorder. *Journal of Affective Disorders, 145,* 386–393. http://dx.doi.org/10.1016/j.jad.2012.05.054

Verheul, R., Van Den Bosch, L. M. C., Koeter, M. W. J., De Ridder, M. A. J., Stijnen, T., & Van Den Brink, W. (2003). Dialectical behaviour therapy for women with borderline personality disorder: 12-month, randomised clinical trial in The Netherlands. *The British Journal of Psychiatry, 182,* 135–140. http://dx.doi.org/10.1192/bjp.182.2.135

Wampold, B. E. (2015). How important are the common factors in psychotherapy? An update. *World Psychiatry, 14,* 270–277. http://dx.doi.org/10.1002/wps.20238

Wampold, B. E. (2019). *Basics of psychotherapy: An introduction to theory and practice* (2nd ed.). Washington, DC: American Psychological Association. http://dx.doi.org/10.1037/0000117-000

Weinberg, I., Ronningstam, E., Goldblatt, M. J., Schechter, M., & Maltsberger, J. T. (2011). Common factors in empirically supported treatments of borderline personality disorder. *Current Psychiatry Reports, 13,* 60–68. http://dx.doi.org/10.1007/s11920-010-0167-x

Weiss, N. H., Tull, M. T., Viana, A. G., Anestis, M. D., & Gratz, K. L. (2012). Impulsive behaviors as an emotion regulation strategy: Examining associations between PTSD, emotion dysregulation, and impulsive behaviors among substance dependent inpatients. *Journal of Anxiety Disorders, 26,* 453–458. http://dx.doi.org/10.1016/j.janxdis.2012.01.007

Wetterborg, D., Dehlbom, P., Långström, N., Andersson, G., Fruzzetti, A. E., & Enebrink, P. (2018). Dialectical behavior therapy for men with borderline personality disorder and antisocial behavior: A clinical trial. *Journal of Personality Disorders, 34,* 1–18. Advance online publication. http://dx.doi.org/10.1521/pedi_2018_32_379

Winter, D., Niedtfeld, I., Schmitt, R., Bohus, M., Schmahl, C., & Herpertz, S. C. (2017). Neural correlates of distraction in borderline personality disorder before and after dialectical behavior therapy. *European Archives of Psychiatry and Clinical Neuroscience, 267,* 51–62. http://dx.doi.org/10.1007/s00406-016-0689-2

Wiser, S., & Telch, C. F. (1999). Dialectical behavior therapy for binge-eating disorder. *Journal of Clinical Psychology, 55,* 755–768. http://dx.doi.org/10.1002/(SICI)1097-4679(199906)55:6<755::AID-JCLP8>3.0.CO;2-R

Yen, S., Johnson, J., Costello, E., & Simpson, E. B. (2009). A 5-day dialectical behavior therapy partial hospital program for women with borderline personality disorder: Predictors of outcome from a 3-month follow-up study. *Journal of Psychiatric Practice, 15,* 173–182. http://dx.doi.org/10.1097/01.pra.0000351877.45260.70

Zanarini, M. C., Frankenburg, F. R., Dubo, E. D., Sickel, A. E., Trikha, A., Levin, A., & Reynolds, V. (1998). Axis I comorbidity of borderline personality disorder. *The American Journal of Psychiatry, 155,* 1733–1739. http://dx.doi.org/10.1176/ajp.155.12.1733

Zanarini, M. C., Frankenburg, F. R., Hennen, J., Reich, D. B., & Silk, K. R. (2004). Axis I comorbidity in patients with borderline personality disorder: 6-year follow-up and prediction of time to remission. *The American Journal of Psychiatry, 161,* 2108–2114. http://dx.doi.org/10.1176/appi.ajp.161.11.2108

Zanarini, M. C., Frankenburg, F. R., Reich, D. B., & Fitzmaurice, G. (2010). Time to attainment of recovery from borderline personality disorder and stability of recovery: A 10-year prospective follow-up study. *The American Journal of Psychiatry, 167,* 663–667. http://dx.doi.org/10.1176/appi.ajp.2009.09081130

Zanarini, M. C., Frankenburg, F. R., Ridolfi, M. E., Jager-Hyman, S., Hennen, J., & Gunderson, J. G. (2006). Reported childhood onset of self-mutilation among borderline patients. *Journal of Personality Disorders, 20,* 9–15. http://dx.doi.org/10.1521/pedi.2006.20.1.9

Index

About the Authors

Alexander L. Chapman, PhD, RPsych, is a professor in the psychology department at Simon Fraser University (SFU), a registered psychologist, and president of the DBT Centre of Vancouver. Dr. Chapman received his BA (1996) from the University of British Columbia and his MS (2000) and PhD (2003) in clinical psychology from Idaho State University, following an internship at Duke University Medical Center. After completing a 2-year postdoc with Dr. Marsha Linehan (developer of DBT) at the University of Washington, he joined the faculty at SFU. Dr. Chapman studies emotion regulation, borderline personality disorder (BPD), self-injury, and related problems. His research has been continuously funded for several years, including a recent grant for the largest randomized controlled trial to date examining DBT for patients with BPD who are suicidal. He has authored or coauthored more than 100 publications, including 12 books and many journal articles. Dr. Chapman has received the Young Investigator's Award of the National Alliance for BPD, the Canadian Psychological Association's Early Career Scientist Practitioner Award, a Career Investigator Award from the Michael Smith Foundation for Health Research, and the Dean's Medal for Academic Excellence (at SFU). Dr. Chapman is a member of the Canadian Institutes of Health Research College of Reviewers and a Fellow of the Association for Behavioral and Cognitive Therapies and the Canadian Association for Cognitive Behavioural Therapies (CACBT).

He cofounded the DBT Centre of Vancouver, regularly trains clinicians and students in effective treatments for complex clinical problems, and has been giving clinical workshops for mental health professionals since 2004. He is board certified in both cognitive behavior therapy (CACBT) and DBT (Linehan Board) and serves on credentialing committees for CBT (CACBT) and DBT (Linehan Board of Certification and Accreditation). In addition, Dr. Chapman has expertise in martial arts and mindfulness and enjoys cooking, hiking, skiing, reading, and spending time with his wonderful wife and two sons.

Katherine L. Dixon-Gordon, PhD, is a clinical psychologist and an assistant professor in the Department of Psychological and Brain Sciences at the University of Massachusetts Amherst (UMass). She received her BSc in psychology from the University of Washington, working with Dr. Marsha Linehan, and her MA and PhD in clinical psychology from Simon Fraser University, working with Dr. Chapman. Dr. Dixon-Gordon directs the DBT program at UMass, as well as the Clinical Affective Science Lab, where she and her team study emotion regulation, BPD, self-injury, and other risky behaviors. She was named a rising star by the Association for Psychological Science and received an early career award from the National Register of Health Service Psychologists. She has published numerous articles and book chapters on DBT and BPD. In addition, Dr. Dixon-Gordon regularly trains clinicians and students in evidence-based treatments for complex clinical problems and is board certified in DBT.

About the Series Editor

Matt Englar-Carlson, PhD, is a professor of counseling and director of the Center for Boys and Men at California State University–Fullerton. A Fellow of the American Psychological Association, Dr. Englar-Carlson's scholarship focuses on training helping professionals to work more effectively with boys and men across the full range of human diversity. His publications and presentations are focused on men and masculinities, social justice and diversity issues in psychological training and practice, and theories of psychotherapy. Dr. Englar-Carlson coedited the books *In the Room With Men: A Casebook of Therapeutic Change, Counseling Troubled Boys: A Guidebook for Professionals, Beyond the 50-Minute Hour: Therapists Involved in Meaningful Social Action*, and *A Counselor's Guide to Working With Men*, and he was featured in the APA-produced video *Engaging Men in Psychotherapy*. He was named Researcher of the Year, Professional of the Year, and he received the Professional Service award from the Society for the Psychological Study of Men and Masculinities, and was one of the core authors of the *APA Guidelines for Professional Psychological Practice With Boys and Men*. As a clinician, Dr. Englar-Carlson has worked with children, adults, and families in school, community, and university mental health settings. He is the coauthor of *Adlerian Psychotherapy*, which is part of the Theories of Psychotherapy Series.